All Things
Made New

*A Comprehensive Outline of
the Bahá'í Faith*

All Things
Made New

*A Comprehensive Outline of
the Bahá'í Faith*

JOHN FERRABY

Ex-Scholar of King's College
Cambridge

Bahá'í Publishing Trust

New Delhi, India

Published with the kind permission of the Bahá'í Publishing Trust,
4 Station Approach, Oakham Rutland, LE15 6QW, United Kingdom

First Indian Edition : 1997
Reprints : 1999, 2000, 2001 & 2004
Second Edition : February 2007

ISBN: 81-86953-01-9

Photograph : Rev. Ronald Royer Science Photo Library,
London Comet West
Cover Design : Getest Ltd. Eynsham, Oxford

Bahá'í Publishing Trust
F-3/6, Okhla Industrial Area, Phase-I
New Delhi-110020, India

Printed at : Brijbasi Art Press, New Delhi-110020

TO

SHOGHI EFFENDI
The Guardian of the Bahá'í Faith

Entrance to the Shrine of Bahá'u'lláh.

PREFACE

This book is an attempt to confine within one volume all the most important teachings of Bahá'u'lláh and the chief facts of Bahá'í history. Since the task is an impossible one, no apology for failure is needed. Much that is important has been omitted; the arrangement of what has been included will not suit all tastes; abstruse matters have been oversimplified and simple matters made abstruse; in fact, the book has all the faults that any book of this kind is bound to have.

It has been written by a Bahá'í, who has not pretended to be anything else; that is to say, he has not filled the book with 'might's' and 'maybe's' to convey a suspended judgment more suited to the reader than the writer of such a book. The author's mind is made up; he is a Bahá'í; there would be nothing objective in presenting the Bahá'í Teaching as though he were not one.

Should any non-Bahá'í reader think some statement of the author's too dogmatic or too confident, he is invited to insert before it the words 'Bahá'ís believe'. The author has himself done so from time to time as a reminder that everything in the book is intended to express Bahá'í belief, but constant repetition of the phrase would be tedious; for the most part it is to be understood.

No attempt has been made to plumb the hidden depths of the Teaching of Bahá'u'lláh. That is a task for future generations of Bahá'ís; in this book no more is attempted than to present words of Bahá'u'lláh and 'Abdu'l-Bahá on every important topic; to outline briefly the history of the Central Figures of the Faith and still more briefly that of the Bahá'í Community; and to present the vision of the Faith conveyed to Bahá'ís by its Guardian.

Nevertheless, since the Teaching of Bahá'u'lláh directly illumines philosophy, psychology, mysticism, biology, medicine and other specialised fields, discussion of some, of their specialised problems has been included. Most of this discussion is in Chapters VIII and IX, which are somewhat more complicated than the rest of the book; they have not been relegated to an appendix because in them will be found much that is simple and important too.

The author wishes to thank all those who so kindly commented on parts of the book before it was finished, and particularly Mr. George Townshend, Hand of the Cause of God, whose suggestions at an early stage changed its form. He thanks Professor Z. N. Zeine for discovering and providing a copy of Sir Justin Sheil's report on the Martyrdom of the Báb, published here for the first time, Mr. H. M. Balyuzi for suggesting and translating from Persian the passage from Zoroastrian Holy Writings quoted in Chapter X and Mr. Rustom Sabit for checking the transliteration of Persian and Arabic names. He thanks the National Spiritual Assembly of the Bahá'ís of the British Isles for decreasing his administrative duties so that he might have time to write, and the National Spiritual Assembly of the Bahá'ís of the United States for permission to quote from *Bahá'u'lláh and the New Era,* by J. E. Esslemont. He thanks his wife for patiently commenting on parts of the book read late at night and for allowing him to write when he might have been doing other things. And last, because his gratitude for this is greatest, he thanks Shoghi Effendi for having encouraged him to start writing. Without his encouragement, this book would never have been written.

CONTENTS

CONTENTS

CONTENTS

CONTENTS

CHAPTER I

Introducing the Bahá'í Faith

All who think must realise that the age we live in is no ordinary age. A new chapter of the history of mankind has opened, a chapter that bears signs of being the first of a new volume.

Man has walked the earth for hundreds of thousands of years, but about the life, thoughts, habits and beliefs of our distant ancestors we know virtually nothing. The little information we possess has been laboriously gleaned from fragments of those substances which resist decay well enough to maintain recognisable shape after the lapse of aeons. These disclose that man's material progress has been very, very slow during most of his existence on earth; for example, he used stone implements right up to the beginning of historical times.

The only legible volume of human history opened about six thousand years ago, which is perhaps one-millionth of the period that has elapsed since our planet came into being and one-hundredth of the period during which man's form has been recognisably human. Six thousand years ago something happened to accelerate man's development, as a result of which he has advanced materially since then at a far greater rate than before. Nearly all the important discoveries enabling him to triumph over nature have been made in the last six thousand years.

Nevertheless, even the new rate was very slow by present standards until the end of the eighteenth century, when there was again a sudden acceleration. So great was this that control of nature has been pushed farther in the last hundred and fifty years than in all previous recorded history. The improvement of means of communication exemplifies the change: encircling the globe now takes less time than was needed to traverse one country before the modern age began. Thus, educated men can now easily obtain whatever information they require about any inhabited place. The known world, which for most people once consisted of a few square miles of familiar ground, has expanded to include the whole earth and is contracting again to a few hours' journey.

With change of circumstance so rapid and so great, it is not surprising that ideas also have suffered revolutionary change in the last hundred years—change prodigious enough to warrant the statement that the mind of civilised man has been turned upside down and shaken. Heresies of a hundred years ago have become the conventional views of today, and ideas for which no one would then have spared a moment's thought are now hailed as the mark of true understanding. At the same time, many assumptions that our grandfathers made without hesitation are being discarded, and many cherished beliefs of former ages are being recognised as mere prejudice. Something that needs explaining has again happened to mankind, a 'something' comparable to, but even greater than, what happened six thousand years ago.

The foreword to the earlier volume of history seems to have been man's gradual assumption of a way of life involving settled communities based upon agriculture and animal husbandry. During several thousand years these communities progressed slowly, with the slowness of Stone Age growth. Then, at the beginning of recorded history, something happened to speed their progress immeasurably. It led to the use of metals, the growth of towns, the inauguration of ordered government, the promotion of learning, wider exchange of ideas; in fact, to all those things that distinguish civilised from primitive man. What happened to enable mankind suddenly to achieve such development? Most explanations come to no more than saying that a chance discovery, or particularly favourable circumstances, set the wagon of mankind in motion and that it gathered speed as it progressed. Reason suggests this is not the way wagons behave, or mankind, or civilisation either. The path lies uphill: a chance discovery or a favourable set of circumstances is like a momentary impetus, which will not carry the wagon far up the hill before friction brings it to rest. The explanation in fact explains nothing.

To account for the change, it is necessary to postulate a major and lasting transformation of the spirit of man; no other motive force could achieve the effect that the book of history records. And since man is a dependent being, such a change could come about only by the Will of God, the Creator, the Omnipotent.* It must have been part of God's plan for mankind that six thousand years ago a new era of human history, a new cycle in the development of the human spirit, should begin.

Such a transformation would affect the whole human race, not merely a single inventive brain or a few pioneers of discovery. It would account for the rapid evolution of city states in several parts of the world at more or less the same time; it would explain why the earliest development was followed by further progress, and why six thousand years ago the organised life of mankind took a sudden turn on to a path leading straight to the world of the eighteenth century; it enables us to appreciate the difference between the life of mankind during those centuries and his unrecorded life before; but it does not enable us to understand the progress of the last hundred and fifty years.

Customary explanations of that progress, like the explanation of man's earlier transformation, present it as the outcome of circumstance and exceptional discovery, but are not convincing. It is easier to show that the artificial, complacent, aristocratic, unreforming age in England at the end of the eighteenth century was unfavourable to progress than to show, why it ushered in the Industrial Revolution. There is more reason to suppose industrial progress would be stifled by the reactionary, repressive mood of the beginning of the nineteenth century than to suppose it would triumph. And although it was clear by the middle of the century that changes in attitudes to fundamental problems were likely, no one could then have foreseen how great and widespread these changes, which, are still proceeding, would be.

---

* For a discussion of reasons for believing in God, see pages 23-25.

Few would deny that we stand at the threshold of a new age. The volume of history that began with the adoption of settled communities has reached its final chapter and a new volume has been started, the details of whose contents cannot yet be guessed. The initial chapter of the new volume deals with those changes which are making possible the unification of the whole human race. For the first time it is possible to contemplate mankind being united in a single world order in which all men will be deemed equal and prejudices of colour, class and creed will have vanished. Reason tells us that in the long run such unification is inevitable and that the only question arising is how long will elapse before it is established. That God will not let man, the glorious crown of His creation, annihilate himself before achieving world unity seems a simple corollary to belief in God.

The consequences of such unification will be comparable in scope and effect to the birth of civilisation, but of even greater importance. Throughout recorded history men have lived in opposition and antagonism to their neighbours and in ignorance of the benefits to be obtained from friendship with distant peoples. The effect upon human development of a change of spirit causing all to live and work in unity is incalculable.

But there is more to the present age even than the spiritual change uniting mankind. The transformation of the human spirit from which civilisation was born was the true source of all the bounties civilisation has bestowed. How significant, then, it is that in this age also there are many signs of a transformation of the human spirit destined to have many important consequences beyond unification. We live in one of the greatest ages man has ever known whose immediate visible greatness is but a pale shadow of the greatness still to come.

This current transformation of the spirit of man must be as much a part of the Divine Purpose as was the one of six thousand years ago. The new era we are entering has not come about by accident. God, Who does not allow a sparrow to fall unseen,[1] controls all things; therefore, so great and wonderful an age must certainly be under His special care. The Plan of God for mankind has determined the present transformation of the human spirit as surely as it determined the last.

In the next chapter the belief will be expounded that from age to age God manifests Himself to man in the form of the Founder of a religion that is both a renewal of former religions and the inspiration of its age. These Manifestations of God are the Channels through which God reveals His sovereignty. They provide the spiritual impetus and sustaining power which is the ultimate cause of progress and from Them streams the river of Everlasting Life.

This heing so, it is logical to suppose that the tremendous events of recent times result from the appearance on earth of yet another Manifestation of God. Logical—yet very difficult for the mind of man to accept. 'The day of miracles is past,' says them mind; 'Such things don't happen any more'; 'A tale for the credulous'; 'Superstitious nonsense'; 'Science proves otherwise'; objections flood into consciousness before the case has even been heard. A moment's contemplation is necessary before the mind can be sufficiently freed from prejudice to form a just judgment.

The appearance of a Manifestation of God is a rare event, which recurs only, at intervals of several hundred years. Moreover, each Messenger has until now gone unrecognised by the grater part of the world's population so that thousands, rather than hundreds, of years have elapsed since the founding of most living religions. A thousand years is a long interval. There is time to forget what happened when God manifested Himself before, to forget that He was treated as a pretender, a madman, an opposed of religion, that the religion He founded was once a heresy and that His followers were regarded by the wise men of His day as misguided fools. There is time to forget that His human body and human needs were as clouds veiling His inner glory from the people of His epoch, that the learning of His day turned men against Him, and that the religious leaders of His day abhorred Him. Time to forget—as people had forgotten when He came before.

The mind of man is liable to be governed by his pride. It is unwilling to accept that a Great One could have appeared on the earth unrecognised by the people the world most admires, hidden from the eyes of all but the most perspicacious of those who heard His name, and unknown for many decades to the vast majority of men. Yet how could it be otherwise? If belief were made so easy that none could refrain from believing, mankind would be deprived of the creative power of hard-won faith. The souls of men could not bear the sudden appearance in full force of the Revelation of the Great One. Moreover, were righteous and evildoers equally enabled to recognise Him, the prophecies and warnings of all the Holy Books would be proved false. His glory is concealed behind the cloud of His human body and soul, which only the pure in heart can pierce while He is still on earth. The learned and those the world admires are not necessarily or usually the pure in heart.

It is hoped that readers of this book will consider with an open mind the Bahá'í belief that God has again manifested Himself upon the earth, however startling this belief may be. Part of the evidence supporting it is described in the book, for example, the history and teachings of the Faith, the growth of its institutions and its spread to virtually every country of the world. But other evidence cannot easily be committed to paper. The diversity of the people who become Bahá'ís, the harmony with which the institutions of the Faith work, the spirit evident at Baha'i gatherings, the effect its acceptance has on ordinary people, are all signs that this is one of the great religions of the world—a vital, soul-stirring religion invigorated by the power of the Holy Spirit.

The Central Figures of the Bahá'í Faith

The One Who is the Manifestation of God for this age is known as BAHÁ'U'LLÁH, which is Arabic for 'The Glory of God.' Born in 1817 of a noble Persian family, He was on this earth until 1892, much of the time as an exile from His native land.

He was preceded by One known as the BÁB, an Arabic word meaning 'Gate', Who lived in Persia from 1819 until His martyrdom in 1850. The Báb also was a Manifestation of God, Whose special mission was to prepare mankind for the coming of Bahá'u'lláh: so great is this Day that it has been blessed by the appearance of two Manifestations of God in quick succession.

The Bahá'í Faith has a third Central Figure, Who, although of a lesser station than the others, is, nevertheless, regarded as the perfect Exemplar of the Bahá'í teachings and the infallible Interpreter of the Words of Bahá'u'lláh. He is known as 'Abdu'l-Bahá, the Servant of the Glory, and was on earth from 1844 to 1921.

The story of these Great Ones and of the spread of the Bahá'í Faith will be sketched later, after teachings of general interest have been expounded; but, in order that these teachings may be seen in better perspective, the main features of the story are outlined here.

The Beginning of the New Era
In the first half of the nineteenth century the world was swept by a religious ferment now forgotten. Bahá'ís regard it as divine preparation for the coming of the Báb and Bahá'u'lláh, parallel to the first stages of the Industrial Revolution, which constituted a similar preparation in the material world. In Europe and America a belief grew that Christ was about to return. It was so strongly held by some people that they left their homes to go to the places where they expected Him to appear; religious bodies founded by such people still exist. In Islám also there was ferment. The leaders of a Persian sect known as the Shaykhis, believing that the Promised One of Islám was already on earth, set out in 1844 to find Him. Unlike their Christian counterparts, they were successful in their search. Eighteen of them independently accepted a young merchant of Shiraz, named 'Ali-Muhammad, a descendant of the Prophet Muhammad, to be the One for Whom they were looking. Bahá'ís believe this event to have introduced the new era and to have marked the beginning of the transformation of the human spirit already commented upon.

Although the Bahá'í Faith and its short-lived precursor the Bábí Faith were founded in the Middle East, it must not be thought that they are mere sects of Islám. Christianity was founded in Israel, but is not a sect of Judaism, though the learned men and the administrators of that day regarded it as one. Each Manifestation of God must appear somewhere upon the earth and spend His youth in some existing society, but He is not a product of that society. Spiritually He comes from an unseen place, the highest heaven of the All-Glorious; the rest is accident, albeit accident controlled by God. Though natural human feeling tempts us all to think the Great One should come in our own continent, or country, or town, or village, or religious society, this is not reasonable. Even if our own belief and mode of life were wholly right, it would not preclude the possibility that God might send His Messenger first to those astray in the maze of error; but if we were so right as that, it would not be necessary for His Messenger to come. The task of redeeming mankind from sin could safely be left to us.

That the *Bábí* and Bahá'í Faiths originated in a Muslim country should not, therefore, hide from us that they constitute independent religions stemming neither from the Muslim teachers of religion nor even from the Prophet Muḥammad Himself, but from God. They have no more and no less in common with the teachings of Muḥammad than with those of Jesus, or Moses, or any other Founder of a great religion. They come from the same family as all, they repeat the basic truths revealed by all, but they do not belong to anyone religion more than to another; they are independent.

The Bábí Dispensation

The Bábí sent His first eighteen disciples to spread throughout Persia the news of His coming. His pure teachings, which set aside the superstructure successive generations of divines had built upon the fundamental truth revealed by Muḥammad, fired the hearts of the oppressed Persians. Very quickly the powerful, bigoted, corrupt Persian divines became alarmed. They maligned Him and His followers and misrepresented His teachings to the masses. Soon, Bábí were being bastinadoed, raped, tortured and murdered and the Bábí Himself was imprisoned.

The poignant story of the Báb and His followers appealed so

strongly to European orientalists of the nineteenth and early twentieth centuries that those who know the Bahá'í Faith only from their writings are liable to receive a quite false impression. They might be tempted to think that the Bábí and not Bahá'u'lláh was the most important Figure in Bahá'í history. This is contrary to the teachings of the Báb Himself. Again and again He declared, both verbally and in writing, that the purpose of His Revelation was to prepare the way for 'Him Whom God shall make manifest,' upon Whose finger, He proclaimed, He was but as a ring. The Bábí and Bahá'í Faiths are two distinct religions, but the purpose of the Bábi Faith has been fulfilled and, in accordance with the Báb's own commands, virtually all the Bábís have become Bahá'ís. It is a sign of the greatness of this Day that a Manifestation of God should have been sent as Forerunner of Bahá'u'lláh to inaugurate a Dispensation that lasted only nine years.

The story of the Báb is indeed a fascinating one. Only when He declared Himself to be from God, He possessed a charming personality, which attracted and overcame all who had dealings with Him. His cruel and corrupt opponents, backed by the power of Church and State, were quite unable to resist the spread of His doctrines. Ever greater violence was used against the Bábís until at last, in desperation, little groups in different parts of the country withdrew to fortified positions to resist attack.

The heroism of these inspired defenders, mere handfuls who resisted for months whole armies, is already legendary; but in the course of the battles nearly all the Bábí leaders were slain. Eventually, the Báb Himself was condemned to death and shot in circumstances that would be incredible were they not so well attested. It seemed as though the opponents of the Faith had triumphed and that the Bábí religion was doomed to rapid extinction.

Bahá'u'lláh

For several years after the martyrdom of the Báb, the apparently leaderless Bábís sank farther in the slough of despond. Their conduct deteriorated. Several of them claimed to be the one promised by the Báb without attracting supporters.

In 1853, three years after the Báb was shot, two half-crazed Bábís attempted unsuccessfully to murder the Sháh, thereby letting loose a wave of persecution that surpassed even the cruelty of the previous years. All the remaining leaders of the Báb's own day were killed in the holocaust, except one—Bahá'u'lláh.

Bahá'u'lláh was named Husayn 'Ali by His father, one of the Ministers of the Sháh. From an early age He showed signs of great character and ability, but on reaching manhood He refused any government office. Instead, He devoted Himself to charitable works to the extent that His friends warned Him He would soon have given away all His vast possessions if He continued such generosity.

As soon as He was told about the claim of the Báb He became a Bábí. He participated actively in spreading the Bábí Faith and in guiding its development during the incarceration of the Báb. After the attempt on the life of the Sháh, He was imprisoned in an underground dungeon holding a hundred and fifty people, which had neither window nor illumination. He was chained in chains of notorious weight and. having been at first deprived of food, later had some of—His food poisoned. In this grim place He became aware that He was the Manifestation of God Whom the Báb had foretold.

On His release He was exiled to Baghdád, where He experienced so much jealousy and opposition from certain of the Bábís that after a year He left the city for the sake of maintaining unity, and lived in the wilderness in seclusion. By the time He returned two years later in response to an urgent plea from the leading members of the Bábí Community, that Community had reached its lowest ebb.

Bahá'u'lláh set Himself to rehabilitate its fortunes with such success that its enemies, who had thought it dying, took fright and worked to achieve His further banishment. Well might they be alarmed! He had transformed the outlook and character of the Bábís by precept and example, gained the respect of the best officials and divines of Baghdád, and become a firm centre round which a revivified Community could gather. In these years the Bahá'í

Community was truly born, although it was not until 1863 that Bahá'u'lláh declared Himself to be the Promised One.

This He did before leaving Baghdád, when His enemies at last succeeded in having Him removed to a place farther from Persia. Before a select group of seventy followers He made his momentous declaration, which none queried, so well was He esteemed.

From Baghdád He went to Constantinople for a few months, whence he was banished to Adrianople and after five years to the prison city of 'Akká (Acre). It was hoped that the notoriously bad climate there would soon end His life, but God willed otherwise. For another twenty-four years He continued to reveal His Message, changing hatred into love and breathing fresh life into the spirit of mankind. As one small sign of His sovereignty and power, it may be related that the Sultan of Turkey, the most powerful monarch of Islám, instructed successive Governors of 'Akká that He should be strictly confined and treated with the utmost severity. This instruction was never countermanded, yet He ended His days in comfort in a pleasant mansion on the plain of 'Akká; respected and loved by all. Governors of 'Akká themselves used humbly to visit their 'prisoner' in His magnificent residence.

While in Adrianople and 'Akká, Bahá'u'lláh openly proclaimed Himself in letters and messages addressed to the leading monarchs of the World, to the divines and followers of its religions, and to many other groups of men. From the notorious prison city of the Turkish Empire, against the will of the two greatest kings of the Middle East in whose territories He spent His whole life on earth, in opposition to one of the most powerful religious hierarchies the world has known, He successfully organised and guided the rapidly growing Bahá'í Community. No merely human being could have so triumphed over such opposition.

During all this time the persecution of the Bahá'ís in Persia continued, sometimes more intensely, sometimes less; it is estimated that twenty thousand martyrs have given their lives for the Faith. Their devotion and their pure conduct is another proof that Bahá'u'lláh, Who inspired them, was a Manifestation of God.

Although Bahá'u'lláh finished His life in comfort; the greater part of it was spent in suffering of an intensity beyond human endurance, as can be appreciated by any man of feeling who ponders the following words:

> *"By the righteousness of God! Every morning I arose from My bed I discovered the hosts of countless afflictions massed behind My door, and every night when I lay down, lo! My heart was torn with agony at what it had suffered from the fiendish cruelty of its foes. With every piece of bread the Ancient Beauty breaketh is coupled the assault of a fresh affliction, and with every drop He drinketh is mixed the bitterness of the most woeful of trials. He is preceded in every step He taketh by an army of unforeseen calamities, while in His rear follow legions of agonising sorrows."*[2]

He had rejected an honoured position as nobleman and courtier and surrendered all His possessions in order to obey the Divine behest to save and revivify mankind. His acceptance of comfort at the end of His life came from no worldly desire, but was solely to demonstrate the powerlessness of those with earthly might in relation to the King of Kings.

'Abdu'l-Bahá

Bahá'u'lláh pronounced His Eldest Son 'Abdu'l-Bahá to be the perfect Exemplar of His teachings, the infallible Interpreter of His word, and His successor as Head of the Faith. Born in 1844 on the day on which the Báb revealed Himself, 'Abdu'l-Bahá had, as a child, recognised His Father's great station. As a young man He increasingly relieved Bahá'u'lláh of lesser responsibilities and at the time of His Father's Ascension was respected only less than Bahá'u'lláh Himself.

On becoming Head of the Faith, 'Abdu'l-Bahá, like Bahá'u'lláh, was at first the victim of much jealousy and opposition. So grave was the danger from His enemies at one time that He wrote in His

Will 'the pope of even an hour's life is lost to me,' and at another He prayed for martyrdom because of the tribulations that rained upon Him. A prisoner in 'Akká for forty years, He was finally liberated when the Young Turk revolution of 1908 deposed the Sultan and set free all in the Turkish Empire who been imprisoned for their religious beliefs.

He was now able to carry the teaching of Bahá'u'lláh to the West, where there was already a small number if Bahá'ís. In 1911-13 He visited Britain, France, Germany, Austria-Hungary and the United States, in which He spent eight months. By this tour He sowed the seeds that have now put out roots and are growing into the flourishing Bahá'í Communities of the Western world.

'Abdu'l-Bahá was knighted by the British for the part He played in alleviating the suffering of the people of the Holy Land during the 1914-18 war, a title He accepted, but never used. He was widely and deeply loved by the people of all religions. One of the distinguished speakers at His funeral, the Governor of Phoenicia, summed up the impression He made on those who were not Bahá'ís: 'Most of us here have, I think, a clear picture of Sir 'Abdu'l-Bahá, of His dignified figure walking thoughtfully in our streets, of His courteous and gracious manner, of His kindness, of His love for little children and flowers, of His generosity and care for the poor and suffering. So gentle was He, and so simple, that in His presence one almost forgot that He was also a great teacher, and that His writings and His conversations have been a solace and an inspiration to hundreds and thousands of people in the East and the West.'[3] A commentator on His American travels has spoken of 'The sense of power mingled with gentleness that invested His whole being with a rare majesty of spiritual exaltation that both set Him apart, and yet that brought Him near to the lowliest soul.'[4]

There is no parallel to 'Abdu'l-Bahá in religious history; one of His titles is 'The Mystery of God' more than a man, He was less than a Divine Manifestation. A Moon to the Sun that was Bahá'u'lláh, He flooded the earth with reflected light after the Sun had set.

The First Guardian of the Bahá'í Faith

'Abdu'l-bahá appointed His grandson, Shoghi Effendi, to head the Faith after Him as the Guardian of the Cause of God, to be followed by a succession of Guardians, each appointed in a prescribed manner. These He proclaimed to be under the direct guidance of the Highly Spirit of Bahá'u'lláh. Shoghi Effendi was the Guardian of the Cause of God for thirty-six years until his death in London on November 4, 1957. At his death he had no lineal descendants nor anyone who fulfilled the requirements laid down in the Will and Testament of 'Abdu'l-Bahá. He therefore could not appoint a successor as Guardian of the Cause of God.

The Guardian alone after 'Abdu'l-Bahá had the right to interpret authoritatively the teachings of Bahá'u'lláh and to state authoritatively their implications. In doing this he received divine guidance that made his interpretation infallible, but nevertheless, his station was human. He was an inspired man, not a 'Mystery of God' like 'Abdu'l-Bahá, still less a Manifestation of God like Bahá'u'lláh and the Báb.

He had no legislative function, except as head of an elective body had he lived until the election of the Universal House of Justice, and in this he differed from the Pope. But the main difference between the Guardian of the Bahá'í Faith and the head of any other religious community is that his appointment can be clearly and unmistakably traced through written records to the authority of the Manifestation of God. No Bahá'í can doubt that the Guardian was the vicegerent of Bahá'u'lláh, a station of great spiritual potency. Discussing this station in His Will; 'Abdu'l-Bahá declares that the shade of the Guardian of the Cause of God 'shadoweth all mankind'.

Spread of the Faith

The first task Shoghi Effendi set himself was to build up the Administrative Order of the Bahá'í Faith, whose principles Bahá'u'lláh had enunciated and whose Charter 'Abdu'l-Bahá had given. With national and local administrative institutions firmly established and becoming sufficiently mature and the international

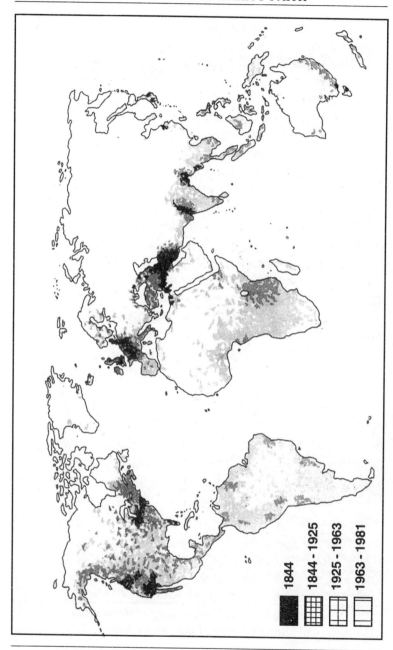

The Growth of the Bahá'í Community 1844-1981.

1844
1844 - 1925
1925 - 1963
1963 - 1981

An example of the handwriting of Bahá'u'lláh:
the first page of the súriy-i-Amr.

institutions continually evolving by the time of Shoghi Effendi's death in 1957, the supreme administrative body of the Bahá'í world, known as the Universal House of Justice, could be elected for the first time in 1963 and has taken up the heavy burden which the Guardian had perforce to carry until his passing.

Under the guidance of Shoghi Effendi, the Bahá'í Faith had spread very rapidly. When 'Abdu'l-Bahá passed on in 1921, the Faith was represented in 35 countries and significant territories. Just before Shoghi Effendi's death it was represented in more than 240, including nearly all the world within its range. Its literature had been translated into 190 languages; valuable endowments had been built up; yet this was still only the beginning of its life. By 1987 there were Bahá'ís in nearly 120,000 centres representing more than 2,100 ethnic groups with literature translated into over 750 languages. The rapidity with which it has spread over the whole globe is further evidence that the Bahá'í Faith is of God, not of man.

The Bahá'í Holy Writings
Those particularly interested in the history of the Faith will find a good deal more about it in the second part of this book. The first part consists in a survey of the Teaching of Bahá'u'lláh, which is given largely in His own words and those of 'Abdu'l-Bahá.

Bahá'ís are particularly fortunate in having available a large quantity of authentic Writings of all three of the Central Figures of their Faith. Most of the Writings of Bahá'u'lláh and 'Abdu'l-Bahá are in the form of letters, known as Tablets, written in Persian or Arabic. By no means all their extant Writings have been collected and of those collected not all have been translated into English.

Only items written in the handwriting of the Founders or items signed by Them, or records of Their spoken words, authenticated either directly or indirectly by the Speaker, are recognised as Scripture. Other records are considered interesting but not authoritative. These are of varying accuracy, depending on the circumstances in which they were recorded, the ability of the note-taker, and often also on the validity of the extempore translation noted. The excerpts in this book have been taken from authentic Scripture whenever possible. When no suitable Scriptural Writing was available in English, only books of verbatim records or of notes 'Abdu'l-Bahá. showed He approved have been used.

Since the original Writings are in Persian and Arabic, accuracy of translation is crucial. English readers are most fortunate in having the translations of Shoghi Effendi, which Bahá'ís are confident convey accurately the sense of the original, because the Guardian was under the guidance of Bahá'u'lláh. If a translation by him of a chosen passage existed, it was used; but when no suitable translation by him was available, recourse had to be made to other translators. Hence the literary quality of excerpts quoted in this book is very variable. Verbatim records of extempore translation are particularly apt to appear unpolished, as they must from their nature be. In general, authenticity has been preferred to literary quality.

Some readers, particularly those acquainted with the works of orientalists interested in the Báb, may wonder why so little use has been made of the Báb's Writings. The reason is that, although they are deemed to be Revelation, they belong to an earlier Dispensation than the one this book is primarily about. Bahá'u'lláh reaffirmed and restated whatever in the Báb's teaching was suited to His own Dispensation, and the rest is of historic interest only.

The Scriptures of other religions are also revered by Bahá'ís, although some are regarded as more authentic than others. The Qur'án is undoubtedly an excellent record of what Muḥammad said; the Gospels contain a good, though fragmentary account of the words of Jesus; the Old Testament is of variable quality since it incorporates very few of Moses' own words, but it has importance also as a record of the teachings of the Prophets of Israel; other Holy Writings are more difficult to evaluate, because most of the material in them was written many hundred years after the Founder gave His Message.

The Status of the Revealed Word
One reason for including in this book so many passages quoted from Holy Writings is that such words have an import beyond the

overt meaning they express. They are holy written with the pen of the spirit, and should accordingly be read with the inner, as well as the outer eye. The heart, as well as the mind, should reconnoiter them. If the phraseology at first seems strange, so too does the phraseology of all Scripture worthy of the name. The strangeness arises from the weight of spiritual meaning the words convey. 'Abdu'l-Bahá said in Paris:

> *"It is easy to read the Holy Scriptures, but it is only with a clean heart and a pure mind that one may understand their true meaning."*[5]

No man has heart clean enough or mind pure enough to exhaust the meaning of Holy Scripture.

PART ONE

THE TEACHINGS
OF BAHÁ'U'LLÁH

CHAPTER II

The Oneness of God and of Religion

So far it has been assumed that the reader believes in God, but
nowadays many people do not. Finding unacceptable the doctrines
of existing religions, particularly those of the one they were taught
as children, they reject altogether both religion and belief in God.
Hence Bahá'u'lláh exclaimed:

> *"The vitality of men's belief in God is dying out in every
> land; nothing short of his wholesome medicine can ever
> restore it. The corrosion of ungodliness is eating into
> the vitals of human society; what else but the Elixir of
> His potent Revelation can cleanse and revive it."*[1]

The Message of Bahá'u'lláh is addressed to unbelievers as
well as to people who already follow a religion, or have maintained
their belief in God without belonging to one. Its relationship to many
kinds of belief and unbelief is shown in this chapter. Bahá'ís hold
that it offers the unbeliever a rational basis for faith and promises to
the believer the fulfilment of his most cherished hopes.

The Existence of God

Although there are many so-called proofs of the existence of God,
to some of which reference will be made, belief does not come
from reasoning alone. It is rather an outcome of a man's whole
experience. Bahá'u'lláh tells us that the signs of the existence of
God are everywhere for those ready to discern them:

> *"Every created thing in the whole universe is but a door
> leading into His knowledge, a sign of His sovereignty,
> a revelation of His names, a symbol of His majesty, a
> token of His power, a means of admittance into His*

straight Path."[2]

Moreover, no man is incapable of discerning these signs:

"He hath endowed every soul with the capacity to recognise the signs of God. How could He, otherwise, have fulfilled His testimony unto men, if ye be of them that ponder His Cause in their. hearts. He will never deal unjustly with anyone, neither will He task a soul beyond its power. He, verily, is the Compassionate, the All-Merciful."[3]

Those seeking faith would be well advised, to search for it in the words of the Founders of religion, through which the winds of certitude blow. The words of Bahá'u'lláh and 'Abdu'l-Bahá, which form so large a part of this book, although consistent with reason bring conviction by other means too.

Their Teaching suggests that contemplation of nature, man, or one's own self, may also be a means of attaining faith. So may the study of the history of religion, if approached with a receptive heart. Reason alone offers less hope of faith than any of these. Nevertheless, for those who demand reasoned arguments, a few based upon Bahá'í Holy Writings will be indicated. Since the author is convinced that the cause of disbelief lies far deeper than mere disagreement with the logic of reasoned proofs, he has not elaborated the arguments, but at least they suggest that belief is consistent with reason, and it could happen that some unbeliever may find amongst them an argument to suit his taste.

The first is derived from analogy with the human body. The action of its various limbs and members is co-ordinated; that which co-ordinates them is the soul. Similarly, the various parts of a machine are caused to work in harmony by the mind of the designer and are made to operate by a single source of power such as steam. The need for the universe to have a co-ordinator and a source of power is analogous.

Another argument is derived from consideration of the purpose of the universe. It is repugnant to our nature and contrary to our experience to believe that so gigantic and well-ordered a system has no purpose.

A third is derived from the evolution of life on this planet. Development has been towards ever higher forms of life; it cannot be due to chance alone that the higher forms are also those which survive.

Yet another argument is derived from the consideration that imperfection can be recognised only if perfection exists. Recognition of ignorance postulates the existence of knowledge and recognition of poverty postulates the existence of wealth. Similarly the recognition that man is a poor, weak creature, incapable of adequately handling his own affairs, postulates the existence of One Who is neither poor nor weak, and Who is capable of handling all things.

A rigidly logical proof of the existence of God can be worked out on the following basis given by 'Abdu'l-Bahá. In a Tablet to Dr. Auguste Forel, the well-known Swiss scientist and humanitarian, who later became a Bahá'í:

"Formation is of three kinds and of three kinds only: accidental, necessary and voluntary. The coming together of the various constituent elements of beings cannot be accidental, for unto every effect there must be a cause. It cannot be compulsory, for then the formation must be an inherent property of the constituent parts and the inherent property of a thing can in no wise be dissociated from it, such as light that is the revealer of things, heat that causeth the expansion of the elements and the (solar) rays which are the essential property of the sun. Thus under such circumstances the decomposition of any formation is impossible, for the inherent properties of a thing cannot be separated from it. The third formation remaineth and that is the voluntary one, that is, an unseen force described as the Ancient Power, causeth the elements

to come together, every formation giving rise to a distinct being."[4]

More important than any such arguments, however, is the feeling of certitude that constitutes true belief. Many have reached it through study of the Bahá'í Writings and association with the Bahá'í Community. The author hopes this book may help others along the same path.

The Essence of God is Unknowable

Some seek refuge from belief in God in the uncomfortable acknowledgment of the fallibility of human reasoning and the affirmation that if God exists He is certainly beyond the comprehension of man. With this view Bahá'ís sympathise; but they do not agree with the inference usually made that it is best to refrain from trying to decide whether or not God exists. People making this inference overlook that God also may realise the magnitude of the gap between Him and His creation and may have provided for the gap to be bridged. This is the Bahá'í belief, which will now be explained.

That God is in His Essence unknowable is a theme continually repeated in the Writings of Bahá'u'lláh. A typical meditation runs:

> *"So perfect and comprehensive is His creation that no mind nor heart, however keen or pure, can ever grasp the nature of the most insignificant of His creatures; much less fathom the mystery of Him Who is the Day Star of Truth, Who is the invisible and unknowable Essence. The conceptions of the devoutest of mystics, the attainments of the most accomplished amongst men, the highest praise which human tongue or pen can render are all the product of man's finite mind and are conditioned by its limitations. . . . From time immemorial He hath been veiled in the ineffable sanctity of His exalted Self, and will everlastingly continue to be wrapt in the impenetrable mystery of His unknowable Essence.*

Every attempt to attain to an understanding of His inaccessible Reality hath ended in complete bewilderment, and every effort to approach His exalted self and envisage His Essence hath resulted in hopelessness and failure."[5]

All we can hope to achieve in describing God is to remind ourselves of the limitations to which we are subject but He is not. Thus 'Abdu'l-Bahá. explains:

"As we consider created things we observe infinite perfections, and the created things being in the utmost regularity and perfection we infer that the Ancient Power on whom dependeth the existence of those beings, cannot be ignorant; thus we say He is All-Knowing. It is certain that it is not impotent, it must be the All-Powerful; it is not poor, it must be the All-Possessing; it is not non-existent, it must be the Ever-Living. The purpose is to show that these attributes and perfections that we recount for that Universal Reality are only in order to deny imperfections rather than to assert the perfections that the human mind can conceive. Thus we say His attributes are unknowable."[6]

Intermediaries between God and Man

The great gap between man and God is bridged by the Holy Spirit, the Face of God, which presents God to man in a way man can apprehend. The Holy Spirit belongs to the world of God, not to His creation. It is like a mirror reflecting His light upon all created things, like the rays of the sun bringing divine light and warmth to His creatures.

From age to age God sends to the earth Messengers, who are possessed of the Holy Spirit and Who manifest God to man. These are the. Founders of the great religions of the world. Through Them the Word of God is diffused and the Water of Life conveyed to humanity. Through Them mankind achieves rebirth and all is made new.

'Abdu'l-Bahá said of the Holy Spirit:

"The Divine Reality may be likened to the sun and the Holy Spirit to the rays of the sun. As the rays of the sun bring the light and warmth of the sun to the earth, giving life to all created beings, so do the Manifestations (of God) bring the power of the Holy Spirit from the divine Sun of Reality to give light and life to the souls of men.

Behold, there is an intermediary necessary between the sun and the earth; the sun does not descend to the earth, neither does the earth ascend to the sun. This contact is made by the rays of the sun which bring light and warmth and heat.

The Holy Spirit is the light from the Sun of Truth, bringing by its infinite power life and illumination to all mankind, flooding all souls with divine Radiance, conveying the blessings of God's Mercy to the whole world. The earth, without the medium of the warmth and light .of the rays of the sun, could receive no benefits from the sun.

Likewise, the Holy Spirit is the very cause of the life of man; without the Holy Spirit he would have no intellect, he would be unable to acquire his scientific knowledge by which his great influence over the rest of creation is gained. The illumination of the Holy Spirit gives to man the power of thought, and enables him to make discoveries by which he bends the laws of nature to his will.

The Holy Spirit it is which, through the mediation of the Prophets of God, teaches spiritual virtues to man and enables him to attain eternal life.

All these blessings are brought to man by the Holy Spirit; therefore we can understand that the Holy Spirit is the intermediary between the Creator and the created. The

*light and heat of the sun cause the earth to be fruitful,
and create life in all things that grow, and the Holy
Spirit quickens the souls of men."*[7]

The Oneness of Religion

Since the Founders of all the world's great religions are
Manifestations of God, possessed of the Holy Spirit and acting as
Intermediaries between God and man, it follows that all the great
religions are in essence one. Bahá'u'lláh says:

*"There can be no doubt whatever that the peoples of
the world, of whatever race or religion, derive their
inspiration from one heavenly Source, and are the
subjects of one God. The difference between the
ordinances under which they abide should be attributed
to the varying requirements and exigencies of the age
in which they were revealed. All of them, except a few
which are the outcome of human perversity, were
ordained of God, and are a reflection of His Will and
Purpose."*[8]

Study of the great religions shows that all teach love, justice,
detachment, honesty, purity, selflessness, wisdom, faithfulness,
humility, forgiveness, charity, respect for parents, contentment,
obedience, mercy, trustworthiness, sincerity, truthfulness,
compassion, righteousness and a host of other virtues. All are
founded on the same ultimate reality; differences between them
arise either from the different needs they were revealed to meet, or
from the failure of the followers of the Manifestations of God to
understand properly the teaching the Manifestation gave.
'Abdu'l-Bahá said in New York:

*"If the religions investigate reality and seek the essential
truth of their own foundations they will agree and no
difference will be found. But inasmuch as religions are
submerged in dogmatic imitations, forsaking the
original foundations, and as imitations differ widely,*

therefore the religions are divergent and antagonistic.
These imitations may be likened to clouds which obscure
the sunrise; but the reality is the sun. If the clouds
disperse, the Sun of Reality shines upon all and no
difference of vision will exist. The religions will then
agree, for fundamentally they are the same."[9]

The Two Parts of Religion

Although the spiritual foundation of all religions is one, each contains elements peculiar to it alone. These are the laws and ordinances each Manifestation of God gives, which are adapted to the particular needs of His own age. They are temporary, contingent, not part of the fundamental spiritual truth at the root of all religion. Circumstances have changed when the next Manifestation of God appears upon the earth, so the laws and ordinances change too. As they have by then served their purpose, God provides for them to give way to new law's suited to the circumstances of the new age. The eternal truths of religion remain what they always were and always will be, but new conditions require new laws for the practical application of the ancient eternal truths.

'Abdu'l-Bahá explained this to a crowded meeting of Jews at a leading Synagogue in San Francisco. After proclaiuning the oneness of the essential part of all religions, He added:

"The second classification or division comprises social
laws and regulations applicable to human conduct. This
is not the essential spiritual quality of religion. It is
subject to change and transformation according to the
exigencies and requirements of time and place. For
instance, in the time of Noah certain requirements made
it necessary that all sea foods be allowable or lawful.
During the time of the Abrahamic prophethood it was
considered allowable because of a certain exigency
that a man should marry his aunt, even as Sarah was
the' sister of Abraham's mother. During the cycle of
Adam it was lawful and expedient for a man to marry

his own sister, even as Abel, Cain and Seth the sons of Adam married their sisters. But in the law of the Pentateuch revealed by Moses, these marriages were forbidden and their custom and sanction abrogated. Other laws formerly valid were annulled during the time of Moses. For example, it was lawful in Abraham's cycle to eat the flesh of the camel, but during the time of Jacob this was prohibited. Such changes and transformations in the teaching of religion are applicable to the ordinary conditions of life but they are not important or essential. His Holiness Moses lived in the wilderness of Sinai where crime necessitated direct punishment. There were no penitentiaries or penalties of imprisonment. Therefore according to the exigency of the time and place it was a law of God that an eye should be given for an eye and a tooth for a tooth. It would not be practicable to enforce this law at the present time; for instance, to blind a man who accidentally blinded you. In the Torah there are many commands concerning the punishment of a murderer. It would not be allowable or possible to carry out these ordinances today. Human conditions and exigencies are such that even the question of capital punishment— the one penalty which most nations have continued to enforce for murder—is now under discussion by wise men who are debating its advisability. In fact, laws for the ordinary conditions of life are only valid temporarily. The exigencies of the time of Moses justified cutting off a man's hand for theft, but such punishment is not allowable now. Time changes conditions, and laws change to suit conditions. We must remember that these changing laws are not the essentials; they are the accidentals of religion. The established ordinances established by a Manifestation of God are spiritual; they concern moralities, the ethical development of man and faith in God. They are ideal and necessarily permanent; expressions of the one foundation and not amenable to change or transformation. Therefore the fundamental basis of the revealed religion of God is immutable, unchanging throughout the centuries, not subject to the varying conditions of the human world."[10]

Cycles of Religion

Unfortunately men are apt to become so attached to the laws of their religion that in the end they regard these as the essential part. A Muslim who disobeys every spiritual teaching of Muḥammad, a Jew who disobeys every spiritual teaching of Moses, may nevertheless consider himself to be one of the favoured of God so long as he punctiliously obeys the ordinances of the Founder of his Faith. All religions experience such retrogression.

When this happens God eventually manifests Himself to man to restore religion and revive mankind. As the warmth of the sun in spring brings fresh life to flowers and trees, the Manifestation of God brings fresh life to the whole of creation. This is a bounty from God, renewed from age to age.

Nevertheless men reject the bounty. All God's Messengers and their early followers have been persecuted, especially at the instigation of the priests and clergy of the old religion. One reason for their persecution is their repeal of the old laws to which people have become so attached. Another is that they teach the pure religion of God, which is unacceptable to those wrapped in the dense-veils of human dogmatism. Another is that the human form of the Manifestation of God blinds people to the spiritual power and might of His inner reality. Another is that at the time the Manifestation of God appears most people have sunk in the depths of self and attachment to worldly pleasures.

At first only very few are attracted to the banner of the Manifestation of God, but since He is God's Representative and His sovereignty is divine, none can gainsay Him. Whatever men do to prevent His achieving ascendancy, even though they imprison, or shoot, or crucify Him, His ultimate triumph is certain.

Gradually more and more people recognise His true station. The influence of His Teaching spreads; the efforts of His opponents are brought to naught by the Divine Will; until eventually the very governments that oppose Him become subject to the sway of His Teaching. A new civilisation arises bringing joy, comfort, and achievement to a large number of people. For a time the new religion experiences a golden age. The new spiritual life of the Revelation flourishes.

Then the veils of human fallibility come between mankind and the light radiated by the Messenger of God. As centuries pass, men reflect it less and less clearly. The veils of idle fancy obscure the truth; the mirror of the human soul becomes clouded; men turn away from virtue to court material satisfaction; self reigns supreme and the laws of religion again become an empty form.

'Abdu'l-Bahá graphically portrayed the cycle by comparing it to the procession of the seasons of the year:

"The day of the appearance of the Holy Manifestations is the spiritual springtime, it is the divine splendour, it is the heavenly bounty, the breeze of life, the rising of the Sun of Reality. Spirits are quickened, hearts are refreshed and invigorated, souls become good, existence is set in motion, human realities are gladdened, and grow and develop in good qualities and perfections. Universal progress takes place, any there are resurrection and lamentation; for it is the day of judgment, the time of turmoil and distress, at the same time that it is the season of joy, of happiness, and of absolute attraction.

Afterwards the life-giving spring ends in fruitful summer. The word of God is exalted, the Law of God is promulgated; all things reach perfection. The heavenly table is spread, the holy things perfume the East and the West, the teachings of God conquer the world, men become educated, praiseworthy results are produced, universal progress appears in the world of humanity, and the divine bounties surround all things. The Sun of Reality rises from the horizon of the Kingdom with the greatest power and heat. When it reaches the meridian it will begin to decline and descend, and the spiritual summer will be followed by autumn when growth and development are arrested. Breezes change into blighting winds, and the unwholesome season dissipates the beauty and freshness of the gardens, plains and bowers. That is to say, attraction and goodwill do not remain, divine qualities are changed, the radiance of hearts is dimmed, the spirituality of souls is altered virtues are replaced by vices, and holiness and purity disappear. Only the name of the religion of God remains, and the exoteric forms of the divine teachings. The foundations of the Religion of God are destroyed and annihilated, and nothing but forms and customs exist. Divisions appear, firmness is changed into instability, and spirits become dead; hearts languish, souls become inert, and winter arrives; that is to say, the coldness of ignorance envelops the world and the darkness of human error prevails. After this come indifference, disobedience, inconsiderateness, indolence, baseness, animal instincts, and the coldness and insensibility of stones. It is like the season of winter when the terrestrial globe, deprived of the effect of the heat of the sun, becomes desolate and dreary. . . .

When the season of winter has had its effect, again the spiritual springtime returns and a new cycle appears. Spiritual breezes blow, the luminous dawn gleams, the divine clouds give rain, the rays of the Sun of Reality shine forth, the contingent world attains unto a new life, and is clad in a wonderful garment. All the signs and the gifts of the past springtime reappear, with perhaps even greater splendour in this new season."[11]

Religion must be a cause of Unity

In the autumn and winter of religion, it may reach a state when it is a cause of dissension, hatred, and strife. This is a sign of the sickness of humanity and the clouding of the human heart, for religion is intended by God to be a source of unity 'Abdu'l-Bahá said in Paris:

> *"Religion should unite all hearts and cause wars and disputes to vanish from the face of the earth, give birth to spirituality, and bring life and light to each heart. If religion becomes a cause of dislike, hatred and division, it were better to be without it, and to withdraw from such a religion would be a truly religious act. For it is clear that the purpose of a remedy is to cure, but if the remedy should only aggravate the complaint it had better be left alone. Any religion which is not a cause of love and unity is no religion, All the holy Prophets were as doctors to the soul.: they gave prescriptions for the healing of mankind; thus any remedy that causes disease does not come from the great and supreme Physician."*[12]

Dual Station of the Manifestations of God

One cause of enmity between religions, and even between the sees of a single religion, has been lack of understanding of the nature of the Manifestations of God. Some claim the Founder of their religion to be an incarnation of God Himself, others consider all the Founders to be but human beings. Bahá'u'lláh affirmed that neither view is correct, although both have some truth. The Manifestations of God partake of humanity, yet possess also an order of spirit higher than human. This is the Holy Spirit, which acts as intermediary between God and man.

Speaking of the station it gives the Manifestations of God, Bahá'u'lláh says:

"The door of the knowledge of the Ancient Being hath ever been, and will continue for ever to be, closed in the face of men. No man's understanding shall ever gain access unto His Holy court. As a token of His mercy, however, and as a proof of His loving kindness, He hath manifested unto men the Day Stars of His divine guidance, the Symbols of His divine unity, and hath ordained the knowledge of these sanctified. Beings to be identical with the knowledge of His own Self. Whoso recogniseth them hath recognised God. Whoso hearkeneth to their call, hath hearkened to the Voice of God, and whoso testifieth to the truth of their Revelation, hath testified to the truth of God Himself. Whoso turneth away from them hath turner away from God, and whoso disbelieveth in them, hath disbelieved in God. Every one of them is the Way of God that connecteth this world with the realms above, and the Standard of His Truth unto everyone in the kingdoms of earth and heaven. They are the Manifestations of God amidst men, the evidences of His Truth, and the signs of His glory."[13]

Nevertheless, even in this station the Manifestations of God are far from being on a level with His Essence. Extolling the greatness of God, Bahá'u'lláh affirms:

"I bear witness with my soul, my spirit, my entire being, that should they Who are the Day-Springs of Thy most holy unity and the Manifestations of Thy transcendent oneness be able to soar so long as Thine own sovereignty endureth and Thine all-compelling authority can last, they will fail in the end to attain unto even the precincts of the court wherein Thou didst reveal the effulgence of but one of Thy most mighty Names. Glorified, glorified be, therefore, Thy wondrous majesty. Glorified, glorified be Thine unattainable loftiness.

Glorified, glorified be the pre-eminence of Thy kingship and the sublimity of Thine authority and power."[14]

When only Their divine station is regarded, the Manifestations of God are ail as one Being; but when Their human personality is regarded, They are seen to be separate entities. Bahá'u'lláh explains fully and clearly in the *Kitáb-i-Íqán:*

"These Manifestations of God have each a twofold station. One is the station of pure abstraction and essential unity. In this respect, if thou callest them all by one name, and dost ascribe to them the same attributes, thou hast not erred from the truth.... If thou wilt observe with discriminating eyes, thou wilt behold Them all abiding in the same tabernacle, soaring in the same heaven, seated upon the same throne, uttering the same speech, and proclaiming the same Faith. Such is the unity of those Essences of Being, those Luminaries of infinite and immeasurable splendour! Wherefore, should one of these Manifestations of Holiness proclaim saying "I am the return of all the Prophets," He, verily, speaketh the truth. In like manner, in every subsequent Revelation, the return of the former Revelation is a fact, the truth of which is firmly established....

The other station is the station of distinction, and pertaineth to the world of creation, and to the limitation thereof. In this respect, each Manifestation of God hath a distinct individuality, a definitely prescribed mission, a predestined revelation, and specially designated limitations. Each one of them is known by a different name, is characterised by a special attribute, fulfils a definite mission, and is entrusted with a particular Revelation. . . .

It is because of this difference in their station and mission that the words and utterances flowing from these Well Springs of Divine knowledge appear to diverge and differ. Otherwise, in the eyes of them that are initiated into the mysteries of Divine wisdom, all their utterances are, in reality, but the expressions of one Truth. As most of the people have failed to appreciate these stations to which We have referred, they, therefore, feel perplexed and dismayed at the varying utterances pronounced by Manifestations that are essentially one and the same.

It hath ever been evident that all these divergencies of utterance are attributable to differences of station. Thus, viewed from the standpoint of their oneness and sublime detachment, the attributes of Godhead, Divinity, Supreme Singleness, and Inmost Essence have been, and are, applicable to those Essences of Being. inasmuch as they all abide on the throne of Divine Revelation, and are established upon the seat of Divine Concealment. Through their appearance the Revelation of God is made manifest, and by their countenance the Beauty of God is revealed. Thus it is that the accents of God Himself have been heard uttered by these Manifestations of the Divine Being.

Viewed in the light of their second station—the station of distinction, differentiation, temporal limitations, characteristics and standards—they manifest absolute servitude, utter destitution, and complete self-effacement. Even as He saith 'I am the servant of God. I am but a man like you.'"[15]

A proper understanding of the Oneness of the Manifestations of God is fundamental for the understanding of religion. Lack of this understanding has cost countless thousands of lives and caused inestimable misery. Bahá'u'lláh stresses it so greatly that He even says there can, in this age, be no true belief in God without it:

"Beware, O believers in the Unity of God, lest ye be tempted to make any distinction between any of the Manifestations of His Cause, or to discriminate against the signs that have accompanied and proclaimed their Revelation. This indeed is the true meaning of Divine Unity, if ye be of them that apprehend and believe this truth. Be ye assured, moreover, that the works and acts of each and every one of these Manifestations of God, nay whatever pertaineth unto them, and whatsoever they may manifest in the future, are all ordained by God, and are a reflection of His Will and Purpose. Whoso maketh the slightest possible difference between their persons, their words, their messages, their acts and manners, hath indeed disbelieved in God, hath repudiated His signs, and betrayed the Cause of His Messengers." [16]

Such a person, to borrow words used by Bahá'u'lláh in the Tablet of Ahmad, 'showeth pride towards God from all eternity to all eternity.' [17]

Progressive Revelation
The Revelation of each of the Divine Educators causes mankind to progress. Through them humanity is enabled to advance along the path ordained by God. Bahá'u'lláh says:

"All men have been created to carry forward an ever-advancing civilisation." [18]

Study of history discloses in varying degrees the progress caused by the various Manifestations of God. For example, traces are found of a Jewish civilisations in Israel after Moses at the time of David and Solomon, of a Buddhist civilisation in India at the time of Asoka, of a Christian civilisation in Europe. The best substantiated record, however, is of the Muslim civilisation that followed Muḥammad. When He came, the Arabs were among the most savage people upon earth; no traveller was safe from being sold into slavery and some tribes even considered it virtuous to bury their daughters alive. Yet within a hundred years of His coming, these savages had founded the most advanced civilisation the world had yet seen, whose foundation can be traced directly to His Teaching. All unbiased historians now agree that the Saracens at the time of the Crusades were more civilised than the Crusaders; indeed, Muslims used to laugh at the primitive ideas of the European invaders, whom they considered barbarian. Muslim Universities were so much admired that the first Christian University, founded in Paris, was founded in imitation of the Muslim Universities of Spain. Our Western civilisation owes to the Muslim civilisation of the Middle Ages no less, and perhaps more, than it does to Greece and Rome.

Such is the power and the sovereignty which the Manifestations of God possess. Their Revelation is the true creative power in the universe. Bahá'u'lláh asserts:

"Every word that proceedeth out of the mouth of God is endowed with such potency as can instill new life into every human frame, if ye be of them that comprehend this truth. All the wondrous works ye behold in this world have been manifested through the operation of His supreme and most exalted Will, His wondrous and inflexible Purpose. Through the mere revelation of the word 'Fashioner,' issuing forth from His lips and proclaiming His attribute to mankind, such power is released as can generate, through successive ages, all the manifold arts which the hands of man can produce. This, verily, is a certain truth. No sooner is this resplendent word uttered, than its animating energies, stirring within all created things, give birth to the means and instruments whereby such arts can be produced and perfected. All the wondrous achievements ye now witness are the direct consequences of the Revelation of this Name. In the days to come, ye will, verily, behold things of which ye have never heard before. Thus hath it been decreed in the Tablet of God,

and none can comprehend it except them whose sight is sharp."[19]

Similarly man's spiritual capacity develops further in each Dispensation. The progress of the human race, both spiritual and material, results from and depends directly upon the potency of the Revelations of the Manifestations of God. Although towards the end of a Dispensation the fire of the love of God ceases to burn in the hearts of men, so that their actions belie the belief they profess in the teachings of the Founder of their religion, nevertheless their spiritual capacity is greater than that of the sincere of former Dispensations. Even though they fail to quaff fully the wine proffered to them, they are potentially more capable spiritually than the purest soul of earlier ages. Their loss in failing to achieve that of which they are capable is therefore also greater.

Mankind in this day of the Revelation of Bahá'u'lláh is capable of greater things than in any previous age. All that the Prophets of the past have revealed, all that the saints and martyrs have achieved, all that those who came close to God longed for, is finding its fruition in this Great Day.

God's Messenger for this Age

The essence of Bahá'í belief is that God has once more sent a Messenger, Bahá'u'lláh, to recreate creation and give fresh life to mankind. Once more the breath of the Holy Spirit has been wafted; once more the Face of God has shone upon the world. All things have been made new. The potency of fonner Revelations has caused humanity to advance to a state in which it is capable of greater things than ever before. It has reached the age of maturity. Bahá'u'lláh has therefore revealed what man is now capable of receiving, those things of which Jesus said:

"I have yet many things to say unto you, but ye cannot bear them now. Howbeit when he, the Spirit of truth, is come, he will guide you into all truth."[20]

Bahá'u'lláh has revealed these things because mankind has

41

progressed enough to be able to bear them, not because He is more knowledgeable, or in any way superior to or different from the Founders of earlier religions. Humanity's need has called forth the Revelation that is now transforming human life.

Just as the Revelations of earlier Manifestations of God brought spiritual and material advancement to mankind, so the Revelation of Bahá'u'lláh is doing the same. As yet, most men do not realise what has caused the revolutionary changes of the last hundred years, changes which are spiritual in origin although manifested also in the material world. That they are sudden and colossal, no one would deny; gradually more and more people are coming to understand their true meaning.

Such has always been the way of God. At first a few only have ears to hear—*"For many are called but few are chosen."*[21] Then the number gradually increases, more and more, faster and faster, until it dawns upon the laggards that a new religion has been born whose followers possess something they would themselves fain have.

This process, which has been repeated again and again in human history, is once more working to its foreordained conclusion. The Word of God has been spoken. Its hidden potency has been revealed. Nothing men can do will prevent it from achieving all that God has willed it should achieve. Therefore Bahá'u'lláh says:

> *"O men! This is a matchless Day. Matchless must, likewise, be the tongue that celebrateth the praise of the Desire of all nations, and matchless the deed that aspireth to be acceptable in His sight. The whole human race hath longed for this Day, that perchance it may fulfil that which well beseemeth its station, and is worthy of its destiny. Blessed is the man whom the affairs of the world have failed to deter from recognising Him Who is the Lord of all things."*[22]

CHAPTER III

Proclamation of the
Message of Bahá'u'lláh

The Nature of the Proclamation

Bahá'u'lláh openly proclaimed His station although He was at the time the victim of religious intolerance, an exile and a prisoner. To the kings and rulers of the earth, its divines and religious leaders, and to a wide variety of special groups of men He addressed His call.

Shoghi Effendi describes this proclamation impressively:

"Kings and emperors, severally and collectively; the chief magistrates of the Republics of the American continent; ministers and ambassadors; the Sovereign Pontiff himself; the Vicar of the Prophet of Islám; the royal Trustee of the Kingdom of the Hidden Imam; the monarchs of Christendom, its patriarchs, archbishops, bishops, priests and monks; the recognised leaders of both the Sunni and Shi'ih sacerdotal orders; the high priests of the Zoroastrian religion; the philosophers, the ecclesiastical leaders, the wise men and the inhabitants of Constantinople—that proud seat of both the Sultanate and the Caliphate; the entire company of the professed adherents of the Zoroastrian, the Jewish, the Christian and Muslim Faiths; the people of the Bayan; the wise men of the world, its men of letters, its poets, its mystics, its tradesmen, the elected representatives of its peoples; His own countrymen— all have, at one time or another, in books, Epistles, and Tablets, been brought directly within the purview of the

43

exhortations, the warnings, the appeals, the declarations and the prophecies which constitute the theme of His momentous summons to the leaders of mankind—a summons which stands unparalleled in the annals of any previous religion, and to which the messages directed by the Prophet of Islám to some of the rulers among His contemporaries alone offer a faint resemblance."[1]

The warnings and the prophecies of these writings will be expounded later in this chapter; exhortations and appeals concerning good government will be referred to in the rest of the book, particularly in the chapter on World Unity.* Our immediate concern is the public declaration of His Mission, which Bahá'u'lláh broadcast in these Tablets.

A typical announcement is contained in the: *Kitáb-i-Aqdas* (The Most Holy Book) addressed to the kings of the collectively:

"O kings of the earth! He Who is the sovereign Lord of all is come The, Kingdom is God's, the omnipotent Protector, the Self subsisting. Worship none but God, and, with radiant hearts lift up, your faces unto your Lord, the Lord of all names. This is a Revelation to which whatever ye possess can never be compared, could ye but know it. We see you rejoicing in that which you have amassed from others, and shutting out yourselves from the worlds which naught except My Guarded Tablet can reckon. The treasures ye have laid up have drawn you far away from your ultimate objective. This ill beseemeth you, could ye but understand it. Wash your hearts from all earthly defilements, and hasten to enter the kingdom of your Lord, the Creator of earth and heaven, Who caused the world to tremble, and all its peoples to wail, except them that have renounced all things and clung to that which the Hidden Tablet hath

---

* See Chapter V.

ordained. . . .

"O kings of the earth! The Most Great Law hath been revealed in this Spot, this Scene of transcendent splendour. Every hidden thing hath been brought to light, by virtue of the Will of the Supreme Ordainer, He Who hath ushered in the last Hour, through Whom the Moon hath been cleft, and every irrevocable decree expounded.

"Ye are but vassals, O kings of the earth! He Who is the King of kings hath appeared, arrayed in His most wondrous glory, and' is summoning you unto Himself, the Help in Peril, the Self subsisting. Take heed lest pride deter you from recognising the Source of Revelation; lest the things of this world shut you out as by a veil from Him Who is the Creator of heaven. Arise, and serve Him Who is the Desire of all nations, Who hath created you through a word from Him, and ordained you to be, for all time, the emblems of His sovereignty."[2]

In this passage Bahá'u'lláh reveals with the Voice of God Himself. To the S̲h̲áh of Persia He explains that He speaks as God wills and not of His own will:

"O king! I was but a man like others, asleep upon My couch, when lo, the breezes of the All-Glorious were wafted over Me, and taught Me the knowledge of all that hath been. This thing is not from Me, but from One who is Almighty, and All-knowing. And He bade Me lift up My voice between earth and heaven, and for this there befell Me what hath caused the tears of every man of understanding to flow. The learning current amongst men I studied not; their schools I entered not. Ask of the city wherein I dwelt, that thou mayest be well assured that I am not of them who speak falsely. This is

but a leaf which the winds of the will of Thy Lord, the Almighty, the All-Praised, have stirred. Can it be still when the tempestuous winds are blowing? Nay, by Him Who is the Lord of all Names and Attributes ! They move it as they list. The evanescent is as nothing before Him Who is the Ever-Abiding. His all-compelling summons hath reached Me, and caused Me to speak His praise amidst all people. I was indeed as one dead when His behest was uttered. The hand of the will of Thy Lord, the Compassionate, the Merciful, transformed Me. Can anyone speak forth of his own accord that for which all men, both high and low, will protest against him? Nay, by Him Who taught the Pen the eternal mysteries, save him whom the grace of the Almighty, the All Powerful, hath strengthened."[3]

Christ and Bahá'u'lláh

This statement is reminiscent of the saying of Jesus when, referring to the coming of the Spirit of Truth, He added:

"For He shall not speak of Himself; but whatsoever He shall hear, that shall He speak; and He will show you things to come."[4]

In a passage addressed to the kings of Christendom, Bahá'u'lláh reminds them of this prophecy. He reminds them also that Christ was to come again 'in the clouds of heaven,' and claims distinctly to be the return of Christ:

"O kings of Christendom I Heard ye not the saying of Jesus, the Spirit of God, 'I go away, and come again unto you.' Wherefore, then, did ye fail, when He did come again unto you in the clouds of heaven, to draw nigh unto Him, that ye might behold His face, and be of them that attained His Presence? In another passage He saith 'When He, the Spirit of Truth, is come, He will guide you into all truth.' And yet, behold how, when He

did bring the truth, ye refused to turn your faces towards Him, and persisted in disporting yourselves with your pastimes and fancies. Ye welcomed Him not, neither did ye seek His Presence, that ye might hear the verses of God from His own mouth, and partake of the manifold wisdom of the Almighty, the All-Glorious, the All-Wise."[5]

Since all the Manifestations of God are as one, Bahá'u'lláh is the return of all the Prophets, Jesus not less than the others. Prophecies of both Old and New Testaments, and of the Qurán too, confirm this; they will be discussed in a later chapter,* which those especially interested in Biblical (or Quráinic) prophecy may like to read before proceeding.

The Greatness of This Day

Prophecies by everyone of the Founders of the great religions foretell the coming of a Great One Who will inaugurate an era of peace and spiritual well-being. Christians expect the return of Christ, Jews the coming of the Lord of Hosts, Muslims of the Shi'ih sect the Qa'im and of the Sunni sect the Mihdí, Buddhists another Buddha, Hindus the return of Krishna, Zoroastrians Sháh-Bahram. What could be more logical and natural than that all these so similar prophecies should refer to a unique age in which a single Messenger of God comes to fulfil them all and to unite mankind in a common Faith?

Although such an event has never before been conceivable, in this age all without prejudice must admit its feasibility. Rapid communication ensures that the Teaching of a Manifestation of God can be quickly introduced to all peoples, and countless millions yearn for a Revelation that will relieve them of a misery they do not fully apprehend. The irreligious may doubt the necessity for faith, but their doubts themselves confirm such prophecies as:

"Because iniquity shall abound, the love of many shall wax cold."[6]

---

* See Chapter X.

Followers of particular sects may wonder that there should be salvation for any who do not share their own long-cherished views; so have they wondered since the world began. Others may be tempted by attachment to the name of the One they revere to turn away from the reality for which the name is a symbol; these sacrifice eternal life for a shadow; attention to a prophecy of Zachariah would save them from their folly.

"In that day shall there be one Lord and his Name One."[7]

However, most people will admit the possibility of all men being united in allegiance to one God through the truth contained in all religions and now revealed again according to the needs of our own age. The claim of Bahá'u'lláh, whether one accepts it or not, must be acknowledged to be rational and suited to the present day. It is so tremendous that its very temerity causes men of sense to ponder deeply what could make One so wise put forward so challenging a claim. If it is true, the age in which we live is greatly exalted. Such a day, prophesied in all Holy Books and unique in the history of mankind, sheds glory on all who live in it. It is not surprising that Bahá'u'lláh should have exclaimed:

"All glory be to this Day, the Day in which the fragrances of mercy have been wafted over all created things, a Day so blest that past ages and centuries can never hope to rival it."[8]

He explains:

"It is evident that every age in which a Manifestation of God hath lived is divinely ordained, and may, in a sense, be characterised as God's appointed Day. This Day, however, is unique, and is to be distinguished from those that have preceded it. The designation "Seal of the Prophets" fully revealeth its high station. The Prophetic Cycle hath, verily, ended. The Eternal Truth

*is now come. He hath lifted up the Ensign of Power,
and is now shedding upon the world the unclouded
splendour of His Revelation."*[8]

Bahá'u'lláh does not claim to be greater than, or intrinsically
different from, the Manifestations of God that preceded Him. He
claims only that mankind has reached a crucial stage in its
development, a statement with which few would disagree. Because
the stage is crucial, an especially intense revelation has been
vouchsafed to man. From Adam to Muḥammad, all the
Manifestations of God foretold this turning-point in the history of
humanity. Their age was the age of prophecy, but Muḥammad was
the Seal of the Prophets. After His Dispensation, the age of fulfilment
began, the age at whose threshold we now stand. To usher it in, the
most powerful of all Revelations has been sent down from the Will
of God.

We who live in this wonderful age have a great opportunity and
a great responsibility. We have the opportunity to act as channels
for the spread of the divine fragrance of this unsurpassed Revelation,
and we have the responsibility of discarding prejudice that might
prevent our recognising the bounties being showered upon us. We
have the opportunity of benefiting from a Revelation whose like
has never been, and the responsibility of deciding whether to turn
towards or away from its Source. We have the opportunity of being
born again, and the responsibility of not letting pride or self-interest,
desire for power or material satisfaction, attachment to the' things
of this world, or its praise, or its fashionable opinions, blind us to the
glory which has shone upon mankind. Bahá'u'lláh indicates the
magnitude of this opportunity and responsibility in such passages as
the following:

*"Verily I say, this is the Day in which mankind can
behold the Face, and hear the Voice, of the Promised
One. The Call of God hath been raised, and the light
of His countenance hath been lifted up upon man. It
behoveth every man to blot out the trace of every idle*

word from the tablet of his heart, and to gaze, with an open and unbiased mind, on the signs of His Revelation, the proofs of His Mission, and the tokens of His Glory.

"Great indeed is this Day! The allusions made to it in all the sacred Scriptures as the Day of God attest its greatness. The soul of every Prophet of God, of every Divine Messenger, hath thirsted for this wondrous Day. All the divers kindreds of the earth have, likewise, yearned to attain it. No sooner, however, had the Day Star of His Revelation manifested itself in the heaven of God's Will, than all, except those whom the Almighty was pleased to guide, were dumbfounded and heedless.

"O thou that hast remembered Me! The most grievous veil hath shut out the peoples of the earth from His glory, and hindered them from hearkening to His call. God grant that the light of unity may envelop the whole earth, and that the seal, 'The Kingdom is God's,' may be stamped upon the brow of all its peoples."[10]

No wonder that He proclaims:

"This is the Voice of God, if ye do but hearken. This is the Day Spring of the Revelation of God, did ye but know it. This is the Dawning-place of the Cause of God, were ye to recognise it. This is the Source of the commandment of God, did ye but judge it fairly. This is the manifest and hidden Secret, would that ye might perceive it. O peoples of the world! Cast away, in My name that transcendeth all other names, the things ye possess, and immerse yourselves in this Ocean in whose depths lay hidden the pearls of wisdom and of utterance, an ocean that surgeth in My name, the All-Merciful. Thus instructeth you He with whom is the Mother Book."[11]

Consequences of the Revelation

The most direct consequences of the Revelation of Bahá'u'lláh are naturally to be found among His followers. The growing world Bahá'í Community is evidence of its power and one of the proofs that Bahá'u'lláh is a Manifestation of God. A mere philosophy, however true, does not change the hearts of men; it does not inspire large numbers of people to accept the suffering which invariably accompanies the founding of a great religion; it cannot evoke the self-forgetfulness essential to true faith.

The living, vital, Bahá'í Community scattered through every country outside the Soviet orbit demonstrates that the Revelation of Bahá'u'lláh is a potent force in the modern world. But there are other effects of the Revelation whose true cause the world does not yet recognise. Throughout this book the reader will find many teachings that seem so much in line with progressive thought as to be unexceptionable. They were given during the nineteenth century by a Middle Eastern exile at a time when they were not current either in the East or in the West: at that time, the stream of opinion was against them. That the attitude and to some extent the practice of progressive peoples have turned, since Bahá'u'lláh gave these Teachings, so markedly in the direction He indicated, is a fact for men of goodwill to ponder. Although the change is not visibly a result of acceptance of Bahá'u'lláh and His Teachings, Bahá'ís believe its formal cause to be the new spirit released by His Revelation. The belief can neither be proved nor disproved; it will be accepted or rejected according as one accepts or rejects that Bahá'u'lláh was a Manifestation of God.

Similarly it can neither be proved nor disproved that the fulfilment of certain prophecies Bahá'u'lláh made was consequence of His Revelation, although it is undeniable that subsequent events have been consistent with what He prophesied. This correspondence provides yet another reason for carefully examining the Faith He founded.

His prophecies are mostly contained in the Tablets in which He proclaimed His Mission and particularly in those addressed to kings and to divines. For example, to kings generally Bahá'u'lláh wrote:

"If ye pay no heed unto the counsels which, in peerless and unequivocal language, we have revealed in this Tablet, Divine chastisement shall assail you from every direction, and the sentence of His justice shall be pronounced against you." [12]

This Tablet was revealed in the 1860's. From then on, kings have gradually lost their power and most of them their thrones as well. The process is not irreversible, but temporarily, at least, kings are playing a decreasing part in managing the world's affairs.

Napoleon III of France

The most powerful monarch at the time Bahá'u'lláh proclaimed His Message was Napoleon III of France. To him Bahá'u'lláh wrote two Tablets—the first meek in tone to test the sincerity of the Emperor, who did not answer it and is reported to have treated it with scorn; the second, sent in 1868, of a different kind altogether. It was translated into French and transmitted to the Emperor by the French resident in 'Akká. In it occurred the following:

"Hadst thou been sincere in thy words, thou wouldst not have cast behind thy back the Book of God [i.e. the previous Tablet], when it was sent unto thee by Him Who is the Almighty, the All-Wise. We have proved thee through it, and found thee other than that which thou didst profess. Arise, and make amends for that which escaped thee. . . . For what thou hast done, thy kingdom shall be thrown into confusion, and thine empire shall pass from thine hands, as a punishment for that which thou hast wrought. Then wilt thou know how thou hast plainly erred. Commotions shall seize all the people in that land, unless thou arisest to help this Cause, and followest Him Who is the Spirit of God (Jesus) in this, the straight Path. Hath thy pomp made thee proud? By My Life! It shall not endure, nay, it shall soon pass

away, unless thou holdest fast by this firm cord. We see abasement hastening after thee, while thou art of the heedless. "[13]

Two years later, in 1870, the French were unexpectedly defeated by the Prussians. Napoleon Ill's army surrendered in the greatest capitulation of modem times, he himself was taken prisoner and exiled, a Republic was formed, to be followed by civil war more terrible than the Franco-Prussian War itself. France fell into confusion. Napoleon's enemy, William I, was proclaimed German Emperor in the Palace of Versailles. The whole world wondered at the sudden collapse of an Empire considered the strongest of its day, whose fall fulfilled to the letter the prophecy of Bahá'u'lláh.

William I of Germany

Addressing William I of Germany, the conqueror of Napoleon III, Bahá'u'lláh wrote in the *Kitáb-i-Aqdas:*

"Do thou remember the one whose power transcended thy power (Napoleon III), and whose station excelled thy station. Where is he? Whither are gone the things he possessed? Take warning, and be not of them that are fast asleep." [14]

In the same Book He also wrote:

"O banks of the Rhine! We have seen you covered with gore, inasmuch as the swords of retribution were drawn against you; and you shall have another turn. And we hear the lamentations of Berlin, though she be today in conspicuous glory." [15]

These prophecies and warnings have been amply justified by the outcome of the two world wars that Germany has lost. William I's grandson was defeated and abdicated. A republic was established whose government had no option but to acquiesce in a Peace Treaty of oppressive severity. A dictatorship, whose doctrines ran counter to all that is best in man, replaced it, leading inevitably to a second war and a second defeat. This time German cities were laid low by heavy bombing. Germany was split into four parts, and Berlin, no longer a capital city, was divided into zones controlled by disagreeing foreign powers.

Alexander II of Russia

Alexander II of Russia was three times warned by Bahá'u'lláh:

> *"Beware lest thy desire deter thee from turning towards the face of thy Lord...Beware, lest thou barter away this sublime station...beware lest thy sovereignty withhold thee from Him Who is the Supreme Sovereign."*[16]

He initiated a reactionary policy, which his successors executed with even greater severity than his own, until suppressed discontent ultimately burst forth as revolution. Civil war; disease and starvation followed; a thoroughgoing materialism enveloped Russia; the Czar and most of his nobles were murdered. Thereafter the people of Russia suffered long continued deprivation to build up industrial capital; part of which was destroyed during the war fought on Russian soil in the 1940'S and had to be rebuilt at the cost of further deprivation.

Francis Joseph of Austria-Hungary

In the *Kitáb-i-Aqdas*, Bahá'u'lláh chided Francis Joseph for having failed to investigate His Cause:

> *"Thou passed Him by, and enquired not about Him... We have been with thee at all times, and found thee clinging unto the Branch and heedless of the Root."*[17]

The empire of the Hapsburgs has since disintegrated. All that remains of the once formidable Holy Roman Empire is a small state, the population of whose capital city, Vienna, is entirely disproportionate to the size of the country. Francis Joseph himself experienced many misfortunes; his brother Maximilian was shot in Mexico; the Crown Prince Rudolph perished in a dishonourable affair; the Empress was assassinated; the Archduke Francis Ferdinand and his wife were murdered in Serajevo, giving rise to one of the most destructive and wide-spread wars the world has known.

'Abdu'l-'Aziz of Turkey

To Sultan 'Abdu'l-'Aziz Bahá'u'lláh wrote:

> *"Bring thyself to account ere thou art summoned to a reckoning."* [18]

And in another place, more specifically:

> *"Soon will He seize you in His wrathful anger, and sedition will be stirred up in your midst, and your dominions will be disrupted. Then will ye bewail and lament, and will find none to help or succour you... Several times calamities have overtaken you, and yet ye failed utterly to take heed... Ere long will ye behold that which hath been sent down from the Pen of My Command."* [19]

It was during the reign of 'Abdu'l-'Aziz that Bahá'u'lláh revealed His Message. Exiled to domains of the Sultan, He was thrice moved by Imperial Decree from place to place within those domains, reaching finally the notorious prison city of 'Akká whose governors received instructions about Him oppressive in their severity. His nephew 'Abdu'l-Hamid II oppressed 'Abdu'l-Bahá similarly.

Imperial Turkey, which under 'Abdu'l-Hamid I had been accepted by the European nations and which had been on the winning side in the Crimean War, fell under 'Abdu'l-'Aziz into a swift decline. He was finally deposed by a palace revolution, denounced as incapable, and assassinated. His imbecile successor was deposed after three months.

During the reign of the next Sultan, the much hated 'Abdu'l-Hamid II, the Turkish Empire began to disintegrate; Serbia,

Montenegro, Rumania, Bulgaria, became independent: Bosnia and Herzegovina were ceded to Austria; the French occupied Tunis, the British Cyprus and Egypt. Eventually hatred of 'Abdu'l-Hamid grew so intense that he was forced to abdicate.

After the 1914-18 war, the Turkish Empire was broken up and Turkey reduced to a minor Asiatic state with no more than a token holding in Europe. Constantinople lost its glory, thus fulfilling another of Bahá'u'lláh's prophecies:

> *"Hath, thine outward splendour made thee vainglorious? By Him who is the Lord of mankind! It shall soon perish, and thy daughters, and thy widows, and all the hundreds that dwell within thee shall lament."*[20]

Once the capital of the most powerful Empire in the world, Constantinople is now no more than a provincial city in a state no longer accounted one of the Great Powers.

Nasiri'd-Din Shah of Iran

Nasiri'd-Din Sháh of Írán, sovereign of Írán in the time of Bahá'u'lláh, instigated at the behest of the Muslim divines the martyrdom of the Báb, the banishment of Bahá'u'lláh, and the persecution of the Bahá'ís. Subsequently his Minister's scheming was instrumental in persuading the Sultan to send Bahá'u'lláh from Baghdád to Constantinople, from Constantinople to Adrianople, and from Adrianople to 'Akká.

Bahá'u'lláh's Tablet to *Nasiri'd-Din Sháh of Írán*, the bearer of which was immediately seized and cruelly martyred, was gentle in tone with many such passages as:

> *"O would that thou wouldst permit Me, O Sháh, to send unto thee that which would cheer the eyes, and tranquillise the souls, and persuade every fair-minded person that with Him is the knowledge of the Book."*[21]

Bahá'u'lláh made no specific prophecy about *Nasiri'd-Din*

Sháh of Írán, possibly to avoid bringing further persecution upon the suffering Íránian Bahá'ís: but the Báb earlier had written:

> _"I swear by God, O Sháh! If thou showest enmity unto Him Who is His Remembrance, God will, on the Day of Resurrection, condemn thee, before the kings, unto hellfire, and thou shall not, in very truth, find on that day any helper except God, the Exalted."_[22]

The Qajar dynasty, of which Nasiri'd-Din Sháh was a member, brought so many troubles to Persia that the particular troubles of the reign of Nasiri'd-Din Sháh and his successors do not stand out so distinctly as do the events reported earlier in this chapter. Chaos, bankruptcy and oppression enveloped the country. He himself was assassinated on the eve of a jubilee which was to inaugurate a new era. His successor was forced to sign a constitution limiting his own powers, and the next two Sháh were deposed. It is noteworthy that grandsons of both Sultan 'Abdu'l-'Aziz and of Nasiri'd-Din Sháh have turned for help to the World Centre of the Faith of Bahá'u'lláh, which offered personal financial assistance to the first and firmly refused political help to the second, as to any other political intriguer.

Pope Pius IX

At the time of Bahá'u'lláh the Pope was a temporal monarch as well as a religious leader. To him Bahá'u'lláh wrote:

> _"Beware lest any name debar thee from God, the creator of earth and heaven. Leave thou the world behind thee, and turn towards thy Lord, through whom the whole earth hath been illumined. ... Dwellest thou in palaces whilst He Who is the King of Revelation liveth in the most desolate of' abodes? Leave them unto such as desire them, and set thy face with joy and delight towards the kingdom."_[23]

The Pope's domain had long been decreasing in size and power.

William I of Germany

Napoleon III of France

'Abdu'l-'Azíz of Turkey

**Some of the Kings and Rulers
addressed by Bahá'u'lláh.**

*Francis Joseph of
Austria-Hungary*

Náṣiri'd-Dín Sháh of Írán

Pope Pius IX

In 1870 it was finally extinguished; even Rome ceased to be under his rule. The decay of the Pope's temporal authority is now complete, but his religious authority decays still, along with the institutions of other religious sects.

Of Divines generally

Bahá'u'lláh has written:

> "*From two ranks amongst men power hath been seized: kings and ecclesiastics.*"[24]

That power has been seized from kings has been demonstrated above; divines also are losing their power. Bahá'ís expect the dignity, although not the power, of kingship eventually to be restored,* but the day of the divines has gone forever. The Bahá'í Faith has no divines. No Bahá'í, other than the Guardian, has the right to interpret Bahá'í writings authoritatively; none has the right to act as intermediary between man and the Holy Spirit. This is one of the signs that the capacity of men in this age is greater than in former ages.

Bahá'u'lláh addressed a number of Tablets to the divines of former religions, to whom He referred in many of His general writings also. He praises the ones who are sincere in their obedience to God.

> "*Those divines... who are truly adorned with the ornament of knowledge and of a goodly character are, verily, as a head to the body of the world, and as eyes to the nations. The guidance of men hath, at all times, been and is dependent upon these blessed souls.*"[25]

But they are few. Most divines lead the people of their religion deeper into error; again and again Bahá'u'lláh condemns them:

> "*Leaders of religion, in every age, have hindered their people from attaining the shores of eternal salvation, inasmuch as they held the reins of authority in their*

---

* See pages 88-89.

mighty grasp. Some for the lust of leadership, others through want of knowledge and understanding, have been the cause of the deprivation of the people. By their sanction and authority, every Prophet of God hath drunk from the chalice of sacrifice, and winged His flight unto the heights of glory. What unspeakable cruelties they that have occupied the seats of authority and learning have inflicted upon the true Monarchs of the world, those Gems of Divine virtue! Content with a transitory dominion, they have deprived themselves of an everlasting sovereignty. "[26]

More forcefully still He says:

"Not one Prophet of God was made manifest Who did not fall a victim to the relentless hate, to the denunciation, denial and execration of the clerics of His day! Woe unto them for the iniquities their hands have formerly wrought! Woe unto them for what they are now doing! What veils of glory more grievous than these embodiments of error! By the righteousness of God! To pierce such veils is the mightiest of all acts, and to rend them asunder the most meritorious of all deeds!" [27]

And He pungently comments:

"The foolish divines have laid aside the Book of God, and are occupied with that which they themselves have fashioned. The Ocean of Knowledge is revealed, and the shrill of the Pen of the most High is raised, and yet they, even as earthworms, are afflicted with the clay of their fancies and imaginings. They are exalted by reason of their relationship to the one true God, and yet they have turned aside from Him! Because of Him have they become famous, and yet they are shut off as by a veil from Him." [28]

Decline of Muslim Institutions

Addressing Muslim Divines, Bahá'u'lláh said:

> *"O concourse of divines! Because of you the people were abased, and the banner of Islám was hauled down, and its mighty throne subverted."*[28]

Since that dire condemnation by Bahá'u'lláh the fortunes of Islám have disintegrated. The Caliphate collapsed and the power of Shi'ih and Sunni divines steadily declined. The corruption of this once great faith led inevitably to the resurgence of strict fundamentalism and today, throughout the Middle East, the faith of Muḥammad is torn by internecine disputes. In Bahá'u'lláh's homeland, Írán, the Shi'ih clergy now wield unconscionable power as leaders of the 'Islámic Republic'. Their tyrannical behaviour has, however, so denigrated the name of Islám that, to many observers, it has become synonymous with blind fanaticism. Regretably, a dark reputation now overshadows the glorious contributions which. Islám has made to human civilisation.

Decline of Christian Institutions

To Christian Divines, Bahá'u'lláh addressed such words as these:

> *"O Concourse of bishops! Ye are the stars of the heaven of My knowledge. My mercy desireth not that ye should fall upon the earth. My justice, however, declareth 'This is that which the Son (Jesus) hath decreed.' And whatsoever hath proceeded out of His blameless, His truthspeaking, trustworthy mouth, can never be altered."*[30]

The decline of Christian institutions is as evident as the decline of Islám. In many countries, empty churches and a disregard of clerical authority speak volubly of their fall. The temporal power of the Pope has vanished; Church and State have been separated in France; the Greek Orthodox Church in Soviet countries has become a shadow of its former self; the dismemberment or one of the most powerful Catholic nations, Austria-Hungary, the opposition to Christian Missions in many countries overseas, and the general tendency towards agnosticism and atheism that has swept Europe, all confirm the decline.

Other Religions

To the divines of other religions also Bahá'u'lláh addressed Himself. To the Jews He proclaims:

> *"The Most Great Law is come, and the Ancient Beauty ruleth upon the throne of David. Thus hath My pen spoken that which the histories of bygone ages have related."* [31]

An these religions share in the general decline, from which only the Bahá'í Faith is free.

Rise of the Bahá'í Faith

That faith has progressed without pause from strength to strength since its foundation. Already it has encircled the earth; the number of localities in which there are Bahá'ís increases yearly and its institutions, still embryonic, continually gather strength. The striking contrast between the declining political and religious institutions of former days and the vital, blossoming institutions of the Bahá'í Faith must make all thoughtful men ponder.

This still very young religion has not yet grown sufficiently to make an easily discernible mark on the world; its counsels are not yet sought in world affairs, But its record is such as to give a foretaste of what is to come. It has energetic life, whose flowering is clearly visible to all who examine its history and development. It's Administrative Order* steadily increases in scope and complexity. Its name becomes increasingly known. Its endowments multiply. Civil authorities become better acquainted with it yearly.

The same vitality that runs through its institutions is evident also in its teachings. These include both the eternal truths present in all religions and specific truths particularly suited to the needs of

---

* See Chapter XV.

our own age and the capacity of our own time. Those teachings of Bahá'u'lláh that repeat teachings given in former ages are restated with a majestic beauty that only a Manifestation of God could provide. They are not mere human re-affirmations of basic truths, but restatements which carry the full, indefinable flavour of the Word of God; as can be seen from the quotations from Bahá'í Writings in this book. Pondering such restatements, perhaps even more than pondering those teachings which are new in this age, brings appreciation of the power that is at once an explanation and a guarantee of the remarkable effect they produce.

Of the teachings new to religion, many have already been adopted by progressive people without knowledge of the Source of their power. Others have not yet been put into effect although many people see them to be reasonable. A few run counter to the opinion of most of humanity. These should be assessed in their context; the man who judges all opinions by whether they agree superficially with the views he already holds will certainly reject them; others may consider it advisable to suspensed judgment until they are ready fully to assess the teachings of Bahá'u'lláh.

If He is a Manifestation of God, His teachings are true, whether we agree with them or not. Should the whole world arise against Him, as virtually it did, His teachings would still be true. Failure of current opinion to connect them would demonstrate only the imperfection of current opinion; fashionable opinions have been wrong before and can be wrong again. The crucial question for each individual is whether to accept the claim Bahá'u'lláh makes that He is a Manifestation of God, for when this has been accepted all else follows. So great a claim can best be assessed by considering the history and teachings of His Faith as a whole.

CHAPTER IV

The Oneness of Mankind

Unity

The central theme of the teaching of Bahá'u'lláh is unity and particularly the oneness of mankind. Bahá'u'lláh says:

> *"The utterance of God is a lamp, whose light is these words: Ye are the fruits of one tree, and the leaves of one branch. Deal ye one with another with the utmost love and harmony, with friendliness and fellowship. He Who is the Day Star of Truth beareth me witness! So powerful is the light of unity that it can illuminate the whole earth. The one true God, He Who knoweth all things, Himself testifieth to the truth of these words."[1]*

In previous Dispensations the brotherhood of man has continually been preached: Malachi, in the Dispensation of Moses, asked, 'Have we not all one Father?',[2] and Jesus said 'All ye are brethren. . . for one is your Father which is in heaven':[3] in the Qur'an, Muḥammad asserts: 'Mankind was but one people';[4] but these were incidental references only. The stress in past ages was on other things, as it had to be when one-half of mankind did not even know the other half existed. The time for the unification of mankind had not then come, whereas now unity is the pivot of human progress.

'Abdu'l-Bahá enlarges in one of His Tablets upon this difference between our age and those gone by. He shows that world unity has become possible and indicates some of its components:

> *"In cycles gone by, though harmony was established, yet owing to the absence of means, the unity of mankind*

could not have been achieved. Continents remained widely divided, nay, even among the peoples of one and the same continent association and interchange of thought were wellnigh impossible. Consequently intercourse, understanding and unity amongst all the peoples and kindreds of the earth were unattainable. In this day, however, means of communication have multiplied, and the five continents of the earth have virtually merged into one.... In like manner all the members of the human family, whether peoples or governments, cities or villages, have become increasingly interdependent. For none is self-sufficiency any longer possible, inasmuch as political ties unite all peoples and nations, and the bonds of trade and industry, of agriculture and education, are being strengthened every day. Hence the unity of all mankind can in this day be achieved. Verily this is none other than one of the wonders of ihis wondrous age, this glorious century. Of this past ages have been deprived, for this century—the century of light—has been endowed with unique and unprecedented glory, power and illumination. Hence the miraculous unfolding of a fresh marvel every day. Eventually it will be seen how bright its candles will burn in the assemblage of man.

"Behold how its light is now dawning upon the world's darkened horizon. The first candle is unity in the political realm, the early glimmerings of which can now be discerned. The second candle is unity of thought in world undertakings, the consummation of which will ere long be witnessed. The third candle is unity in freedom which will surely come to pass. The fourth candle is unity in religion which is the corner-stone of the foundation itself, and which, by the power of God, will be revealed in all its splendour. The fifth candle is

the unity of nations—a unity which in this century will be securely established, causing all the peoples of the world to regard themselves as citizens of one common fatherland. The sixth candle is unity of races, making of all that dwell on earth peoples and kindred's of one race. The seventh candle is unity of language, i.e., the choice of a universal tongue in which all peoples will be instructed and converse. Each and everyone of these will inevitably come to pass, inasmuch as the power of the Kingdom of God will aid and assist in their realisation." [5]

Love for Mankind

The principle of the oneness of mankind is stressed again and again in the Holy Writings of the Bahá'í Faith, with many picturesque illustrations.

"The Tabernacle of unity hath been raised; regard ye not one another as strangers. Ye are the fruits of one tree, and the leaves of one branch's." [6]

"They are the waves of one sea, the drops of one river, the stars of one heaven, the rays of one sun, the trees of one orchard, the flowers of one garden." [7]

'Abdu'l-Bahá, in His *Will and Testament*, urged the Bahá'ís to make their deeds express this oneness:

"In this sacred Dispensation, conflict and contention are in no wise permitted. Every aggressor deprives himself of God's grace. It is incumbent upon everyone to show the utmost love, rectitude of conduct, straightforwardness and sincere kindliness unto all the peoples and kindreds of the world, be they friends or strangers. So intense must be the spirit of love and lovingkindness, that the stranger may find himself a friend, the enemy a true brother, no difference whatsoever existing between them. For universality is

*of God and all limitations earthly. Thus man must strive
that his reality may manifest virtues and perfections,
the light whereof may shine upon everyone. The light
of the sun shineth upon all the world and the merciful
showers of Divine Providence fall upon all peoples.
The vivifying breeze reviveth every living creature and
all beings endued with life obtain their share and
portion at His heavenly board. In like manner, the
affections and loving kindness of the servants of the
One True God must be bounti fully and universally
extended to all mankind. Regarding this, restrictions
and limitations are in no wise permitted.*"[8]

It is not easy always to love one's fellow-men; human
imperfection sometimes arouses in us feelings that conflict with
love. Moreover, our own imperfection may cause us to recoil from
what ought to attract us. Such obstacles to universal love vanish if
we look upon all we meet as embodiments of spiritual qualities
emanating from God. Therefore 'Abdu'l-Bahá tells us:

*"When you love a member of your family or a
compatriot, let it be with a ray of the Infinite Love, Let
it be in God, and for God! Wherever you find the
attributes of God love that person, whether he be of
your family or of another. Shed the light of a boundless
love on every human being whom you meet, whether of
your country, your race, your political party, or of any
other nation, colour or shade of political opinion.*"[9]

Such boundless love enables us to appreciate the truth of
'Abdu'l-Bahá's statement:

*"The only difference between members of the human
family is that of degree. Some are like children who are
ignorant, and must be educated until they arrive at
maturity, some are like the sick and must be treated
with tenderness and care. None are bad or evil! We*

must not feel repelled by these poor children. We must treat them with great kindness, teaching the ignorant and tenderly nursing the sick."[10]

Diversity in Unity

Viewed like this, the diversity of the human race is seen to be one of its glories. Its variety enchants, as does a garden of varied flowers. Unity does not require uniformity. Just as the varied limbs and members of the human body are co-ordinated and united by the soul of man, so the varied peoples of the world can be co-ordinated arid united by the power of God. 'Abdu'l-Bahá elaborates these ideas in one of His Tablets:

"Consider the flowers of a garden. Though differing in kind, colour, form and shape, yet, inasmuch as they are refreshed by the waters of one spring, revived by the breath of one wind, invigorated by the rays of one sun, this diversity increaseth their charm, and addeth unto their beauty, How unpleasing to the eye if all the flowers and plants, the leaves and blossoms, the fruits, the branches and the trees of that garden were all of the same shape and colour! Diversity of hues, form and shape, enricheth and adorneth the garden, and heighteneth the effect thereof. In like manner, when divers shades of thought, temperament and character are brought together under the power of one central agency, the beauty and glory of human perfection will be revealed and made manifest. Naught but the celestial potency of the Word of God, which ruleth and transcendeth the realities of all things, is capable of harmonising the divergent thoughts, sentiments, ideas and convictions of the children of men."[11]

Overcoming Prejudices

Formerly these differences gave rise to prejudices of race, colour, class, creed and nation, which sowed the seed of strife. 'Abdu'l-Bahá. wrote in His Tablet to the Central Organisation for a Durable Peace held at The Hague in 1919:

> *"As long as these prejudices prevail, the world of humanity will not have rest. For a period of 6,000 years history informs us about the world of humanity. During these 6,000 years the world of humanity has not been free from war, strife, murder and bloodthirstiness. In every period war has been waged in one country or another and that war was due to either religious prejudice, racial prejudice, political prejudice or patriotic prejudice. It has therefore been ascertained and proved that all prejudices are destructive of the human edifice. As long as these prejudices persist, the struggle for existence must remain dominant, and bloodthirstiness and rapacity continue. Therefore, even as was the case in the past, the world of humanity cannot be saved from the darkness of nature and cannot attain illumination except through the abandonment of prejudices and the acquisition of the morals of the Kingdom."*[12]

In this age prejudice is to prevail no longer. The power released by the Revelation of Bahá'u'lláh will be sufficient to eliminate all that has divided men and kept them apart. Bahá'u'lláh proclaims:

> *"O ye that dwell on earth! The distinguishing feature that marketh the pre-eminent character of this Supreme Revelation consisteth in that We have, on the one hand, blotted out from the pages of God's holy Book whatsoever hath been the cause of strife, of malice and mischief amongst the children of men, and have, on the other, laid down the essential prerequisites of concord, of understanding, of complete and enduring unity. Well is it with them that keep My statutes."*[13]

Gradually men are realising the folly and absurdity of ancient prejudices. They are awakening to the knowledge that the oneness of mankind requires them to abandon all such barriers to unity. One by one the prejudices are being exposed for what they are—fantasies which the insecure of spirit concoct to bolster their self-esteem by disparaging others.

The World One Country

Of all the prejudices which hold men apart, the most potent in recent times has been that of nation. Few people wholly evade its grasp. Although the extreme form, dear to the hearts of dictators, has been widely discredited, too many still regard as paramount the interests of those belonging to the same nation as themselves.

To do so is to deny the oneness of mankind. A sane and moderate patriotism is harmless enough, or even beneficial in encouraging local public spirit, but such patriotism must always be subordinate to the wider loyalty to mankind, which is the foundation of world unity. Bahá'u'lláh states categorically:

> *"The earth is but one country and mankind its citizens."*[14]

Elsewhere He says:

> *"Of old it hath been revealed: 'Love of one's country is an element of the Faith of God.' The Tongue of Grandeur hath, however, in the day of His manifestation proclaimed: 'It is not his to boast who loveth his country, but it is his who loveth the world.' Through the power released by these exalted words He hath lent a fresh impulse, and set a new direction, to the birds of men's hearts, and hath obliterated every trace of restriction and limitation from God's holy Book."*[15]

'Abdu'l-Bahá explains in greater detail:

> *"As to the patriotic prejudice, this is also due to absolute ignorance, for the surface of the earth is one native land. Everyone can live in any spot on the terrestrial globe.... These boundaries and outlets have been*

71

devised by man. In the creation, such boundaries and outlets were not assigned. Europe is one continent, Asia is one continent, Africa is one continent, Australia is one continent, but some of the souls, from personal motives and selfish interests, have divided each one of these continents and considered a certain part as their own country. God has set up no frontier between France and Germany; they are continuous. Yea, in the first centuries, selfish souls, for the promotion of their own interests, have assigned boundaries and outlets and have, day by day, attached more importance to these, until this led to intense enmity, bloodshed and rapacity in subsequent centuries. In the same way, this will continue indefinitely and if this conception of patriotism remains limited within a certain circle, it will be the primary cause of the world's destruction. No wise and just person will acknowledge these imaginary distinctions. Every limited area which we call our native country we regard as our motherland, whereas the terrestrial globe is the motherland of all, and not any restricted area. In short, for a few days we live on this earth and eventually we are buried in it; it is our eternal tomb. Is it worth while that we should engage in bloodshed and tear one another to pieces for this eternal tomb? Nay, far from it, neither is God pleased with such conduct nor would any sane man approve of it."[16]

A natural corollary is that all should devote themselves to the interests of mankind rather than to the interests of any limited section of it. Bahá'u'lláh states:

"That one indeed is a man who, today, dedicateth himself to the service of the entire human race. The Great Being saith: Blessed and happy is he that ariseth to promote the best interests of the peoples and kindreds of the earth."[17]

Rulers, as well as peoples, should try to promote the wellbeing of the whole of mankind.* Were they to do this, the world's sickness would quickly be healed. Bahá'u'lláh proclaims:

"If the rulers and kings of the earth, the symbols of the power of God, exalted be His glory, arise and resolve to dedicate themselves to whatever will promote the highest interests of the whole of humanity, the reign of justice will assuredly be established amongst the children of men, and the effulgence of its light will envelop the whole earth." [18]

But rulers are unlikely for a long, long time to obey this behest. They are as unskilled physicians, powerless to diagnose the sickness or to prescribe its cure. Until the advice of the True Physician is followed, the world's sickness will not be healed.

Race and Colour Prejudice
One of the most dangerous and longest lived of prejudices is that arising from difference of race or skin colour. It is exhibited flagrantly by some of the white-skinned dominant minority; but those whose skin is black, yellow, or brown are not wholly free from it either. Already it threatens civil strife in some parts of the world, and if unchecked it will undoubtedly be responsible for much bloodshed. Bahá'u'lláh exhorts mankind to reject this prejudice especially:

"O ye discerning ones! Verily the words which have descended from the heaven of the Will of God are the source of unity and harmony for the world. Close your eyes to racial differences, and welcome all with the light of oneness." [19]

'Abdu'l-Bahá says still more explicitly:

"God maketh no distinction between the white and the black. If the hearts are pure both are acceptable unto

* See page 89.

Him. God is no respecter of persons on account of either colour or race. All colours are acceptable unto Him, be they white, black or yellow. Inasmuch as all were created in the image of God, we must bring ourselves to realise that all embody divine possibilities."[20]

For some, it is particularly difficult to realise that skin colour does not connote superiority or inferiority of spirit. Reasons are given for presuming one's own race better than any other, which carry conviction until an objective examination of the scientific evidence show them to be false. The evidence of scientific research weighs heavily against skin colour being associated with either mental or spiritual superiority. Nevertheless, since man is not governed by reason alone, effort is needed to overcome this deep-seated prejudice. 'Abdu'l-Bahá exhorted both white and coloured races in the United States:

"Strive earnestly and put forth your greatest endeavour toward the accomplishment of this fellowship and the cementing of this bond of brotherhood between you. Such an attainment is not possible without will and effort on the part of each; from one, expressions of gratitude and appreciation; from the other, kindliness and recognition of equality. Each one should endeavour to develop and assist the other toward mutual advancement."[21]

When racial prejudice has been overcome, no difference between the races of mankind is felt. True Bahá'ís are no more and no less conscious that someone comes from another continent than that he comes from another town. An all-embracing love causes them to *"consort with all men... in a spirit of friendliness and fellowship."*[22]

Intermarriage of the races, far from being frowned upon, is warmly approved because it smooths the path to racial harmony.*

---

* But consent of parents is necessary. See page 323-24.

Unity of East and West

Some differences of custom and upbringing are sufficiently marked for goodwill to be needed to achieve harmony. People from the East and people from the West have backgrounds so different that they need to guard against misunderstanding each other. 'Abdu'l-Bahá exhorted those who came to hear Him in Paris:

"Oh, you of the Western nations, be kind to those who come from the Eastern world to sojourn among you. Forget your conventionality when you speak with them; they are not accustomed to it. To Eastern peoples this demeanour seems cold, unfriendly. Rather let your manner be sympathetic. Let it be seen that you are filled with universal love. When you meet a Persian, or any other stranger, speak to him as to a friend; if he seems lonely, try to help him, give him of your willing service; if he be sad, console him, if poor succour him, if oppressed rescue him, if in misery comfort him. In doing so you will manifest that not in words only, but in deed and in truth, you think of all men as your brothers."[23]

To those from the East, Westerners sometimes seem irreverent because they show their reverence less openly than Easterners. Hospitality and formal courtesy are also stressed more in the East than the West. On the other hand, some of the virtues which have enabled the West to achieve its great material progress receive scant attention in the East. Both East and West can learn from the other's virtues. Hence 'Abdu'l-Bahá said:

"The East and West must unite to give to each other what is lacking. This union will bring about a true civilisation, where the spiritual is expressed and carried out in the material."[24]

The Coming of Age of Mankind

There are some who think it impossible for mankind to be united, basing their belief either on the presumed unalterable selfishness of man, or on the deep-seated prejudices which have so far held men apart. To render selfish people unselfish and to disperse prejudice are indeed beyond human ability, but God is competent to accomplish both. He alone, through His Messengers, can change hearts, turn dross into gold, and banish from the human spirit *"whatsoever hath been the cause of strife, of malice and mischief amongst the children of men."*[25]

Whenever a Manifestation of God brings new life to humanity, those who recognise Him are united by a band strong enough to resist the dispersive forces of prejudice and selfishness. The early Christians were of no one country or ancestry, but after the fall of the Roman Empire only such unity as remained among Christians held together the peoples of Europe. Later, Muslim unity made it possible for a Muslim to travel from Spain to India among men who would treat him as their brother. The history of those times and what little is known of the early followers of other Messengers are clear evidence of the power of the Word of God to unite mankind.

Likewise, the Bahá'í Community is evidence that the Word of God is again exerting a unifying influence. Already the Community includes white, black, brown and yellow races from more than 350 countries and significant territories, from every religious background and from every class. At each big Bahá'í Conference, many of these diverse groups are represented and the spirit of unity generated is felt by Bahá'ís and non Bahá'ís alike.

The unity which exists among Bahá'ís resembles, but is stronger than, that of the early Christians and the early Muslims; for the elements united are more diverse. We live in a peerless age when, for the first time in the history of the human race, mankind can be recognised as one. According to Bahá'u'lláh, the Divine Plan of Creation requires the process of unification to culminate at this stage in human history; all that has gone before has been leading to the present age. in which the oneness of mankind is to be realised in world unity The family, the tribe, the city state, the nation has each played its unifying part in man's development. Each form of organisation was appropriate to a particular phase of this, but none suits his condition now. We have entered a new era, in which the unification of mankind can be adequately organised only by a world state.

The achievement of world-wide unity is an event of unsurpassed significance in human history. No event of former ages can compare with it. It marks the coming of age of the human race, and none who believes in a merciful God can surely suppose that He would leave men to their own poor devices at so important a time. God has released through Bahá'u'lláh the forces necessary to unite mankind, to weld it together and to set it in the path to its ultimate goal of being *"as one soul and one body."*[26]

The limbs and members of the human body work together in perfect concord as a single unit; in the aeons ahead, mankind must aim at developing a similar concord between individuals, which will enable all to progress together along the path of God as harmoniously and effectively as though they were the limbs and members of the body of mankind. *"Be ye as the fingers of one hand, the members of one body,"*[27] said Bahá'u'lláh to His followers. A most important step towards this ultimate goal is the unification of mankind in the present age.

Accordingly, the spirit of unity released by Bahá'u'lláh is more intense than any released in former ages. Its first fruits are visible in the Bahá'í Community today; tomorrow its spiritual power will overwhelm mankind. More progress towards unity has been made in the last hundred years than was conceivable a hundred years ago. The flame of each of the seven candles mentioned by 'Abdu'l-Bahá* is burning brightly. The minds of men are receptive. The spirit of unity is around us, more noticeable because the resistance offered by racialism, nationalism and materialism is causing so much suffering. As in the past the power of unity has always been triumphant, as family feuds gave way to tribal loyalty and city pride became immersed in pride of nation, so in this age the spirit of unity is causing loyalty to mankind gradually to overcome all narrower allegiances.

---

* See page 66.

World unity is willed by God in this age and nothing human beings can do will prevent it. The hearts of men are changing: deep-rooted, age-long prejudices are vanishing; the maturity of mankind is at hand. 'Abdu'l-Bahá, echoing Bahá'u'lláh proclaims the change which is taking place in the spirit of mankind:

"All created things have their degree or stage of maturity. The period of maturity in the life of a tree is the time of its fruit bearing.... The animal attains a stage of full growth and completeness and in the human kingdom man reaches his maturity when the light of his intelligence attains its greatest power and development. ... Similarly there are periods and stages in the collective life of humanity. At one time it was passing through its stage of childhood, at another its period of youth, but now it has entered its long-predicted phase of maturity, the evidences of which are everywhere apparent.... That which was applicable to human needs during the early history of the race can neither meet nor satisfy the demands of this day, this period of newness and consummation. Humanity has emerged from its former state of limitation and preliminary training. Man must now become imbued with new virtues and powers, new moral standards, new capacities. New bounties, perfect bestowals, are awaiting and already descending upon him. The gifts and blessings of the period of youth, although timely and sufficient during the adolescence of mankind, are now incapable of meeting the requirements of its maturity."[28]

At such a time, with such events happening and clearly visible to all, how can anyone say it is impossible for mankind to be united?

CHAPTER V

World Unity

Disintegration of the Old Order

In Chapter III it was shown that kings and divines have brought
about their own downfall by turning aside from the spirit of the new
age. Mankind as a whole shares the rejection and its penalties.

Resistance to the spirit of the new age is causing great suffering.
Bahá'u'lláh bewailed the plight of mankind:

*"Witness how the world is being afflicted with a fresh
calamity every day. Its tribulation is continually
deepening. From the moment the Suriy-i-Ra'is (Tablet
to Ra'is) was revealed until the present day, neithet hath
the world been tranquillised, nor have the hearts of its
peoples been at rest. At one time it hath been agitated
by contentions and disputes, at another it hath been
convulsed by wars, and fallen a victim to inveterate
diseases. Its sickness is approaching the stage of utter
hopelessness, inasmuch as the true Physician is
debarred from administering the remedy, whilst unskilled
practitioners are regarded with favour, and are
accorded full freedom to act."*[1]

So far has mankind strayed from the path of God that, only
through tribulation can it be led back again. At a time when Western
nations seemed set firmly towards ever-increasing prosperity,
Bahá'u'lláh wrote:

*"The world is in travail, and its agitation waxeth day
by day. Its face is turned towards waywardness and
unbelief. Such shall be its plight, that to disclose it now*

*would not be meet and seemly. Its perversity will long
continue. And when the appointed hour is come, there
shall suddenly appear that which shall cause the limbs
of mankind to quake. Then, and only then, will the
Divine Standard be unfurled, and the Nightingale of
Paradise warble its melody."*[2]

Jesus, in His Day, explained that you cannot put new wine into
old bottles, for the old bottles will burst, We are now witnessing the
bursting of old bottles unfitted to contain the wine of the new
Revelation. Bahá'u'lláh explains:

*"The world's equilibrium hath been upset through the
vibrating influence of this most great, this new World
Order. Mankind's ordered life hath been revolutionised
through the agency of this unique, this wondrous
System—the like of which mortal eyes have never
witnessed."*[3]

Two processes are proceeding simultaneously, disintegration
of the old order as its inefficacy under current conditions becomes
ever more marked, and the creation of a new order, still embryonic,
but destined to constitute eventually the pattern and the nucleus of
a future world government.

The bankruptcy of the order is visible both in the impotence of
statesmanship to harmonise conflicting views of national
governments or provide a sure basis for international co-operation,
and in the decline of ecclesiastical institutions. Fear stalks humanity,
a fear only too well-grounded since it stems from growing recognition
of a state of affairs it is too late to alter without suffering.

Religion, which formerly was the chief source of order in the
world, is now unable to deter men from foolishness and worse than
foolishness. The canker of materialism has long been eating into
the heart of East and West alike. Racialism and nationalism progress
beside lawlessness, drunkenness, and sexual immorality. The sins
of the people, as well as those of their rulers, call down the wrath of
heaven, without which but few in our day are ready to attain

salvation. Bahá'u'lláh pointed unequivocally to the consequences of irreligion:

> *"Religion is a radiant light and an impregnable stronghold for the protection and welfare of the peoples of the world, for the fear of God impelleth man to hold fast to that which is good, and shun all evil. Should the lamp of religion be obscured, chaos and confusion will ensue, and the lights of fairness, of justice, of tranquillity and peace cease to shine."*[4]

Only the fire of tribulation can now lead mankind back to the impregnable stronghold of religion and to recognition of the Will of God for this age. Whatever befalls to purify the human spirit will inevitably carry farther the process that has already deposed kings, disrupted empires, and greatly weakened the influence of ecclesiastical institutions. At the same time, by preparing the way for the spiritualisation of the mass of mankind it will hasten the second process, the creation of a New World Order.

New World Order

This new order will not reach full flower for many hundreds of years. It will attain its finest development only when mankind accepts, and sincerely tries to apply, all the teachings of Bahá'u'lláh. To those who cannot see beyond the chaos and the limitations of the present day, a statement of this goal of a new world order must seem the fruitless dream of an idealist. So also the vision of Islám seemed unreal to the contemporaries of Muḥammad; but had they lived a hundred or more years later, they would have witnessed the dream made actuality. The New World Order of Bahá'u'lláh is being built today in thousands of small communities where the Bahá'í Administrative Order is taking form.[*] It does not, and never will, bring Bahá'ís into conflict with existing governments, for Bahá'u'lláh stressed firmly the principle of obedience to those in authority.[**] But when the inability of the old order to provide any adequate

---

[*] See Chapter XV.
[**] See pages 93-4.

means of organising mankind in this day has been so fully demonstrated that none can deny it, the world will find ready to hand the pattern and nucleus of a proved and workable new world order in the administrative institutions the Bahá'ís are building.

When this new order has been universally adopted, humanity will at last be free to move on towards the world organisation implicit in the teaching of Bahá'u'lláh, so attractively portrayed by Shoghi Effendi:

"The unity of the human race, as envisaged by Bahá'u'lláh, implies the establishment of a world commonwealth in which all nations, races, creeds and classes are closely and permanently united, and in which the autonomy of its state members and the personal freedom and initiative of the individuals that compose them are definitely and completely safeguarded. This commonwealth must, as far as we can visualise it, consist of a world. legislature, whose members will, as the trustees of the whole of mankind, ultimately control the entire resources of all the component nations, and will enact such laws as shall be required to regulate the life, satisfy the needs and adjust the relationships of all races and peoples. A world executive, backed by an international Force, will carry out the decisions arrived at, and apply the laws enacted by, this world legislature, and will safeguard the organic unity of the whole commonwealth. A world tribunal will adjudicate and deliver its compulsory and final verdict in all and any disputes that may arise between the various elements constituting this universal system. A mechanism of world inter-communication will be devised, embracing the whole planet, freed from national hindrances and restrictions, and functioning with marvellous swiftness and perfect regularity. A world metropolis will act as the nerve centre of a world civilisation, the focus towards which the unifying forces of life will converge and from which its energising influences will radiate. A world language will either be invented or chosen from among the existing languages and will be taught in the schools of all the federated nations as an auxiliary to their mother tongue. A world script, a world literature, a uniform and universal system of currency, of weights and measures, will simplify and facilitate intercourse and understanding among the nations and races of mankind. In such a world society, science and religion, the two most potent forces in human life will be reconciled, will co-operate, and will harmoniously develop. The press will, under such a system, while giving full scope to the expression of the diversified views and convictions of mankind, cease to be mischievously manipulated by vested interests, whether private or public, and will be liberated from the influence of contending governments and peoples. The economic resources of the world will be organised, its sources of raw materials will be tapped and fully utilised, its markets will be co-ordinated and developed, and the distribution of its products will be equitably regulated."[5]

At present the New World Order of Bahá'u'lláh is still embryonic. The Bahá'í Administrative Order is concerned only with the affairs of a comparatively small community, and the day when the peoples of the world shall voluntarily instal it as a World Order of their own choosing is yet far distant. While the irresistible forces of the age are bringing the downfall of the old order and creating the new, some intermediate form of organisation is needed to preserve outward peace and to hasten the day when a world commonwealth can be established.

Collective Security

Many years before the idea of a League of Nations found favour with the world's most advanced political and sociological thinkers, Bahá'u'lláh urged the adoption of a system of collective security, based upon principles that He indicated. In a Tablet to Queen Victoria written about 1870, He enjoined the world's rulers:

"Be united, O kings of the earth, for thereby will the

tempest of discord be stilled amongst you, and your peoples find rest, if ye be of them that comprehend. Should any one among you take up arms against another, rise ye all against him, for this is! naught but manifest justice."[6]

'Abdu'l-Bahá explains how such a system should be instituted:

"True civilisation will unfurl its banner in the midmost heart of the world whenever a certain number of its distinguished and high-minded sovereigns—the shining exemplars of devotion and determination—shall, for the good and happiness of all mankind, arise, with firm resolve and clear vision, to establish the Cause of Universal Peace. They must make the Cause of Peace the object of general consultation, and seek by every means in their power to establish a Union of the nations of the world. They must conclude a binding treaty and establish a covenant, the provisions of which shall be sound, inviolable and definite. They must proclaim it to all the world and obtain for it the sanction of all the human race. This supreme and noble undertaking— the real source of the peace and well being of all the world—should be regarded as sacred by all that dwell on earth. All the forces of humanity must be mobilised to ensure the stability and permanence of this Most Great Covenant. In this all-embracing Pact the limits and frontiers of each and every nation should be clearly fixed, the principles underlying the relations of governments towards one another definitely laid down, and all international agreements and obligations ascertained. In like manner, the size of the armaments of every government should be strictly limited, for if the preparations for war and the military forces of any nation should be allowed to increase, they will arouse the suspicion of others. The fundamental principle

underlying this solemn Pact should be so fixed that if any government later violate anyone of its provisions, all the governments on earth should arise to reduce it to utter submission, nay the human race as a whole should resolve, with every power at its disposal, to destroy that government. Should this greatest of all remedies be applied to the sick body of the world, it will assuredly recover from its ills and will remain eternally safe and secure."[7]

In any system of collective security, a crucial question is how to decide matters of international law, such as whether a treaty has been violated; Bahá'u'lláh prescribes a Supreme Tribunal for the purpose. 'Abdu'l-Bahá outlines the features of this Supreme Tribunal in a Tablet He wrote in 1919:

"Although the League of Nations has been brought into existence, yet it is incapable of establishing Universal Peace. But the Supreme Tribunal which His Holiness Bahá'u'lláh has described will fulfil this sacred task with the utmost might and power. And His plan is this: that the national assemblies of each country and nation—that is to say parliaments—should elect two or three persons who are the choicest men of that nation, and are well informed concerning international laws and the relations between governments and aware of the essential needs of the world of humanity of this day. The number of these representatives should be in proportion to the number of inhabitants of that country. The election of these souls who are chosen by the national assembly, that is, the parliament, must be confirmed by the upper house, the congress and the cabinet and also by the president or monarch so these persons may be the elected ones of all the nation and the government. From among these people the members of the Supreme Tribunal will be elected, and all mankind

will thus have a share therein, for every one of these delegates is fully representative of his nation. When the Supreme Tribunal gives a ruling on any international question, either unanimously or by majority rule, there will no longer be any pretext for the plaintiff or ground of objection for the defendant. In case any of the governments or nations in the execution of the irrefutable decision of the Supreme Tribunal be negligent or dilatory, the rest of the nations will rise up against it, because all the governments and nations of the world are the supporters of this Supreme Tribunal. Consider what a firm foundation this is! But by a limited and restricted League the purpose will not be realised as it ought and should. This is the truth about the situation which has been stated."[8]

Comparison of the method by which Bahá'u'lláh would establish peace with the inadequate attempts at international organisation the nations have so far made discloses many shortcomings of the present system—the United Nations. Interpreting the teaching of Bahá'u'lláh on the subject, Shoghi Effendi has said:

"What else could these weighty words signify if they did not point to the inevitable curtailment of unfettered national sovereignty as an indispensable preliminary to the formation of the future Commonwealth of all the nations of the world? Some form of a world Super-State must needs be evolved, in whose favour all the nations of the world will have willingly ceded every claim to make war, certain rights to impose taxation and all rights to maintain armaments, except for the purposes of maintaining internal order within their respective dominions. Such a state will have to include within its orbit an International Executive adequate to enforce supreme and unchallengeable authority on every recalcitrant member of the commonwealth; a World

Parliament whose members shall be elected by the people in their respective countries and whose election shall be confirmed by their respective governments; and a Supreme Tribunal whose judgment will have a binding effect even in such cases where the parties concerned did not voluntarily agree to submit their case to its consideration."[9]

There are some who regard even the form of collective security prescribed by Bahá'u'lláh as an unattainable ideal. The counsel of such as these has led mankind from war to war without alleviating its lot one iota. Who are they to declare impossible what the Pen of Might has revealed? They would do well to ponder these words uttered by the Tongue of Grandeur:

"The All-Knowing Physician hath his finger on the pulse of mankind. He perceiveth the disease, and prescribeth, in His unerring wisdom, the remedy... We can well perceive how the whole human race is encompassed with great, with incalculable afflictions. We see it languishing on its bed of sickness, sore tried and disillusioned. They that are intoxicated by self-conceit have interposed themselves between it and the Divine and infallible Physician. Witness how they have entangled all men, themselves included, in the mesh of their devices. They can neither discover the cause of the disease nor have they any knowledge of the remedy. They have conceived the straight to be crooked, and have imagined their friend an enemy. Incline your ears to the sweet melody of this Prisoner. Arise, and lift up your voices, that haply they that are fast asleep may be awakened. Say: O ye who are as dead! The Hand of Divine bounty proffereth unto you the Water of Life. Hasten and drink your fill. Whoso hath been reborn in this Day, shall never die; whoso remaineth dead, shall never live."[10]

International Auxiliary Language

Another important step towards mutual understanding of the peoples of the world is agreement by their governments on some language to be taught in all schools. This language might be newly invented or one already existing; either will do, providing the choice is agreed by a large enough number of governments.

Instruction in the chosen language will not replace instruction in anyone's mother tongue. The international language is to be auxiliary to the various national ones and to exist alongside of them. Everyone will speak two languages, so that even if the number of living languages remains as great as it is now, all people will have one in common. Of the importance of this Bahá'u'lláh said:

> *"The day is approaching when all the peoples of the world will have adopted one universal language and one common script. When this is achieved, to whatsoever city a man may journey, it shall be as if he were entering his own home. These things are obligatory and absolutely essential. It is incumbent upon every man of insight and understanding to strive to translate that which hath been written into reality and action."*[11]

'Abdu'l-Bahá praised Esperanto highly and urged Bahá'ís to learn it at that time. However, He indicated that it would need to be modified before it could become widely accepted in the East, since its structure was Western. Bahá'ís value the efforts Esperantists are making to establish this tongue as an inter nationally agreed auxiliary language and will be very glad if these efforts are successful; but they will be glad also if some other language is agreed instead. Bahá'ís supporters of the idea of a universal language rather than of the claims to universality made on behalf of any particular one.

Good Government

In spite of the present lowering of the prestige of kings, brought on by their disregard of the warnings of Bahá'u'lláh, Bahá'ís do not expect kingship to vanish permanently. Eventually, its dignity, though not its power, will be restored. Bahá'u'lláh taught his followers to pay due regard to the dignity of kingship:

"Regard for the rank of sovereigns is divinely ordained, as is clearly attested by the words of the Prophets of God and His chosen ones."[12]

The station of a just king is very high:

"A just king is the shadow of God on earth. All should seek shelter under the shadow of his justice, and rest in the shade of his favour. This is not a matter which is either specific or limited in its scope, that it might be restricted to one or another person, inasmuch as the shadow telleth of the One Who casteth it."[13]

Bahá'u'lláh even says:

"A just king enjoyeth nearer access unto God than anyone."[14]

But He does not approve absolute monarchy. In His Tablet to Queen Victoria He praised the British system of government and at the same time indicated how Members of Parliament should approach their great responsibility. He wrote:

"We have also heard that thou hast entrusted the reins of counsel into the hands of the representatives of the people. Thou, indeed, hast done well, for thereby the foundations of the edifice of thine affairs will be strengthened, and the hearts of all that are beneath thy shadow, whether high or low, will be tranquillised. It behoveth them, however, to be trustworthy among his servants, and to regard themselves as the representatives of all that dwell on earth. This is what counselleth them, in this Tablet, He Who is the Ruler, the All-Wise.... Blessed is he that entereth the assembly for the sake of God, and judgeth between men with pure justice. He, indeed, is of the blissful."[15]

To those in authority Bahá'u'lláh commends moderation:

"It is incumbent upon them who are in authority to exercise moderation in all things. Whatsoever passeth beyond the limits of moderation will cease to exert a beneficial influence. Consider, for instance, such things as liberty, civilisation and the like. However much men of understanding may favourably regard them, they will, if carried to excess, exercise a pernicious influence upon men."[16]

Of excessive material civilisation, He says:

"The civilisation, so often vaunted by the learned exponents of arts and sciences, will, if allowed to overlap the bounds of moderation, bring great evil upon men. Thus warneth you He who is the All-Knowing. If carried to excess, civilisation will prove as prolific a source of evil as it had been of goodness when kept within the restraints of moderation. Meditate on this, O people, and be not of them that wander distraught in the wilderness of error. The day is approaching when its flame will devour the cities, when the Tongue of Grandeur will proclaim: 'The Kingdom is God's, the Almighty, the All-Praised!'"[17]

In these days of hydrogen bombs and other horrors, the evil of immoderate civilisation is only too apparent. Were spiritual development more advanced, the same degree of material civilisation would not be excessive; but when material civilisation outstrips spiritual development, the danger to mankind is as great as the danger of a loaded gun to an infant.

Excessive liberty, too, is dangerous. Most people will agree that men should not be so unconstrained as to be free to harm others; Bahá'u'lláh says they must also be kept from harming themselves, through the restraint imposed by obedience to divine commandments. As man needs the guidance of the Manifestations of God to enable him to decide what is right and what is wrong, so he needs the restraint Their Laws impose. Man should be stayed by submission to the Divine Will from harming either himself or others. Therefore Bahá'u'lláh revealed:

> *"Liberty must, in the end, lead to sedition, whose flames none can quench. Thus wameth you He Who is the Reckoner, the All-Knowing. Know ye that the embodiment of liberty and its symbol is the animal. That which beseemeth man is submission unto such restraints as will protect him from his own ignorance, and guard him against the harm of the mischief maker. Liberty causeth man to overstep the bounds of propriety, and to infringe on the dignity of his station. It debaseth him to the level of extreme depravity and wickedness. Regard men as a flock of sheep that need a shepherd for their protection. This, verily, is the truth, the certain truth. We prove of liberty in certain circumstances, and refuse to sanction it in others. We, verily, are the All-Knowing."*[18]

In the Tablets He wrote to kings and rulers of His day, Bahá'u'lláh gave much wise guidance on the art of government. All that is implicit in these gems of wisdom will be properly appreciated only by later generations. Their substance is exemplified by this extract from a Tablet addressed to the kings of the earth jointly:

> *"Lay not aside the fear of God, O kings of the earth, and beware that ye transgress not, the bounds which the Almighty hath fixed. Observe the injunctions laid upon you in His Book, and take good heed not to overstep their limits. Be vigilant, that ye may not do injustice to anyone, be it to the extent of a grain of mustard seed. Tread ye the path of justice, for this, verily, is the straight path.*

Compose your differences, and reduce your armaments, that the burden of your expenditures may be lightened, and that your minds and hearts may be tranquillised. Heal; the dissensions that divide you, and ye will no longer be, in need of any armaments except what the protection of your cities and territories demandeth. Fear ye God, and take heed not to outstrip the bounds of moderation, and be numbered among the extravagant.

We have learned that you are outlay every year, and are laying the burden thereof on your subjects. This, verily, is more than they can bear, and is a grievous injustice. Decide justly between men, and be ye the emblems of justice amongst them. This, if ye judge fairly, is the thing that behoveth you, and beseemeth your station.

Beware not to deal unjustly with anyone that appealeth to you, and entereth beneath your shadow. Walk ye in the fear of God, and be ye of them that lead a godly life. Rest not on your power, your armies and treasures. Put your whole trust and confidence in God, Who hath created you, and seek ye His help in all your affairs. Succour cometh from Him alone. He succoureth whom He will with the hosts of the heavens and the earth.

Know ye that the poor are the trust of God in your midst. Watch that ye betray not His trust, that ye deal not unjustly with them and that ye walk not in the ways of the treacherous. Ye will most certainly be called upon to answer for His trust on the day when the Balance of Justice shall be set, the day when unto every one shall be rendered his due, when the doings of all men, be they rich or poor, shall be weighed:"[19]

Obedience to Government
The Bahá'í Faith teaches that one should be obedient to the

government of the area in which one lives. This is to preserve unity and is very important. Bahá'u'lláh said:

"Give a hearing ear, O people, to that which I, in truth, say unto you. The one true God, exalted be His glory, hath ever regarded, and will continue to regard, the hearts of men as His own, His exclusive possession. All else, whether pertaining to land or sea, whether riches or glory, He hath bequeathed unto the Kings and rulers of the earth. From the beginning that hath no beginning the ensign proclaiming the words 'He doeth whatsoever He willeth' hath been unfurled in all its splendour before His Manifestation. What mankind needeth in this day is obedience to them that are in authority, and a faithful adherence to the cord of wisdom. The instruments which are essential to the immediate protection, the security and assurance of the human race have been entrusted to the hands, and lie in the grasp, of the governors of human society. This is the wish of God and His decree."[20]

Jesus also spoke of this when He said *"Render therefore unto Caesar the things that are Caesar's; and unto God the things that are God's."*[21] 'Abdu'l-Bahá says even more specifically in His *Will and Testament*:

"We must obey and be the well-wishers of the governments of the land, regard disloyalty unto a just king as disloyalty to God Himself and wishing evil to the government a transgression of the Cause of God."[22]

A true Bahá'í is justified in disobeying His government only if it requires him to do something contrary to the fundamental teachings of Bahá'u'lláh, so that obedience to the government would amount to a denial of Faith. Thus, if a government tries to make a Bahá'í say he is a Muslim, or a Christian, or a Buddhist, or a Jew, he does not obey; but if the laws of a country require all able-bodied men to

serve in the armed forces and admit no exceptions, Bahá'ís obey
their government even to the extent of fighting. Where exceptions
are permitted, they apply for non-combatant service, but if their
application is rejected even after appeal, they serve in the combatant
forces like Bahá'ís in countries whose laws make no allowance for
conscience.

The Lesser Peace and the Most Great Peace

Properly regarded the Revelation of Bahá'u'lláh is seen to usher in
a period whose significance is unsurpassed in human history. Neither
the unification of mankind, nor the establishment of world peace,
nor even the inauguration of a World commonwealth, completes
the story of man's coming of age. There remains for the world to
achieve a particular condition that all the great Prophets have
unequivocally praised. It is to be reached in a golden period when
men will live harmoniously together in a society inspired by the
Grace of God. Each religion has its particular name for the golden
period; Christians know it as the Millennium and the condition as
the Kingdom of God on earth, which is to be *full of the knowledge
of the Lord as the waters cover the sea.*"²³

Bahá'u'lláh came to engender this condition, named by Him
the 'Most Great Peace.' It will blossom when His New World Order
has emerged and given birth to a new world civilisation, whose like
mankind has never experienced. That civilisation, initially nurtured
by the Most Great Peace, will continue to grow in coming ages and
eras until, many thousands of years hence, it reaches its maturity;
but in this age and in this era, the foundation is being laid. What
happens in distant eras is dependent on what happens now, while
mankind is coming of age and the New World Order is being
formed.

Had the world's rulers and leaders, and after them the generality
of mankind, recognised and accepted Bahá'u'lláh when He
announced Himself, the golden age would be with us now.
Unfortunately, men had strayed so far from the path laid down by
the Messengers of God that they missed their opportunity. They
can now regain the path only through suffering. The Millennium is

at hand, the Kingdom of God is to be established on earth in this Dispensation, the Most Great Peace is nigh, but the way to glory lies through trial and sorrow.

In the end, the Most Great Peace will unfailingly appear, because the whole history and purpose of mankind demands it. The Will of God has shaped history to prepare for this Great Day of Unity and no human acts can frustrate His intention. But men can hinder what men cannot prevent. The coming of the Most Great Peace has been postponed because of man's iniquity, so Bahá'u'lláh offers an alternative as a stepping-stone to better things. He introduced the passage on collective security, already quoted from His Tablet to Queen Victoria,* by this statement:

> *"Now that ye have refused the Most Great Peace, hold ye fast unto this, the Lesser Peace, that haply ye may in some degree better your own condition and that of your dependents."*[24]

It is towards the Lesser Peace that the world's rulers must now strive while the Bahá'ís prepare the way for the Most Great Peace by diffusing the fragrances of Bahá'u'lláh and by building the Bahá'í Administrative Order. These two processes can, and indeed must, progress simultaneously, so that humanity may be freed as soon as possible from the curse of war, and so that the Day when the Most Great Peace will dawn may be hastened instead of hindered by the deeds of men.

---

* See pages 83-84.

CHAPTER VI

Social and Economic Teachings

Equal Status for Men and Women

The world civilisation destined to grow out of the New World Order will incorporate various social and economic features delineated by Bahá'u'lláh. A very important one is the acknowledgment of the equal status of men and women, which is really implicit in the belief that mankind is one. Division into a superior and an inferior sex is inconsistent with this belief.

Equality of status of men and women does not imply equality of function, in which they clearly differ. Some jobs are best done by men, some by women, and some equally well by either. What matters is that neither men nor women should deem the other sex inferior because of its different function. The two sexes can contribute equally to the progress of the human race.

'Abdu'l-Bahá often spoke of this. In Philadelphia He said:

"In proclaiming the oneness of mankind, He (Bahá'u'lláh) taught that men and women are equal in the sight of God and there is no distinction to be made between them. The only difference between them now is due to lack of education and training. If woman is given equal opportunity of education, distinction and estimate of inferiority will disappear. The world of. humanity has two wings as it were, one is the female, the other is the male. If one wing is defective the strong perfect wing will not be capable of flight. The world of humanity has two hands. If one be imperfect, the capable hand is restricted and unable to perform its duties. God is the creator of mankind. He has endowed both sexes

with perfections and intelligence, given them physical members and organs of sense, without differentiation or distinction as to superiority; therefore, why should women be considered inferior? This is not according to the plan and justice of God. He has created them equal; in His estimate there is no question of sex. The one whose heart is purest, whose deeds are most perfect is acceptable to God, male or female. Often in history women have been the pride of humanity; for example, Mary the mother of Jesus. She was the glory of mankind. Mary Magdalene, Asíyih, daughter of Pharaoh, Sarah wife of Abraham and innumerable others have glorified the human race by their excellences.... Furthermore, the education of women is of greater importance than the education of men, for they are the mothers of the race and mothers rear the children. The first teachers of children are the mothers. Therefore they must be capably trained in order to educate both sons and daughters. There are many provisions in the words of Bahá'u'lláh in regard to this. He promulgated the adoption of the same course of education for man and woman. Daughters and sons must follow the same curriculum of study, thereby promoting unity of the sexes. When all mankind shall receive the same opportunity of education and the equality of men and women be realised the foundations of war will be utterly destroyed. Without equality this will be impossible because all differences and distinction are conducive to discord and strife. Equality between men and women is conducive to the abolition of warfare for the reason that women will never be willing to sanction it. Mothers will not give their sons as sacrifices upon the battlefield after twenty years of anxiety and loving devotion in rearing them from infancy, no matter what cause they are called upon to defend. There is no doubt that when women obtain equality of rights war will entirely cease among mankind."[1]

Education

The great importance of education is stressed by 'Abdu'l-Bahá in *The Secret of Divine Civilisation,* formerly known as *The Mysterious Forces of Civilisation.* Urging Persian leaders at the end of the nineteenth century to promote education in Persia, He showed by arguments likely to appeal to His audience that all progress depends upon it:

> *"The primary, the most urgent requirement is the promotion of education. It is inconceivable that any nation should achieve prosperity and success unless this paramount, this fundamental concern is carried forward. The principal reason for the decline and fall of peoples is ignorance....*

> *"Observe to what a degree the lack of education will weaken and degrade a people. Today (1875) from the standpoint of population the greatest nation in the world is China, which has something over four hundred million inhabitants. On this account, its government should be the most distinguished on earth, its people the most acclaimed. And yet on the contrary, because of its lack of education in cultural and material civilization, it is the feeblest and the most helpless of all weak nations. Not long ago, a small contingent of English and French troops went to war with China and defeated that country so decisively that they took over its capital Peking. Had the Chinese government and people been abreast of the advanced sciences of the day, had they been skilled in the arts of civilization, then if all the nations on earth had marched against them the attack would still have failed, and the attackers would have returned defeated whence they had come.*

"Stranger even than this episode is the fact that the government of Japan was in the beginning subject to and under the protection of China, and that now for some years, Japan has opened its eyes and adopted the techniques of contemporary progress and civilization, promoting sciences and industries of use to the public, and striving to the utmost of their power and competence until public opinion was focussed on reform. This government has currently advanced to such a point that, although its population is only one sixth, or even one tenth, that of China, it has recently challenged the latter government, and China has finally been forced to come to terms. Observe carefully how education and the arts of civilization bring honour, prosperity, independence and freedom to a government and its people."[2]

Now, for the first time in human history, it is credible that all mankind may receive some measure of formal education. This is another sign that the maturity of mankind is at hand. In all previous ages, the educated have belonged to a small privileged class and sometimes only the priests were literate. Now God, through Bahá'u'lláh, has ordained that all, without exception, should be educated. 'Abdu'l-Bahá says in His Tablet to the Hague:

"And among the teachings of Bahá'u'lláh is the promotion of education. Every child must be instructed in sciences as much as is necessary. If the parents are able to provide the expenses of this education, it is all right, otherwise the community must provide the means for the teaching of that child."[3]

Such education will ensure both progress in understanding the laws of nature and a sufficiently widespread knowledge of applied science for scientific research to bear the fruit of higher material civilisation.

Bahá'u'lláh also speaks of education in a wider sense than formal education in schools. For example, He says:

"The fear of God hath ever been the prime factor in the education of His creatures."[4]

In this sense, education means aiding acquisition of the Knowledge of God.* The supreme Educators are the Founders of the great religions, Who convey to men the power to rise above wordly desire and cause them to be spiritually reborn. Explaining this in the United States in 1912, 'Abdu'l-Bahá indicates the true nature of all education:

"The people of Europe and America have been uplifted by education and training from the world of defects and have ascended toward the realm of perfection, whereas the people of Africa, denied educational development, remain in a natural condition of illiteracy and deprivation; for nature is incomplete and defective. Education is a necessity. If a piece of ground be left in its natural and original state, it will either become a thorny waste or be covered by worthless weeds. When cleared and cultivated, this same unproductive field will yield plentiful harvests of food for human sustenance.

"This same difference is noticeable among animals; some have been domesticated, educated, others left wild. The proof is clear that the world of nature is imperfect, the world of education perfect. That is to say, man is rescued from the exigencies of nature by training and culture; consequently education is necessary, obligatory. But education is of various kinds. There is a training and development of the physical body which ensures strength and growth. There is intellectual education or mental training for which schools and

---

* See pages 137-38.

colleges are founded. The third kind of education is that of the spirit. Through the breaths of the Holy Spirit, man is uplifted into the world of moralities and illumined by the lights of divine bestowals. The moral world is only attained through the effulgence of the Sun of Reality and the quickening life of the divine spirit. For this reason the holy Manifestations of God appear in the human world. They come to educate and illuminate mankind, to bestow spiritual susceptibilities, to quicken inner perceptions and thereby adorn the reality of man—the human temple—with divine graces.... For this reason the holy divine Manifestations are the first Teachers and Educators of humanity."[5]

Thus education should be both spiritual and intellectual. Bahá'u'lláh says:

"Schools must first train the children in the principles of religion, so that the promise and the threat, recorded in the Books of God, may prevent them from the things forbidden and adorn them with the mantle of the commandments. But this in such a measure that it may not injure the children by resulting in ignorant fanaticism and bigotry."[6]

On the other hand He also says.

"To acquire knowledge is incumbent on all, but of those sciences which may profit the people of the earth, and not such sciences as begin in mere words, and end in mere words. The possessors of sciences and arts have a great right among the people of the world."[7]

Hence Bahá'í education will avoid both the extreme of religious fanaticism and the extreme of scientific narrow-mindedness. Combining spiritual and ethical instruction with the study of arts and sciences, it will fittingly prepare the children of the future to uphold and exploit the Most Great Peace.

Work

The ultimate object of all learning is the Knowledge of God,* but education should also fit a child to earn its living when it grows up, for according to Bahá'í Teaching all must work. Even the rich should not be idle. Bahá'u'lláh revealed:

> *"O My servants! Ye are the trees of My garden; ye must give forth goodly and wondrous fruits, that ye yourselves and others may profit therefrom. Thus it is incumbent on everyone to engage in crafts and professions, for therein lies the secret of wealth, O men of understanding! For results depend upon means, and the grace of God shall be all sufficient unto you. Trees that yield no fruit have been and will ever be for the fire."*[8]

Work, whether paid or voluntary, should be done in a spirit of service to mankind. So executed, it is in this age equivalent to worship. 'Abdu'l-Bahá said in Paris:

> *"The man who makes a piece of notepaper to the best of his ability, conscientiously, concentrating all his forces on perfecting it, is giving praise to God. Briefly, all effort and exertion put forth by man from the fullness of his heart is worship, if it is prompted by the highest motives and the will to do service to humanity. This is worship: to serve mankind and to minister to the needs of the people. Service is prayer. A physician ministering to the sick, gently, tenderly, free from prejudice and believing in the solidarity of the human race, he is giving praise."*[9]

These teachings are important now, but will be even more needed in the world of the future from which want will have been banished

---

* See pages 137-38.

and in which a high standard of living will be available to all for little exertion. Without the attitude to work inculcated by Bahá'u'lláh, this prosperity might be imperilled by reluctance to work of men grown soft from good living.

Limitation of Wealth and Poverty

Just as there will be no idle rich in the Bahá'í world of the future, so also there will be none whose riches are excessive by the standards of the age. Bahá'u'lláh ordains that both riches and poverty shall be limited. None will fall below the subsistence level; all will be ensured a minimum level comfort, which may vary from age to age, and possibly from country to country too, according to the degree of prosperity attained. 'Abdu'l-Bahá spoke more forcefully about the need to eliminate poverty than about most things. In Paris He said:

"The arrangement of the circumstances of the people must be such that poverty shall disappear, that everyone, as far as possible, according to his rank and position, shall share in comfort and well-being.

We see amongst us men who are overburdened with riches on the one hand, and on the other those unfortunate ones who starve with nothing; those who possess several stately palaces, and those who have not where to lay their head.

This condition of affairs is wrong, and must be remedied. Now the remedy must be carefully undertaken. It cannot be done by bringing to pass absolute equality between men.

Equality is a chimera! It is entirely impracticable! Even if equality could be achieved it could not continue— and if its existence were possible, the whole order of the world would be destroyed. The law of order must always obtain in the world of humanity. Heaven has so decreed in the creation of man.

Certainly, some being enormously rich and others lamentably poor, an organisation is necessary to control and improve this state of affairs. It is important to limit riches as it is also important to limit poverty. Either extreme is not good. To be seated in the mean is most desirable. If it be right for a capitalist to possess a large fortune, it is equally just that his workman should have a sufficient means of existance."[10]

Industry

The only true solution of economic problems is spiritual, although specific governmental action is also necessary. This general attitude is indicated by the following fragments taken from different talks of 'Abdu'l-Bahá quoted in *Star of the West*:

"The secrets of the whole economic question are divine in nature and are concerned with the world of the heart and spirit.

The disease which afflicts the body politic is lack of love and absence of altruism.... The solution of economic questions, for instance, will not be accomplished by array of labour against capital and capital against labour in strife and conflict, but by the voluntary attitude of sacrifice on both sides. Then a real and lasting justness of conditions will be brought about."[11]

Neither Bahá'u'lláh nor 'Abdu'l-Bahá specified in detail the governmental action that will be needed; this is a secondary matter to be worked out by the future Houses of Justice in accordance with general principles laid down in the Bahá'í Holy Writings. The system can be varied to suit the varied need of different places and periods, a far more practicable method than trying to apply a single unchanging master-plan to diverse circumstances. 'Abdu'l-Bahá often spoke of the principles of the system in passages similar to the following:

"Laws and regulations should be established which would permit the workmen to receive from the factory owner their wages and a share in the fourth or the fifth part of the profits,* according to the capacity of the factory; or in some other way the body of workmen and the manufacturers should share equitably the profits and advantages. Indeed, the direction and administration of affairs come from the owner of the factory, and the work and labour from the body of the workmen. In other words, the workmen should receive wages which assure them an adequate support, and when they cease to work, becoming feeble or helpless, they should receive from the owner of the factory a sufficient pension. The wages should be high enough to satisfy the workmen with the amount they receive, so that they may be able to put a little aside for days of want and helplessness.

When matters will be thus fixed, the owner of the factory will no longer put aside daily a treasure which he has absolutely no need of.... And the workmen and artisans will no longer be in the greatest misery and want, they will no longer be submitted to the worst privations at the end of their life. . . . It would be well, with regard to the social rights of manufacturers, work men and artisans, that laws be established giving moderate profits to manufacturers, and to workmen the necessary means of existence and security for the future. Thus, when they become feeble and cease working, get old and helpless and die leaving children underage, these children will not be annihilated by excess of poverty.

---

* The proportion mentioned is for illustration only. Elsewhere other proportions are mentioned.

And it is from the income of the factory itself to which they have a right, that they will derive a little of the means of existence.

In the same way, workmen should no longer rebel and revolt, nor demand beyond their rights; they should no longer go out on strike, they should be obedient and submissive, and not ask for impudent wages. But the mutual rights of both associated parties will be fixed and established according to custom by just and impartial laws. In case one of the two parties should transgress, the courts of justice would have to give judgment, and by an efficacious fine put an end to the transgression; thus order will be re-established, and the difficulties settled."[12]

In the future, such a system of regulation will ensure the harmonious exploitation of the physical resources of the world to the greatest mutual benefit of capital and labour, but the time to apply the system has not yet come. Before the economic ills of mankind can be healed, whether in this way or in any other, current injustices must be rectified and the generality of mankind must be sufficiently spiritualised to apply goodwill to economic relations. The world is sick and Acts of Parliament alone, no matter how wise, cannot heal it. Good government and perfect planning can make no headway against greed, prejudice, selfishness, materialism, and the other evils that now cause economic unrest. Only when people are able to appreciate 'Abdu'l-Bahá's dictum that 'the secrets of the whole economic question are divine in nature and are concerned with the world of heart a spirit' will they have achieved a condition that renders possible the solution of their problems.

They will then also realise that agriculture is the most important industry, upon which the life of mankind depends. The day of great cities will pass, and with the cities many of the pressing problems of our own time.

Voluntary Giving

Bahá'u'lláh greatly stresses the virtue and benefit of voluntary giving which is more fruitful than compulsory sharing. He exhorts:

"O Children of Dust! Tell the rich of the midnight sighing of the poor, lest heedlessness may lead them into the path of destruction, and deprive them of the Tree of wealth. To give and to be generous are attributes of Mine: well is it with him that adorneth himself with My virtues."[13]

That sharing should be voluntary is in the interest of both the donor and the recipient. It is a sign of true civilisation, and provides a surer basis for re-apportioning wealth than any other means. Of it 'Abdu'l-Bahá said:

"The time will come in the near future when humanity will become so much more sensitive than at present that the man of great wealth will not enjoy his luxury, in comparison with the deplorable poverty about him. He will be forced, for his own happiness, to expend his wealth to procure better conditions for the community in which he lives."[14]

Eventually these voluntary contributions will pass through official channels and will constitute an important part of the income of Local Houses of Justice.*

Public Finance

J. E. Esslemont sums up in Bahá'u'lláh and the New Era the Bahá'í teachings about public finance as follows: 'Abdu'l-Bahá suggests that each town and village or district should be entrusted as far as possible with the administration of fiscal matters within its own area and should contribute its due pro portion for the expenses of the general government. One of the principal sources of revenue should be graduated income tax. If a man's income does not exceed

---

* See pages 301-3.

his necessary expenditure he should not be required to pay any tax, but in all cases where income exceeds the necessary expenditure a tax should be levied, the percentage of tax increasing as the surplus of income over necessary expenditure increases.

"On the other hand, if a person, through illness, poor crops, or other cause for which he is not responsible, is unable to earn an income sufficient to meet his necessary expenses for the year, then what he lacks for the maintenance of himself and his family should be supplied out of public funds.

"There will also be other sources of public revenue, e.g. from intestate estates, mines, treasure-trove and voluntary contributions, while among the expenditures will be grants for the support of the infirm, of orphans, of schools, of the deaf and blind, and for the maintenance of public health. Thus the welfare and comfort of all will be provided for."[15]

Bequest and Inheritance

About bequest and inheritance J. E. Esslemont writes in the same book: 'Bahá'u'lláh states that a person should be free to dispose of his possessions during his lifetime in any way he chooses, and it is incumbent on everyone to write a will stating how his property is to be disposed of after his death. When a person dies without leaving a will, the value of the property should be estimated and divided in certain stated proportions among seven classes of inheritors, namely, children, wife or husband, father, mother, brothers, sisters arid teachers, the share of each diminishing from the first to the last. In the absence of one or more of these classes, the share which would belong to them goes to the public treasury.

"There is nothing in the law of Bahá'u'lláh to prevent a man from leaving all his property to one individual if he pleases, but Bahá'is will naturally be influenced, in making their wills, by the model Bahá'u'lláh had laid

down for the case of intestate estates, which ensures distribution of the property among a considerable number of heirs."[16]

Of Crime and Criminals

Asked whether a criminal should be punished, or forgiven and disregarded, 'Abdu'l-Bahá said:

"There are two sorts of retributory punishments. One is vengeance, the other chastisement. Man has not the right to take ven geance, but the community has the right to punish the criminal; and this punishment is intended to warn and to prevent, so that no other person will dare to commit a like crime. This punishment is for the protection of man's rights, but it is not vengeance; vengeance appeases the anger of the heart by opposing one evil to another. This is not allowable; for man has not the right to take vengeance. But if criminals were entirely for given, the order of the world would be upset. So punishment is one of the essential necessities for the safety of communities; but he who is oppressed by a transgressor has not the right to take vengeance: on the contrary, he should forgive and pardon, for this is worthy of the world of man.

The communities must punish the oppressor, the murderer, the malefactor, so as to warn and restrain others from committing like crimes. But the most essential thing is that the people must be educated in such a way that no crimes will be committed; for it is possible to educate the masses so effectively that they will avoid and shrink from perpetrating crimes, so that the crime itself will appear to them the greatest chastisement, the utmost condemnation and torment. Therefore no crimes which require punishment will be committed.

Communities are day and night occupied in making

*penal laws and in preparing and organising instruments
and means of punishment. They build prisons, make
chains and fetters, arrange places of exile and
banishment, and different kinds of hardship and
tortures, and think by these means to discipline
criminals; whereas, in reality, they are causing
destruction of morals and perversion of characters.
The community, on the contrary, ought day and night
to strive and endeavour with the utmost zeal and effort
to accomplish the education of men, to cause them day
by day to progress and to increase in science and
knowledge, to acquire virtues, to gain good morals and
to avoid vices, so that crimes may not occur. At the
present time the contrary prevails; the community is
always thinking of enforcing penal laws, and of
preparing means of punishment, instruments of death
and chastisement, places for imprisonment and
banishment; and they expect crimes to be committed.
This has a demoralising effect.*

*But if the community would endeavour to educate the
masses, day by day knowledge and sciences would
increase, the understanding would be broadened, the
sensibilities developed, customs would become good,
and morals normal; in one word, in all these classes of
perfection, there would be progress, and there would
be fewer crimes."*[17]

Of the Press
Bahá'u'lláh wrote:

*"In this Day the mysteries of this earth are unfolded
and visible before the eyes, and the pages of swiftly
appearing newspapers are indeed the mirror of the
world; they display the doings and actions of the
different nations: they both illustrate them and cause*

them to be heard. Newspapers are as a mirror which is endowed with hearing, sight and speech; they are a wonderful phenomenon and a great matter. But it behoveth the writers thereof to be sanctified from the prejudice of egotism and desire and to be adorned with the ornament of equity and justice; they must enquire into matters as much as possible, in order that they may be informed of the real facts, and commit the same to writing."[18]

Material and Spiritual Civilisation

It will be noted that most of the teachings introduced in this chapter involve action by governments. Such teachings are complementary to those invoking individual action. They are much needed in the age in which we live.

In the time of Jesus, men thirsted for individual guidance under a regime which gave scant attention to individual rights. Jesus provided what the world then required, a religion primarily concerned with the deeds, faith and salvation of individuals.

But in our age, another need is evident; individual faith and action must be supplemented by the right kind of govern mental organisation. Bahá'u'lláh therefore addressed His teachings to governments as well as to individuals.

Nevertheless, right governmental organisation without spiritual rebirth of the generality of mankind will not heal the world's ills. Only a regenerated humanity can benefit from or adequately administer the New World Order of Bahá'u'lláh. At present mankind is immersed in materialism, so that most people's desire is for material, not spiritual, things. One man wants wealth, another power, another the material happiness of sensual satisfaction; few have as their prior aim doing the Will of God.

The intellectual and scientific achievements of man in this new age have so outrun his spiritual development that he himself acknowledges his incompetence to control the effects of his discoveries. Only when he progresses spiritually will he be able to reap the full benefit of his material achievements. Until then, each advance in material civilisation will bring fresh problems, fresh dangers and fresh unhappiness. 'Abdu'l-Bahá explained this piquantly in one of His addresses in the United States in 1912:

"No matter how far the material world advances it cannot establish the happiness of mankind. Only when material and spiritual civilisation are linked and co-ordinated will happiness be assured. Then material civilisation will not contribute its energies to the forces of evil in destroying the oneness of humanity, for in material civilisation good and evil advance together and maintain the same pace. For example, consider the material progress of man in the last decade. Schools and colleges, hospitals, philanthropic institutions, scientific academies and temples of philosophy have been founded, but hand in hand with these evidences of development, the invention and production of means and weapons for human destruction have correspondingly increased. In early days the weapon of war was the sword; now it is the magazine rifle. Among the ancients men fought with javelins and daggers; now they employ shells and bombs. Dreadnoughts are built, torpedoes invented and every few days a new ammunition is forthcoming.

All this is the outcome of material civilisation; therefore although material advancement furthers good purposes in life, at the same time it serves evil ends. The divine civilisation is good because it cultivates morals.... If the moral precepts and foundations of divine civilisation become united with the material advancement of man, there is no doubt that the happiness of the human world will be attained and from every direction the glad-tidings of peace upon earth will be announced. Then humankind will achieve extraordinary progress, the sphere of human intelligence will be immeasurably enlarged, wonderful inventions will appear and the spirit of God will reveal itself; all men will consort with joy and fragrance, and life eternal will be conferred upon the children of the kingdom. Then will the power of the divine make itself effective and the breath of the Holy Spirit penetrate the essence of all things. Therefore the material and the divine or merciful civilization must progress together until the highest aspirations and desires of humanity shall become realised."[19]

CHAPTER VII

Personal Conduct

Faith and Deeds

Praiseworthy moral conduct is the surest evidence of spiritual development. Bahá'u'lláh wrote:

> *"The essence of faith is fewness of words and abundance of deeds; he whose words exceed his deeds, know verily his death is better than his life."*[1]

Thus true faith requires works for its proper expression and until faith is so expressed it is merely potential. When a religion is vital and creative, the moral conduct of its followers provides evidence of its living power.

The conduct of the early Christians was such that Galen, a celebrated physician and philosopher of the second century A.D., wrote of them: "Today we see a people called Christians who believe in rewards and punishments, and this sect show forth beautiful actions like those which a true philosopher performs."[2] Similarly, each of the great religions in its period of creative growth has inspired its followers to show forth all good actions. Only as they gradually lose touch with the spirit of the Founder's Teaching does the stress gradually change to observance of ritual and verbal acknowledgment of doctrine—doctrine that the Founder would not recognise as His own. Whatever good is done in the name of most religions today is done in spite of such misplaced stress.

Jesus Himself indicated an unfailing test of the sincerity of those who profess religion when He proclaimed *"By their fruits ye shall know them."*[3] Bahá'u'lláh confirms and elaborates this test, saying:

> *"The Day Star of Truth that shineth in its meridian*

---

splendour beareth Us witness! They who are the people of God have no ambition except to revive the world, to ennoble its life, and regenerate its peoples. Truthfulness and goodwill have, at all times, marked their relations with all men. Their outward conduct is but a reflection of their inward life, and their inward life a mirror of their outward conduct. No veil hideth or obscureth the verities on which their faith is established."[4]

But others besides the teachers of religion must be righteous. Bahá'u'lláh urges:

"O Son of My Handmaid! Guidance hath ever been given by words, and now it is given by deeds. Everyone must show forth deeds that are pure and holy, for words are the property of all alike, whereas such deeds as these belong only to Our loved ones. Strive then with heart and soul to distinguish yourselves by your deeds. In this wise We counsel you in this holy and resplendent Tablet."[5]

Addressing a gathering of Bahá'ís in New York in 1912, 'Abdu'l-Bahá exclaimed:

"I desire distinction for you. The Bahá'ís must be distinguished from others of humanity. But this distinction must not depend upon wealth—that they should become more affluent than other people. I do not desire for you financial distinction. It is not an ordinary distinction I desire, not scientific, commercial, industrial distinction. For you I desire spiritual distinction; that is, you must become eminent and distinguished in morals. In the love of God you must become distinguished from all else. You must become distinguished for loving humanity; for unity and accord; for love and justice. In brief you must become distinguished in all the virtues of the human world; for

faithfulness and sincerity; for justice and fidelity; for
firmness and steadfastness; for philanthropic deeds and
service to the human world; for love toward every
human being; for unity and accord with all people; for
removing prejudices and promoting international peace.
Finally, you must become distinguished for heavenly
illumination and acquiring the bestowals of God. I
desire this distinction for you. This must be the point of
distinction among you."[6]

Ethical Teachings of Bahá'u'lláh

The teachings of Bahá'u'lláh regarding personal conduct reaffirm many teachings of earlier Manifestations of God, but in reaffirming them, He renews their creative force and gives mankind a deeper insight into their true meaning. His system is not a mere synthesis of the ethical teachings of former Messengers of God; Bahá'u'lláh uncovers afresh the springs of righteousness and illumines the eyes of men with the light of Divine Guidance.

To some degree, all the teachings of Bahá'u'lláh influence personal conduct; for example, those on the Oneness of Mankind require Bahá'í to adopt an attitude towards their fellow-men affecting every human relationship. But in this chapter, the teachings which reaffirm the fundamental ethical principles promulgated by all the Messengers of God will be expounded, so that the reader may judge for himself what new life Bahá'u'lláh has given even to these eternal truths.

The flavour of His Revelation can be savoured from an inimitable summary which He Himself provided in a Tablet addressed to one of His sons:

"Be generous in prosperity, and thankful in adversity.
Be worthy of the trust of thy neighbour, and look upon
him with a bright and friendly face. Be a treasure to the
poor, an admonisher to the rich, an answerer of the cry
of the needy, a preserver of the sanctity of thy pledge.
Be fair in thy judgment, and guarded in thy speech. Be

*unjust to no man, and show all meekness to all men. Be
as a lamp unto then that walk in darkness, a joy to the
sorrowful, a sea for the thirsty, a haven for the
distressed, an upholder and defender of the victim of
oppression. Let integrity and uprightness distinguish
all thine acts. Be a home for the stranger, a balm to the
suffering, a tower of strength for the fugitive. Be eyes
to the blind, and a guiding light unto the feet of the
erring. Be an ornament to the countenance of truth, a
crown to the brow of fidelity, a pillar of the temple of
righteousness, a breath of life to the body of mankind,
an ensign of the hosts of justice, a luminary above the
horizon of virtue, a dew to the soil of the human heart,
an ark on the ocean of knowledge, a sun in the heaven
of bounty, a gem on the diadem of wisdom, a shining
light in the firmament of thy generation, a fruit upon
the tree of humility."*[7]

These teachings are joyous and should be followed joyfully.
Bahá'u'lláh commands:

*"O Son of Man! Rejoice in the gladness of thine heart,
that thou mayest be worthy to meet Me and to mirror
forth my beauty."*[8]

Sadness and despondency act as veils between the Beauty of
God and the mirror of the human heart, whereas joy helps us to
soar to the heights of detachment. 'Abdu'l-Bahá loved laughter;
often instead of enquiring after the health of someone He met, He
would ask 'Are you happy?' He said people should seek to acquire
'radiant acquiescence,' an attitude whose rank is evident from
Bahá'u'lláh's statement that:

*"The source of all good is trust in God, submission
unto His command, and contentment in His holy will
and pleasure."*[9]

Attainment to this state will be discussed further in Chapter
VIII where some of the mystical teachings of the Bahá'í Faith are
mentioned.* It suffices here to quote one simple rule for self-
improvement given by Bahá'u'lláh which can be profitably followed
even by those least interested in the pursuit of mystical knowledge:

> *"O Son of Being! Bring thyself to account each day ere
> thou art summoned to a reckoning; for death,
> unheralded, shall come upon thee and thou shalt be
> called to give account for thy death."*[10]

Love

The Biblical word 'love' covers a multitude of virtues that are
conveniently indicated, although not exactly specified, by this one
word; for many people, its meaning embraces all virtue.

Using the word thus, it may truly be said that Bahá'u'lláh
teachings are the most perfect expression of love the world has yet
been granted; man's spiritual capacity has advanced since the days
of Jesus or Muhammad, so that we in our day can receive a fuller
expression of the Love of God than could the men of those times.

In another sense also, His Teachings express perfect love. Like
all the Manifestations of God He suffered—both in ways men can
understand and in ways they cannot—to release that spiritual power
that regenerates souls and creates the world anew. Through His
suffering, as through theirs, the banner of divine sovereignty has
been raised and the gate to the path of salvation opened.

Some people regard love for mankind as the most important
kind of love: a number of Bahá'u'lláh's teachings on this have
already been given.** 'Abdu'l-Bahá summarises them thus in His
Will:

> *"Wherefore, O my loving friends! Consort with all the
> peoples, kindreds and religions of the world with the
> utmost truthfulness, uprightness, faithfulness,*

---

* See pages 139-42.
**See Chapter IV.

*kindliness, goodwill arid friend liness; that all the world
of being may be filled with the holy ecstasy of the grace
of Bahá, that ignorance, enmity, hate and rancour may
vanish from the world and the darkness of estrangement
amidst the peoples and kindreds of the world may give
way to the Light of Unity. Should other peoples and
nations be unfaithful to you show your fidelity unto
them, should they be unjust toward you show justice
toward them, should they keep aloof from you attract
them to yourself, should they show their enmity be
friendly toward them, should they poison your lives
sweeten their souls, should they inflict a wound upon
you be a salve to their sores. Such are the attributes of
the sincere! Such are the attributes of the truthful."*[11]

This kind of love is expressed in friendliness, compassion, and
service. 'Abdu'l-Bahá, the perfect Exemplar Whose example Bahá'í
try to follow, showed all these qualities to a degree no one can hope
to emulate until the next Manifestation of God comes. His whole
life is evidence of His great love. The following description of Him
in old age, when His physical powers were failing, illustrates how
perfectly He manifested these qualities: 'During the winter of
1919-20 the writer [J. E. Esslemont] had the great privilege of
spending two and a half months as the guest of 'Abdu'l-Bahá at
Haifa and intimately observing His daily life. At that time, although
nearly 76 years of age, He was still remarkably vigorous, and
accomplished daily an almost incredible amount of work. Although
often very weary He showed wonderful powers of recuperation,
and His services were always at the disposal of those who needed
them most. His unfailing patience, gentleness, kindliness and tact
made His presence like a. benediction. It was His custom to spend
a large part of each night in prayer and meditation. From early
morning until evening, except for a short siesta after lunch, He was
busily engaged in reading and answering letters from many lands
and in attending to the multitudinous affairs of the household and of

the Cause. In the afternoon He usually had a little relaxation in the form of a walk or drive, but even then He was usually accompanied by one or two, or a party, of pilgrims with whom He would converse on spiritual matters, or He would find opportunity by the way of seeing and ministering to some of the poor. After His return He would call the friends to the usual evening meeting in His salon. Both at lunch and supper He used to entertain a number of pilgrims and friends, and charm His guests with happy and humorous stories as well as precious talks on a great variety of subjects. '*My home is the home of laughter and mirth,*' He declared, and indeed it was so. He delighted in gathering together people of various races, colours, nations and religions in unity and cordial friendship around His hospitable board. He was indeed a loving father not only to the little community at Haifa, but to the Bahá'í Community throughout the world."[12]

A no less important kind of love is the love of man for God, which is the key to the Divine Kingdom. Of it Bahá'u'lláh says:

"*O Son of Being! Love Me, that I may love thee. If thou lovest Me not, My love can in no wise reach thee. Know this, O servant.*"[13]

Love for God requires love of whatever belongs to the heavenly world, such as the qualities discussed in this chapter, and detachment from whatever belongs to the human world, such as material satisfaction and personal prestige. Thus Bahá'u'lláh says:

"*O Son of Man! If thou lovest Me, turn away from thyself; and if thou seekest. My pleasure, regard not thine own; that thou mayest die in Me and I may live eternally in thee.*"[14]

Detachment

The Writings of Bahá'u'lláh abound in exhortations to detachment, to achieve which is one of the purposes of our life on this earth. He says:

"O My Servants! Were ye to discover the hidden, the shoreless oceans of My incorruptible wealth, ye would, of a certainty, esteem as nothing the world, nay the entire creation. Let the flame of search burn with such fierceness within your hearts as to enable you to attain your supreme and most exalted goal— the station at which ye can draw nigh unto, and be united with, your Best-Beloved."[15]

"O My servant! Free thy self from the fetters of this world, and loose thy soul from the prison of self. Seize thy chance, for it will come to thee no more."[16]

The mystic path, which seekers have trodden under the guidance of every Manifestation of God, is truly the path of detachment, by which designation Bahá'u'lláh Himself refers to it in His epilogue to *The Hidden Words.*

Detachment does not imply complete renunciation. Asceticism and self-torment have no place on the path to God illumined by Bahá'u'lláh. Explaining the meaning of detachment from the world, He says:

"Know ye that by 'the world' is meant your unawareness of Him Who is your Maker, and your absorption in aught else but Him. The 'life to come', on the other hand, signifieth the things that give you a safe approach to God, the All-Glorious, the Incomparable. Whatsoever deterreth you, in this Day, from loving God is nothing but the world. Flee it, that ye may be numbered with the blest. Should a man wish to adorn himself with the ornaments of the earth, to wear its apparels, or partake of the benefits it can bestow, no harm can befall him, if he alloweth nothing whatever to intervene between him and God, for God hath ordained every good thing, whether created in the heavens or in the earth, for such of His servants as truly believe in Him. Eat ye, O people,

*of the good things which God hath allowed you and
deprive not yourselves from His wondrous bounties.
Render thanks and praise unto Him, and be of them
that are truly thankful."*[17]

Justice

Bahá'u'lláh's explanation of detachment indicates that middle way
which so often is the way of justice. Extremes are rarely defensible
Bahá'u'lláh comments:

*"Whoso cleaveth to justice, can, under no
circumstances, transgress the limits of moderation."*[18]

Justice is especially important in the present age of the unification
of mankind because, says Bahá'u'lláh:

*"That which traineth the world is justice, for it is upheld
by two pillars, reward and punishment. These two pillars
are the sources of life to the world."*[19]

It is clear that Bahá'u'lláh means by justice something very
different from the apportionment of legal punishment, which is all
the word conveys to some people justice is an Attribute of God, a
spiritual quality that all must seek: One who has this quality will deal
with others justly, whether or not he possesses worldly power.
Speaking of the need for all to be just, 'Abdu'l-Bahá said:

*"Justice is not limited, it is a universal quality. Its
operation must be carried out in all classes, from the
highest to the lowest. Justice must be sacred, and the
rights of all the people must be considered. Desire for
others only what you desire for your selves. Then shall
we rejoice in the sun of Justice which shines from the
Horizon of God. Each man has been placed in a post
of honour, which he must not desert. A humble workman
who commits an injustice is as much to blame as a
renowned tyrant. Thus we all have our choice between
justice and injustice."*[20]

The quality of justice is manifested in apportionment of reward and punishment according to deserts; upon such manifest justice any stable world order must be built. Should men be assured that reward and punishment would always and unavoidably be justly apportioned, crime would cease and the conduct of all men would be greatly improved. The World Order of Bahá'u'lláh will embody justice as no political order has yet done, encouraging men correspondingly to live as God would have them live. Hence 'Abdu'l-Bahá exclaims:

> *"God be praised! The sun of justice hath risen above the horizon of Bahá'u'lláh. For in His Tablets the foundations of such a justice have been laid as no mind hath, from the beginning of creation, conceived."*[21]

However even these comments do not portray the full significance of the quality of justice. A just judgment is one which is influenced neither by the judge's own desire, nor his personal views, nor self-interest, nor pre-conceived expectation, nor any of the factors which might deflect a judgment from true justice. Only one who is suitably detached can achieve wholly just judgments. If he is intellectually detached, he achieves what is sometimes called 'scientific detachment', the kind of detachment that enables scientists to assess evidence and make discoveries; a similar attitude in different circumstances enables a legal judge to guide a jury to a just decision. But these are both limited forms of justice, since the scientist may be an unjust employer, the judge a tyrant in his home, and both may support unjust governmental policies. True justice ensures that all judgments are just, whether scientific or legal, political, religious or personal. Those who possess this quality are enabled to understand divine truths, because the veils of self and attachment to the world have been lifted. Their souls are receptive to the Word of God and their lives reflect His commandments. No wonder Bahá'u'lláh exclaims:

> *"O Son of Spirit! The best beloved of all things in My*

sight is Justice; turn not away therefrom if thou desirest Me, and neglect it not that I may confide in thee. By its aid thou shalt see with thine own eyes and not through the eyes of others, and shalt know of thine own knowledge and not through the knowledge of thy neighbour. Ponder this in thy heart, how it behoveth thee to be. Verily justice is My gift to thee and the sign of My loving-kindness. Set it then before thine eyes."[22]

Mercy and Forgiveness

Justice does not preclude mercy and forgiveness. True justice is merciful, although the mercy may not be evident to those affected. The Mercy of God is not always apparent to men, to whom His Justice may at first appear unjust. Our limited human viewpoint enables us to see only part of the picture and our limited human understanding enables us to understand only part of what we see. It is not, then, surprising that Divine Justice is beyond our comprehension, nor that many people are unwilling to admit this limitation; a young child is similarly unable always to appreciate the merciful justice of its parents, or to admit that they are better able to judge what is to its own best advantage.

Forgiveness, as well as mercy, is enjoined by Bahá'u'lláh as a personal obligation:

"He should forgive the sinful, and never despise his low estate, for none knoweth what his own end shall be."[23]

But this does not mean that society should forgive those that sin against it. 'Abdu'l-Bahá asserts:

"The canopy of existence resteth upon the pole of justice, and not of forgiveness, and the life of mankind dependeth on justice and not on forgiveness."[24]

And He explains:

"If someone oppresses, injures, and wrongs another,

and the wronged man retaliates, this is vengeance and is censurable.

...If 'Amru dishonours Zaid, the latter has not the right to dishonour 'Amru; if he does so, this is vengeance, and it is very reprehensible. No, rather he must return good for evil, and not only forgive, but also, if possible, be of service to his oppressor.... But the community has the right of defence and of self- protection; moreover, the community has no hatred nor animosity for the murderer; it imprisons or punishes him merely for the protection and security of others. . . . If the community and the inheritors of the murdered one were to forgive and return good for evil, the cruel would be continually ill-treating others, and assassinations would continually occur. Vicious people, like wolves, would destroy the sheep of God. The community has no ill-will and rancour in the infliction of punishment, and it does not desire to appease the anger of the heart; its purpose is by punishment to protect others, so that no atrocious actions may be committed."[25]

Trustworthiness

The need for personal integrity is greatly stressed by Bahá'u'lláh:

"A good character is, verily, the best mantle for men from God. With it He adorneth the temples of His loved ones. By My life! The light of a good character surpasseth the light of the sun and the radiance thereof."[26]

Of trustworthiness, Bahá'u'lláh writes:

"Verily, this is the door of tranquillity to all in the world, and the sign of glory from the presence of the Merciful One. Whosoever attains thereto has attained to treasuries of wealth and affluence. Trustworthiness is

the greatest door to the security and tranquillity of mankind. The stability of every affair always depends on it, and the worlds of honour, glory and affluence are illuminated by its light. "[27]

Trustworthiness implies utter truthfulness, which is strongly enjoined. Nevertheless, 'Abdu'l-Bahá explains that too great a rigidity about such matters may be harmful, since exceptional circumstances may arise, in which obedience to one of the commands of God involves modifying obedience to another:

"Consider that the worst of qualities and most odious of attributes, which is the foundation of all evil, is lying. No worse or more blameworthy quality than this can be imagined to exist; it is the destroyer of all human perfections, and the cause of in numerable vices. There is no worse characteristic than this; it is the foundation of all evils. Notwithstanding all this, if a doctor consoles a sick man by saying; 'Thank God you are better, and there is hope of your recovery', though these words are contrary to the truth, yet they may become the consolation of the patient and turning-point of the illness. This is not blame worthy."[28]

Purity
Bahá'u'lláh stresses the need for purity, which in its ultimate spiritual meaning refers to purity of motive, and detachment from self and the desires of the world. He explains:

"He hath chosen out of the whole world the hearts of His servants and made them each a seat for the revelation of His glory. Wherefore, sanctify them from every defilement, that the things for which they were created may be engraven upon them. This indeed is a token of God's bountiful favour."[29]

The heart of man must be pure, that the Love of God may

manifest itself therein; it must be kindly, that it may attract others to that love; and it must be radiant, that Divine Love may be transmitted to those who are attracted. Hence Bahá'u'lláh says:

"O Son of Spirit! My first counsel is this: Possess a pure, kindly and radiant heart, that thine may be a sovereignty ancient, imperishable and everlasting."[30]

Such purity is closely allied to detachment from the things of the world and particularly from its lusts. Bahá'u'lláh proclaims:

"We, verily, have decreed in Our Book a goodly and bountiful reward to whosoever will turn away from wickedness, and lead a chaste and godly life. He, in truth, is the Great Giver, the All-Bountiful."[31]

Bahá'u'lláh enjoins all to be chaste, especially women:[*]

"Purity and chastity have been, and still are, the most great ornaments for the handmaidens of God. God is My Witness! The brightness of the light of chastity sheddeth its illumination upon the worlds of the spirit, and its fragrance is wafted even unto the Most Exalted Paradise."[32]

Cleanliness, although only physical, aids the achievement of purity. 'Abdu'l-Bahá wrote:

"My meaning is this, that in every aspect of life, purity and holiness, cleanliness and refinement, exalt the human condition and further the development of man's inner reality. Even in the physical realm, cleanliness will conduce to spirituality, as the Holy Writings clearly state. And although bodily cleanliness is a physical thing, it hath, nevertheless, a powerful influence on the life of the spirit."[33]

Association with those who obey the commands of God is also

---

[*] For the teaching of Bahá'u'lláh on marriage, see pages 321-22.

a useful aid to purity. Bahá'u'lláh says:

"The company of the ungodly increaseth sorrow, whilst fellowship with the righteous cleaneth the rust from off the heart."[34]

But an even more potent means of purifying the heart is prayer and meditation. Bahá'u'lláh exclaims:

"O Son of Glory! Be swift in the path of holiness and enter the heaven of communion with Me. Cleanse thy heart with the burnish of the spirit, and hasten to the Court of the Most High."[35]

Most potent of all, without which neither purity, nor detachment, nor love, nor justice is obtainable, is obedience to the commands of the Manifestation of God. Such obedience enables man to advance along the path of detachment to that purity of heart which allows him to see with the eye of justice and to receive the Love of God into his heart. No wonder Bahá'u'lláh proclaims:

"All must adhere to and practise that which hath been revealed from the Supreme Pen. The True One testifies and the atoms of the universe bear witness that We have spoken and revealed in Tablets and Epistles from the Supreme Pen that which is conducive to the exaltation, elevation, training, protection, and progress of the people of the earth. We beg of God to strengthen the servants."[36]

Unity

The Revelation of Bahá'u'lláh centres in the Oneness of Mankind with its many implications, so that His whole Revelation concerns unity. Several chapters of this book, notably Chapters IV and V, explain how His Word promotes it. Nevertheless, a few specific teachings, not mentioned elsewhere, are indicated here.

Bahá'u'lláh vehemently exhorts the believers in His Revelation to maintain unity amongst themselves and to promote it among others, saying:

> *"Every eye, in this Day, should seek what will best promote the Cause of God. He, Who is the Eternal Truth, beareth Me witness! Nothing whatever can, in this Day, inflict a greater harm upon this Cause than dissension and strife, contention, estrangement and apathy, among the loved ones of God. Flee them, through the power of God and His sovereign aid, and strive ye to knit together the hearts of men, in His Name, the Unifier, the All-Knowing, the All-Wise."*[37]

One of the greatest enemies of unity is gossip which Bahá'u'lláh strongly discourages. He says:

> *"Well is it with the righteous that mock not the sinful, but rather conceal: their misdeeds, so that their own shortcomings may remain veiled to men's eyes."*[38]

and proclaims forcefully:

> *"O Son of Man Breathe not the sins of others so long as thou art a sinner. Shouldst thou transgress this command, accursed wouldst thou be, and to this I bear witness."*[39]

Should mankind as a whole ever come to obedience to this commnand, much misery would be avoided. Gossip degrades both him who speaks and him who listens. Bahá'u'lláh explains:

> *"Backbiting quencheth the light of the heart, and extinguisheth the life of the soul."*[40]

Indeed, He adds that any excess of speech is a deadly poison:

> *"Material fire consumeth the body, whereas the fire of the tongue devoureth both heart and soul. The force of the former lasteth but for a time, whilst the effects of the latter endure a century."*[41]

Miscellaneous Teachings

A few other ethical teachings of Bahá'u'lláh are too important to be omitted from this chapter. Humility and reverence are greatly praised:

"They who are the beloved of God, in whatever place they gather and whomsoever they may meet, must evince, in their attitude towards God, and in the manner of the celebration of His praise and glory, such humility and submissiveness that every atom of the dust beneath their feet may attest the depth of their devotion."[42]

Courtesy is given a high station:

"We, verily, have chosen courtesy, and made it the true mark of such as are nigh unto Him. Courtesy is, in truth, a raiment which fitteth all men, whether young or old. Well is it with him that adorneth his temple therewith, and woe unto him who is deprived of this great bounty."[43]

Kindness to animals is enjoined. 'Abdu'l-Bahá says:

"Sensibility is the same whether you harm man or animal. There is no difference. Nay, rather, cruelty to the animal is more painful because man has a tongue and he sighs, complains and groans when he receives an injury and complains to the government and the government protects him from cruelty; but the poor animal cannot speak, it can neither show its suffering nor is it able to appeal to the government.... Therefore one must be very considerate towards animals and show greater kindness to them than to man. Educate the children in their infancy in such a way that they may become exceedingly kind and merciful to the animals. If an animal is sick, they should endeavour to cure it; if it is hungry, they should feed it; if it is thirsty, they should

satisfy its thirst; if it is tired, they should give it rest. "[44]

Both the taking of drugs and the consumption of alcohol is forbidden by Bahá'u'lláh in His Book of Laws, *the Kitáb-í Aqdas (The Most Holy Book)*. 'Abdu'l-Bahá explains:

"The drinking of wine is, according to the text of the Most Holy Book, forbidden; for it is the cause of chronic diseases, weakeneth the nerves, and consumeth the mind."[45]

A growing body of medical men is coming to realise the truth of this statement.

The Creative Power of Righteous Deeds

Putting into practice these teachings of Bahá'u'lláh on individual conduct has a creative power so wonderful that it could be termed miraculous were it not available to everybody Bahá'u'lláh says of it:

"Through the power of the words He hath uttered the whole of the human race can be illumined with the light of unity, and the remembrance of His Name is able to set on fire the hearts of all men, and burn away the veils that intervene between them and His glory. One righteous act is endowed with a potency that can so elevate the dust as to cause it to pass beyond the heaven of heavens. It can tear every bond asunder, and hath the power to restore the force that hath spent itself and vanished."[46]

Righteous deeds attract divine confirmation to the one who acts and to all mankind. Expressing faith, they purify the heart of man and enable him to draw near to God. Through them, he achieves his true station; through them his love for God and his fellow-men is made manifest; through them is expressed obedience of which Bahá'u'lláh wrote:

"The beginning of all things is the knowledge of God, and the end of a things is strict observance of whatsoever hath been sent down from the empyrean of the Divine Will that pervadeth all that is in the heavens and all that is on the earth."[47]

Man's first duty is to recognise the Manifestation of God for the age in which he lives; his second duty is to be obedient to the commands the Divine Messenger chooses to reveal. All who accept these two obligations have placed their feet firmly on the path of spiritual progress and will receive increasingly the reward God gives to those who make efforts for His sake—the Knowledge and the Love of God.

CHAPTER VIII

Science and the Knowledge of God

The Independent Investigation of Truth

From time immemorial man has sought the Knowledge and the Love of God. He has travelled in search of it along many roads and down countless byways. Sometimes the search has led him nearer to truth, sometimes it has taken him further from it. Often those who prided themselves on their knowledge have been very far from true understanding; often those who were scorned by men of learning have been roses in the garden of truth. Jesus was an unlettered carpenter; Caiaphas was a learned High Priest; but the knowledge of Jesus was to the knowledge of Caiaphas as the light of the sun is to the light of a candle. Caiaphas was honoured and revered by the learned men of Israel because his learning was of the same kind as theirs—acceptance of errors made by generation upon generation of Jewish Rabbis, each adding its own particular errors to those of earlier generations. Clearly, study of the opinions and beliefs commonly held by the learned men of a particular age is no sure path to the Knowledge of God. Any study made must be critical and not mere blind endorsement of the opinions of those temporarily possessing prestige.

Still less is blind acceptance of the views of one's ancestors assure path to the Knowledge of God. Such uncritical believes responsible for much of the world's trouble; for a man who blindly is unable either to defend his belief by reason of adopt it to unfamiliar knowledge. When he meets new truth, he must either reject it or discard his belief. It is not surprising that this unthinking acceptance has led to much suffering and bloodshed even within the short span covered by historical records. 'Abdu'l-Bahá spoke in New York of the enmity that exists between 'nations,' i.e. the followers of different religions, as a result of it:

> *"The darkness of imitations encompasses the world.*
> *Every nation is holding to its traditional religious forms.*
> *The light of reality is obscured. Were these various*
> *nations to investigate the reality, there is no doubt they*
> *would attain to it. As reality is one, all nations would*
> *then become as one nation. So long as they adhere to*
> *various imitations and are deprived of the reality, strife*
> *and warfare will continue and rancour and sedition*
> *prevail. If they investigate the reality, neither enmity*
> *nor rancour will remain and they will attain to the utmost*
> *concord among themselves."*[1]

This independent investigation of truth is of the utmost
importance both to society and to the individual. The nature of man
is such that he must investigate to fulfil his own being; blind
acceptance is as death to the soul. One of the ways in which God
separates the righteous from the unrighteous at the coming of a
Manifestation of God is so to manifest Himself that the clouds of
idle fancy conceal Him from all except those whose sight is sharp
and who investigate truth independently. Speaking in Boston,
'Abdu'l-Bahá said:

> *"God has given man the eye of investigation by which*
> *he may see and recognise truth. He has endowed man*
> *with ears that he may hear the message of reality and*
> *conferred upon him the gift of reason by which he may*
> *discover things for himself. This is his endowment and*
> *equipment for the investigation of reality. Man is not*
> *intended to see through the eyes of another, hear*
> *through another's ears nor comprehend with another's*
> *brain. Each human creature has individual endowment,*
> *power and responsibility in the creative plan of God.*
> *Therefore depend upon your own reason and judgment*
> *and adhere to the outcome of your own investigation;*
> *otherwise you will be utterly submerged in the sea of*

ignorance and deprived of all the bounties of God. Turn to God, supplicate humbly at His threshold, seeking assistance and confirmation, that God may rend asunder the veils that obscure your vision. Then will your eyes be filled with illumination, face to face you will behold the reality of God and your heart become completely purified from the dross of ignorance, reflecting the glories and bounties of the kingdom."[2]

Until a man has detached himself from preconceived opinions inherited from his ancestors, he has not taken the first step in search of truth. Prejudice weighs him down and prevents his turning towards the light. To cut himself free from prejudice may be a long and wearisome undertaking, but it is essential for all truth-seekers, whether the search be religious or scientific.

Harmony of Science and Religion

It should not surprise anyone that the essential prerequisite for both kinds of search is the same, because truth is one. Science does not seek a specifically scientific truth inconsistent with true religion unless it is faulty science; and religion does not seek a specifically religious truth inconsistent with true science, unless it is faulty religion. 'Abdu'l-Bahá said in Pittsburgh:

"Any religious belief which is not conformable with scientific proof and investigation is superstition, for true science is reason and reality, and religion is essentially reality and pure reason; therefore the two must correspond. Religious teaching which is at variance with science and reason is human invention and imagination unworthy of acceptance, for the antithesis and opposite of knowledge is superstition born of the ignorance of man. If we say religion is opposed to science we either lack of true science or true religion, for both are founded the premises and conclusions of reason and both must bear its test."[3]

Many superstitions inconsistent with true science have been taught, in the name of religion; such beliefs are among the prejudice that must be discarded by all who seek God. They are as veils obscuring the way of truth. But in this age another kind of prejudice is also apparent—the prejudice of pseudo. Scientific materialism, the belief that the only reality is that experienced through the senses.

Materialism is no more consistent with true science than it is with true religion. Current scientific knowledge of the nature of matter offers no basis for materialism; experiments on telepathy, clairvoyance, and prediction provide strong scientific evidence against it. Its addicts, however, are convinced neither by logic nor by experiment; they are entrenched against reason in the pit dug by their prejudices and as unshakable in their conviction as the most ignorant, fear-ridden devotee of superstition. 'Abdu'l-Bahá used good-natured ridicule to induce them to see their error. For example, in Montreal He said:

"All the animals are materialists. They are deniers of God and without realisation of a transcendent power in the universe. They have no knowledge of the divine prophets and holy books; mere captives of nature and the sense world. In reality they are like the great philsophers of this day who are not in touch with God and the Holy Spirit; deniers of the prophets, ignorant of spiritual susceptibilities, deprived of the heavenly bounties and without belief in the supernatural. The animal lives this kind of life blissfully and untroubled whereas the material philosophers labour and study for ten or twenty years in schools and colleges, denying God, the Holy Spirit and divine inspirations. The animal is even a greater philosopher, for it attains the ability to do this without labour and study. For instance, the cow denies God and the Holy Spirit, knows nothing of divine inspirations, heavenly bounties or spiritual emotions and is a stranger to the world of hearts. Like the philosophers, the cow is a captive of nature and

knows nothing beyond the range of the senses. The philosophers, however, glory in this, saying 'We are not captives of superstitions; we have implicit faith in the impressions of the senses and know nothing beyond the realm of nature which contains and covers everything!' But the cow without study or proficiency in the sciences, modestly and quietly views life from the same standpoint, living in harmony with nature's laws in the utmost dignity and nobility. This is not the glory of man. The glory of man is in the knowledge of God, spiritual susceptibilities, attainment to transcendent powers and the bounties of the Holy Spirit. The glory of man is in being informed of the teachings of God. This is the glory of humanity. Ignorance is not glory but darkness."[4]

Superstition and materialism are the twin morasses into which religion and science fall when religion is divorced from reason and science from inspiration. 'Abdu'l-Bahá said when in Paris:

"Religion and science are the two wings upon which man's intelligence can soar into the heights, with which the human soul can progress. It is not possible to fly with one wing alone. Should a man try to fly with the wing of religion alone he would quickly fall into the quagmire of superstition, whilst on the other hand, with the wing of science alone he would also make no progress, but fall into the despairing slough of materialism."[5]

Knowledge

Both religion and science include within their field the search for knowledge. The pure scientist does not reckon the use to which his discoveries may be put; to the extent that he does consider these, he ceases to be a pure scientist. His object is knowledge—knowledge of that particular part of creation with which his research deals, and of the laws that govern it.

The religious seeker also seeks knowledge, a knowledge which may fittingly be described as spiritual. This is the same in essence as the knowledge the scientist seeks, a different mode of the one knowledge that is the source of all others, the Knowledge of God. All creation is but an expression of the Knowledge of God, and study of creation is but study of His Knowledge. Bahá'u'lláh expresses this by saying:

"All things in their inmost reality, testify to the revelation of the names and attributes of God within them. Each according to its capacity indicateth, and is expressive of, the knowledge of God. So potent and universal is this revelation, that it hath encompassed all things visible and invisible."[6]

Similarly, study of the laws governing creation is in the last resort study of the Will of God. No wonder, then, that Bahá'u'lláh proclaims:

"The source of all learning is the knowledge of God, exalted be His Glory, and this cannot be attained save through the knowledge of His Divine Manifestation."[7]

Thus God is both the Source and the Object of all knowledge; but since there can be no direct intercourse between Him and His creation, He manifests Himself in the Holy Spirit, the Intermediary between God and Creation* to whom the term 'source and Object of all knowledge' may justly be applied.

It may be that scientific and religious seekers will pay more attention to each other's methods in the future than they have done in the past. In our own age, the great prestige of science ensures scientific method at least a hearing from most religious seekers, but an assertion that science can learn from religion risks ridicule from those influenced by materialism. The author will, therefore, illustrate his point by a suggestion of his own, which scientists to whom he has made it privately have thought worth considering.

---

* See pages 27-28.

Most people qualified to judge will agree that scientific discoveries are not made by means of rigid deduction of the kind discussed in text-books on logic. The human mind does not work that way. In practice what happens is that thinking about relevant facts leads, either gradually or suddenly, to the formation of a hypothesis, which is then tested by reason and observation. The hypothesis is a kind of inspired guess, an idea only partly accounted for by preliminary reasoning and observation; its ultimate emergence is more akin to intuition than text-book logic.

If any way could be found of arriving at better, truer, more accurate, more fundamental hypotheses, there can be no doubt that science would benefit. The search for religious truth provides just the methods needed to attain this end. Prayer, meditation, the study of Holy Writings, obedience to the commands of God, detachment, purity, drawing near to God, may prove as fruitful conditions for the emergence of such hypotheses in scientific minds as they are for the attainment of spiritual knowledge in the minds of those who seek religious truth.

Should this ever be generally recognised, the paths of science and religion would draw closer and their harmony become visible to all.

The Path to God
For seekers after spiritual knowledge, an early step must be to realise the difference between knowledge and learning. Knowledge is a ray of understanding the sun of Truth, whereas learning is only an accumulation of supposed facts. A man of great learning may have less true knowledge than a labourer, and a labourer may have more true knowledge than the most learned of men. Indeed, learning is apt to become a veil obscuring the Sun of Truth, so that scholars must be wary that their learning does not lead them astray. Thus Bahá'u'lláh instructs:

"Oh my brother, when a true seeker determines to take the step of search in the path leading to the knowledge of the Ancient of Days, he must, before all else, cleanse

and purify his heart, which is the seat of the revelation
of the inner mysteries of God, from the obscuring dust
of all acquired knowledge, and the allusions of the
embodiments of satanic fancy. He must purge his breast,
which is the sanctuary of the abiding love of the
Beloved, of every defilement, and sanctify his soul from
all that pertaineth to water and clay, from all shadowy
and ephemeral attachments." [8]

Only when he has stepped on to this path will the seeker for the first time become conscious of the Love of God. He may have the experience, sometimes described as 'conversion,' in which the Love of God becomes his constant aim and the object of his yearning desire; but he must not think that because he has this experience he has achieved his goal. It signifies only that the path has led him to a particular valley on the route; if he presses on resolutely with his search he will pass through many more. Should he persevere, and should his journey be blessed, he may eventually reach that green land where he achieves the goal of his endeavour by entering the Presence of the Manifestation of God.

The first entry into the Presence is described by Bahá'u'lláh as follows:

"This station is the dying from self and the living in
God, the being poor in self and rich in the Desired
One. Poverty as here referred to signifieth being poor
in the things of the created world, rich in the things of
God's world. For when the true lover and devoted friend
reacheth to the presence of the Beloved, the sparkling
beauty of the Loved One and the fire of the lover's
heart will kindle a blaze and burn away all veils and
wrappings. Yea, all he hath, from heart to skin, will be
set aflame, so that nothing will remain save the Friend." [9]

It is not to be expected that a guide to those searching for spiritual knowledge, such as the Tablet from which this quotation comes, should be easy to understand. Everyone must discover truth for himself; Bahá'u'lláh provides the means for the journey, but the journey must be made by each soul separately. Thus Bahá'u'lláh exclaims:

> *"O my servants! My holy, My divinely ordained Revelation may be likened unto an ocean in whose depths are concealed innumerable pearls of great price, of surpassing lustre. It is the duty of every seeker to bestir himself and strive to attain the shores of this ocean, so that he may, in proportion to the eagerness of his search and the efforts he hath exerted, partake of such benefits as have been pre-ordained in God's irrevocable and hidden tablets."*[10]

Mysticism and the Bahá'í Faith

This search for spiritual knowledge is the true mysticism, and in this sense of the word the Bahá'í Faith is a mystical religion; but the word has connotations that do not apply to the Bahá'í Faith. Thus, some mystics believe they can become one with God, a belief Bahá'í's consider blasphemous, implying as it does that God is of the same substance as His creation.

Possibly the great mystics did not hold this belief, even though it is attributed to most of them; their failure to find words adequately to convey experiences that the garment of words cannot contain may have led to misunderstanding. A similar misunderstanding could easily have arisen from certain passages revealed by Bahá'u'lláh Himself, for example:

> *"Let the flame of search burn with such fierceness within your hearts as to enable you to attain your supreme and most exalted goal—the station in which ye can draw nigh unto, and be united with, your Best-Beloved."*[11]

This must be read in conjunction with such explanations as:

> *"It behoveth thee to consecrate thyself to the Will of God. Whatsoever hath been 'revealed in His Tablets is*

but a reflection of His Will. So complete must be thy
consecration, that every trace of worldly desire will be
washed from thine heart. This is the meaning of true
unity." [12]

Be that as it may, it is beyond doubt that most of even the great
mystics advocated methods condemned by Bahá'u'lláh. Asceticism
and self-torment were for them standard procedure. Mortifying the
flesh was a painful but necessary way of opening the inward eye.
Rapture and ecstasy became technical terms signifying particular
trance-like states in which the mystic believed himself to draw close
to or be united with God.

The method of Bahá'u'lláh is quite different. It consists of
purification of the heart by obedience to the commandments of
God, so that the light God has placed within it can shine unobscured.
When the mirror of the heart has been sufficiently polished, and the
obscuring veils burnt away by the fire of love, the soul is enabled to
enter the Presence of the Manifestation of God and drink from the
Chalice of Everlasting life.

This is a mysticism from which none need feel revulsion. It is
no woolly substitute for lack of true understanding, nor an emotional
device for evading thought. It is an ally and associate of reason,
opening the door to realms that reason cannot enter. It is a worthy
companion for science. It is a means to the Knowledge of God.

Meditation
Flashes of spiritual insight may come at any time, but they come
most often in periods of deliberate meditation. Meditation is the
highest kind of prayer, to which it is more closely allied than it is to
thinking. In thinking, one actively directs one's mind to relevant
facts, drawing conclusions from the relations between them; in
meditation, one turns one's soul passively to the world of spirit,
concentrating on a problem and courting what God may disclose.
Thinking is directed by the will of man, which guides the mind;
meditation requires subordination of man's will to the Will of God.
The mind is at rest in meditation; but just as the will of man is never

wholly subjected to the Will of God, so the mind of man is never wholly at rest. Meditation and mental activity alternate causing traces of meditation to illumine thought processes and thought to aid understanding of knowledge acquired in meditation.

The station given to meditation in the Bahá'í Faith is high. 'Abdu'l-Bahá extolled it thus:

> *"Through the faculty of meditation man attains to eternal life; through it he receives the breath of the Holy Spirit—the bestowal of the Spirit is given in reflection and meditation.*
>
> *The spirit of man is itself informed and strengthened during meditation; through it affairs of which man knew nothing are unfolded before his view. Through it he receives Divine inspiration, through it he receives heavenly food.*
>
> *Meditation is the key for opening the doors of mysteries. In that state man . . . withdraws himself from all outside objects; in that subjective mood he is immersed in the ocean of spiritual life and can unfold the secrets of things-in-themselves. To illustrate this, think of man as endowed with two kinds of sight; when the power of insight is being used the outward power of vision does not see.*
>
> *This faculty of meditation frees man from the animal nature, discerns the reality of things, puts man in touch with God."*[13]

However, meditation is no substitute for action. Addressing the Christian monks in His Tablet to Napoleon III, Bahá'u'lláh says:

> *"O concourse of monks! Seclude not yourselves in your churches and cloisters. Come ye out of them by My leave, and busy, then, yourselves with what will profit you and others. Thus corn mandeth you He Who is the*

Lord of the Day of Reckoning. Seclude yourselves in the stronghold of My love. This, truly, is the seclusion that befitteth you, could ye but know it. He that secludeth himself in his house is indeed as one dead. It behoveth man to show forth that which will benefit mankind. He that bringeth forth no fruit is fit for the fire. "[14]

That work done in a spirit of service is equivalent to worship and may, therefore, be regarded as a form of prayer was explained earlier.[*]

Prayer

True prayer is a good deal subtler than merely making requests to God. It is so closely related to meditation that when Bahá'u'lláh makes such behests as:

"O Son of Light! Forget all save Me and commune with My spirit. This is of the essence of My command, therefore turn unto it." [15]

The behest may be satisfied either by prayer or by meditation. The nature of prayer is illumined by the following excerpt from a Tablet of 'Abdu'l-Bahá:

"The wisdom of prayer is this: that it causeth a connection between the servant and the True One, because in that state man with all heart and soul turneth his face towards His Highness the Almighty, seeking His association and desiring His love and compassion. The greatest happiness for a lover is to converse with his beloved, and the greatest gift for a seeker is to become familiar with the object of his longing; that is why with every soul who is attracted to the Kingdom of God, his greatest hope is to find an opportunity to entreat and supplicate before his Beloved, appeal for His mercy

---

[*] See page 102.

*and grace and be immersed in the ocean of His
utterance, goodness and generosity. Besides all this,
prayer and fasting* is the cause of awakening and
mindfulness and conducive to protection and
preservation from tests.* "[16]

In all prayer, man seeks to communicate with his Loved One.
Words may be used to focus attention and to direct the mind and
soul towards God, but the true orison is the prayerful attitude they
engender and not the specific verbal requests made. That God
permits men to pray to Him in words of supplication is a great
bounty and a mercy granted to human weakness.

The power of prayer should be used to further the Will of God,
not the will of man. Bahá'u'lláh commands:

*"O Son of Spirit! Ask not of Me that which we desire
not for thee, then be content with what We have ordained
for thy sake, for this is that which profiteth thee, if
therewith thou dost content thyself."* [17]

The attitude of prayer attracts confirmation; if we supplicate
those things God desires, either on our own behalf or on behalf of
others, our prayer will be confirmed. Praying for heavenly qualities
helps us to acquire them, and our prayers for others aid their spiritual
progress. Even if we pray for things God does not desire, our prayer
is not wasted; the breeze of heavenly confirmation is wafted upon
us, helping us to want the right things instead of those we prayed
for. The answer to our prayer may not be to give us what we asked
for, but it will for the Bahá'í teaching on fasting, certainly be 'that
which profiteth' us, with which we should be content.

Bahá'u'lláh and 'Abdu'l-Bahá both revealed many prayers,
which illustrate for us the kind of request God would have us make
of Him. Only their prayers and the few still available of those
revealed by other Divine Manifestations are used by the Bahá'ís at
their meetings. Most of them are anthems of praise. They have the

---

* For the Bahá'í teaching on fasting, see pages 327-28.

power, to a far, far greater extent than any supplication devised by man, of calling forth the attitude of true adoration. A few examples are given at the end of this chapter.

Bahá'u'lláh revealed also many meditations in which He addresses Himself to God in praise proclaiming His devotion to the Divine Will and praying for Himself and for others. Reading them has much the same effect as prayer in drawing the soul nearer to God. Examples of these meditations also are given at the- end of this chapter.

Prayers and meditations of the Messengers of God have a special potency because their words clothe spiritual truths, lying far deeper than the apparent meaning of the words. They carry the breaths of the Holy Spirit, which are wafted not only over the hearts of all who read them, but over the hearts of all mankind. Bahá'u'lláh exhorts:

> *"Intone, O my servants, the verses of God that have been received by thee, as intoned by them who have drawn nigh unto Him, that the sweetness of thy melody may kindle thine own soul, and attract the hearts of all men. Whoso reciteth, in the privacy of his chamber, the verses revealed by God, the scattering angels of the Almighty shall scatter abroad the fragrance of the words uttered by his mouth, and shall cause the heart of every righteous man to throb. Though he may, at first, remain unaware of its effect, yet the virtue of the grace vouchsafed unto him must needs sooner or later exercise its influence upon his soul. Thus have the mysteries of the Revelation of God been decreed by virtue of the will of Him Who is the Source of power and wisdom."* [18]

Although Bahá'u'lláh states that even words recited in privacy have this effect, He encourages Bahá'ís to come together to pray, saying:

> *"He that seeketh to commune with God, let him betake himself to the companionship of His loved ones."* [19]

Such communal worship has greater power than isolated devotion, but in the Bahá'í Dispensation there are to be no congregational prayers except for one revealed by Bahá'u'lláh to be said in unison at funerals. All others are recited by one person on behalf of everyone present. A Bahá'í devotional programme consists of prayers and readings from the Holy Writings, selected in advance and apportioned to different readers. Chanting instead of reading is customary in the Middle East, but Western languages are not suitable for chanting. The Holy Writings are sometimes sung in these languages, and this may later become more usual, but for the present it is rare.

Know Thyself

In the course of one of His meditations, Bahá'u'lláh reveals the following:

> *"Far, far from Thy glory be what mortal man can affirm of Thee, or attribute unto Thee, or the praise with which he can glorify Thee! Whatever duty Thou has prescribed unto Thy servants of extolling to the utmost Thy majesty and glory is but a token of Thy grace unto them, that they may be enabled to ascend unto the station conferred upon their own inmost being, the station of the knowledge of their own selves."*[20]

Throughout the ages men have realised that one path to the Knowledge of God lay through self-knowledge. The traditional Jewish story of the creation of man in the image of God implies it. Hindu and Buddhist philosophy advocates it. The Ancient Greeks were so well aware of it that they inscribed on stone the injunction 'Know thyself.' All the great religions have confirmed it, and in this age Bahá'u'lláh has given mankind a fresh understanding of it and a new approach to it. He even says:

> *"True loss is for him whose days have been spent in utter ignorance of his true self."*[21]

The Teachings of Bahá'u'lláh concerning the nature of man are very important. In their depths lie hidden truths that no one has yet uncovered; future generations will gradually come to understand their implications better, and meanwhile each can find in them daily fresh truth for himself.

They contain much of interest to psychology and psychiatry, awaiting elucidation by such psychologists and psychiatrists as appreciate their value. In the study of man, science and religion can unite, for this is a field in which both methods of acquiring knowledge can be used profitably.

Nevertheless, the self-knowledge of which Bahá'u'lláh speaks is not identical with the knowledge that the scientific study of man leads to. It can be reached only by the pure in heart, who Jesus said would see God. They see Him by becoming conscious of their own inmost selves about which Bahá'u'lláh stated:

"O My servants! Could ye apprehend with what wonders of My munificence and bounty I have willed to entrust your souls, ye would, of a truth, rid yourselves of attachment to all created things, and would gain a true knowledge of your own selves—a knowledge which is the same as the comprehension of Mine own Being. Ye would find yourselves independent of all else but Me, and would perceive, with your inner and outer eye, and as manifest as the revelation of My effulgent Name, the seas of My loving kindness and bounty moving within you. Suffer not your idle fancies, your evil passions, your insincerity and blindness of heart to dim the lustre, or stain the sanctity, of so, lofty a station."[22]

No wonder then that Bahá'u'lláh has said:

"The Purpose of the one true God, exalted be His glory, in revealing Himself unto men is to lay bare those gems that lie hidden within the mine of their true and inmost selves."[23]

Some Prayers of Bahá'u'lláh

"O my God! O my God! Unite the hearts of Thy servants, and reveal to them Thy great purpose. May they follow Thy commandments steps by and abide in Thy law. Help them, O God their endeavour, and grant them strength to serve Thee O God, leave them not to themselves, but guide their step by the light of Thy knowledge and cheer their hearts by Thy love Verily, Thou art their Helper and their Lord."[24]

"Glorified art Thou, O Lord my God! I implore Thee by the onrushing winds of Thy grace, and by Them Who are the Day-Springs of Thy purpose and the Dawning-Places of Thine inspiration, to send down upon me and upon all that have sought Thy face that which beseemeth Thy generosity and bountiful grace, and is worthy of Thy bestowals and favours. Poor and desolate I am, O my Lord! Immerse me in the ocean of Thy wealth; athirst, suffer me to drink from the living waters of Thy loving-kindness.

I beseech Thee, by Thine own Self and by Him Whom Thou hast appointed as the Manifestation of Thine own Being and Thy discriminating Word unto all that are in heaven and on earth, to gather together Thy servants beneath the shade of the Tree of Thy gracious providence. Help them, then, to partake of its fruits, to incline their ears to the rustling of its leaves, and to the sweetness of the voice of the Bird that chanteth upon its branches. Thou art, verily, the Help in Peril, the Inaccessible, the Almighty, the Most Bountiful."[25]

"Suffer me, O my God, to draw nigh unto Thee, and to abide within the precincts of Thy court, for remoteness from Thee hath well nigh consumed me. Cause me to rest under the shadow of the wings of Thy grace, for

the flame of my separation from Thee hath melted my heart within me. Draw me nearer unto the river that is life indeed, for my soul burneth with thirst in its ceaseless search after Thee. My sighs, O my God, proclaim the bitterness of mine anguish, and the tears I shed attest my love for Thee.

I beseech Thee, by the praise wherewith Thou praisest Thyself and the glory wherewith Thou glorifiest Thine own Essence, to grant that we may be numbered among them that have recognised Thee and acknowledged Thy sovereignty in Thy days. Help us then to quaff, O my God, from the fingers of mercy the living waters of loving-kindness, that we may utterly forget all else except Thee, and be occupied only with Thy Self. Powerful art Thou to do what Thou willest. No God is there beside Thee, the Mighty, the Help in Peril, the Self-Subsisting.

Glorified be Thy name, O Thou Who art the King of all Kings!"[26]

"O my Lord! Make Thy beauty to be my food, and Thy presence my drink, and Thy pleasure my hope, and praise of Thee my action, and remembrance of Thee my companion, and the power of Thy sovereignty my succourer, and Thy habitation my home, and my dwelling place the seat Thou has sanctified from the limitations imposed upon them who are shut out as by a veil from Thee.

Thou art, verily, the Almighty, the All-Glorious, the Most Powerful."[27]

Some Prayers of 'Abdu'l-Bahá

"He is the Compassionate, the All-Bountiful!

O God, my God! Thou seest me, Thou knowest me; Thou

*art my Haven and my Refuge. None have I sought nor
any will I seek save Thee, no path have I trodden nor
any will I tread but he path of Thy love. In the darksome
night of despair, my eye turneth expectant and full of
hope to the morn of Thy boundless favour and at the
hour of dawn my drooping soul is refreshed and
strengthened in remembrance of Thy beauty and
perfection. He whom the grace of Thy mercy aideth,
though he be but a drop, shall become the boundless
ocean, and the merest atom which the outpouring of
Thy loving kindness assisteth, shall shine even as the
radiant star.*

*Shelter under Thy protection, O Thou. Spirit of Purity,
Thou Who art the All-Bountiful Provider, this enthralled,
enkindled servant of Thine. Aid him in this world of
being to remain steadfast and firm in Thy love and grant
that this broken-winged bird may attain a refuge and
shelter in Thy Divine Nest, that abideth upon the
Celestial Tree."*[28]

*"O God, refresh and gladden my spirit. Purify my heart.
Illumine my mind. I lay all my affairs in Thy hand. Thou
art My Guide and My Refuge. I will no longer be
sorrowful and grieved, I will be happy and joyful. O
God, I will no longer be full of anxiety, nor will I let
trouble harass me. I will not dwell on the unpleasant
things of life. O God, Thou art kinder to me than I am
to myself. I dedicate myself to Thee, O Lord."*[29]

Some Meditations of Bahá'u'lláh

*"God testifieth to the unity of His and to the singleness
of His own Being. On the throne of eternity, from the
inaccessible heights of His station, His tongue
proclaimeth that there is none other God but Him. He
Himself, independently of all else, hath ever been a*

witness unto His own oneness, the revealer of His own nature, the glorifier of His own Essence. He, verily, is the All-Powerful, the Almighty, the Beauteous. He is supreme over His servants and standeth over His creatures. In His hand is the source of authority and truth. He maketh men alive by His signs, and causeth them to die through Thy wrath. He shall not be asked of His doings and His might is equal unto all things. He is the Potent, the All-Subduing. He holdeth within His grasp the empire of all things, and on His right hand is fixed the Kingdom of His Revelation. His power, verily, embraceth the whole of creation. Victory and overlordship are His; all might and dominion are His; all glory and greatness are His. He, of a truth, is the All-Glorious, the Most Powerful, the unconditioned."[30]

"Glorified art Thou, O Lord my God! Every man of insight confesseth Thy sovereignty and Thy dominion, and every discerning eye perceiveth the greatness of Thy majesty and the compelling power of Thy might. The winds of tests are powerless to hold back them that enjoy near access to Thee from setting their faces towards the horizon of Thy glory, and the tempest of trials must fail, to draw away and hinder such as are wholly devoted to Thy will from approaching Thy court.

Methinks, the lamp of Thy love is burning in their hearts, and the light of Thy tenderness is lit within their breasts. Adversities are incapable of estranging them from Thy Cause, and the vicissitudes of fortune can never cause them to stray from Thy pleasure.

I beseech Thee, O my God, by them and by the sighs which their hearts utter in their separation from Thee, to keep them safe from the mischief of their adversaries, and to nourish their souls with what Thou has ordained for Thy loved ones on whom shall come no fear and who shall not be put to grief."[31]

"Thou dost witness, O my God, how He Who is Thy splendour calleth Thee to remembrance, notwithstanding the manifold troubles that have touched Him, troubles which none except Thee can number. Thou beholdest how, in His prison-house, He recounteth Thy wondrous praises with which Thou didst inspire Him. Such is His fervour that His enemies are powerless to deter him from mentioning Thee, O Thou Who art the Possessor of all names!

Praised be Thou that Thou hast so strengthened Him with Thy strength, and endowed Him by Thine almighty power with such potency, that aught save Thee is in His estimation but a handful of dust.

The light of unfading splandour have so enveloped Him that all else but Thee in His eyes but a shadow. And when Thine irresistable summons reached me, I arose, fortified by Thy strength, and called all that are in Thy heaven and all that are on Thy earth to turn in the direction of Thy favours and the horizon of Thy bounties. Some caviled at me, and determined to hurt me and slay me. Others drank to the full of the wine of Thy grace, and hastened towards the habitation of Thy throne.

I beseech Thee, O Thou Who art the Creator of earth and heaven and the Source of all things, to attract Thy servants through the fragrances of the Robe of Thine Inspiration and Thy Revelation, and to help them attain the Tabernacle of Thy behest and power. From eternity Thou wert by Thy transcendent might supreme over all things, and Thou wilt be exalted unto eternity in Thy Godhead and surpassing sovereignty.

Let Thy mercy, then, be upon Thy servants and Thy creatures. Thou art, in truth, the Almighty, the Inaccessible, the All-Glorious, the Unconditioned."[32]

"Glory to Thee, O my God! But for the tribulations which, are sustained in Thy path, how could Thy true lovers be recognised; and were it not for the trials which are borne for love of Thee, how could the station of such as yearn for Thee be revealed? Thy might beareth me witness! The companions of all who adore Thee are the tears they shed, and the comforters of such as seek Thee are the groans they, utter, and the food of them who haste to meet Thee is the fragments of their broken hearts. How sweet to my taste is the bitterness of death suffered in Thy path, and how precious in my estimation are the shafts of Thine enemies when encountered for the sake of the exaltation of Thy word! Let me quaff in Thy Cause, O my God, whatsoever Thou didst desire, and send down upon me in Thy love all Thou didst ordain. By Thy glory! I wish only what Thou wishest, and cherish what Thou cherishest. In Thee have I, at all times, placed my whole trust and confidence.

Raise up, I implore Thee, O my God, as helpers to this Revelation such as shall be counted worthy of Thy name and of Thy sovereignty, that they may remember me among Thy creatures, and hoist the ensigns of Thy victory in Thy land.

Potent art Thou to do what pleaseth Thee. No God is there but Thee, the Help in Peril, the self-Subsisting."[33]

CHAPTER IX

Man and the Universe

Man's True Nature

Man's true nature is spiritual, not physical. It is one of the mysteries of the universe, for the mind and soul of man can never fully comprehend his own inner reality.. Nevertheless, a great deal can be learn about it and the first and most important thing is that man is a dependent being. His destiny, and the destiny of all men, depends upon God, even though he has been endowed with free-will with which to achieve it. Thus, Bahá'u'lláh explains:

> "Know thou that all men have been created in the nature made by God, the Guardian, the Self-Subsisting. Unto each one hath been prescribed a pre-ordained measure, as decreed in God's mighty and guarded Tablets. All that which ye potentially possess can, however, be manifested only as a result of your own volition."[1]

Free-Will

Although the will of man is free, might and power belong to God alone Consequently man's freedom can only be relative.

'Abdu'l-Bahá says clearly:

> "Some things are subject to the free-will of man, such as justice, equity, tyranny, and injustice, as well as all the good and evil actions; it is evident and clear that these actions are, for the most part, left to the will of man. But there are certain things to which man is forced and compelled: such as sleep, death, sickness, decline of power, injuries and misfortunes; these are not subject to the will of man, and he is not responsible for them,

*for he is compelled to endure them. But in the choice of
good and bad actions he is free, and he commits them
according to his own will.* "[2]

Throughout his life man is at every moment faced with a choice
between alternatives; his actions bear witness to the decisions he
has taken. These decisions are not necessarily made at the highest,
clearest level of consciousness; they may not be the outcome of
cogitation, or of any mental activity whatsoever. Nevertheless they
reflect the state of the soul and largely determine its future
development. A man who impulsively rushes into a burning house
to save a strange child may not stop to think before doing so, but his
action springs from the effect of his experience on the nature with
which he has been endowed by God; and his noble action will
influence both the development of his soul and his future experience.

The Two Natures of Man
The choice which each of us makes at every moment is between
the various urges to which we are subject. We cannot do anything,
either good or bad, unless we first desire to do it. Bahá'u'lláh refers
to the receptacle of desire as the human heart, for it is the heart of
the spiritual man analogous to the physical heart of man's body.

Desire may be directed towards heavenly or towards earthly
things; that is to say, to divine qualities such as love, justice, mercy,
radiance, or to things of this world such as material satisfaction,
self aggrandisement, and earthly power. At all times, the will of
man has to choose between these urges, acting as a kind of filter
which passes some and suppresses others. The desire passing
through may not belong wholly either to heaven or to earth; it is
more likely to be composite, since human motives are seldom wholly
pure. But to the extent that the will accepts heavenly urges, the
heart and soul are purified. The desire of the heart becomes more
heavenly, less earthly, and the soul itself is readier next time to
accept the heavenly alternative. Speaking in Paris of this process,
'Abdu'l-Bahá said:

"In man there are two natures; his spiritual or higher

nature and his material or lower nature. In one he approaches God, in the other he lives for the world alone. Signs of both these natures are to be found in man. In his material aspect he expresses untruth, cruelty and injustice; all these are the outcome of his lower nature. The attributes of his divine nature are shown forth in love, mercy, kindness, truth and justice, one and all being expressions of his higher nature. Every good habit, every noble quality belongs to man's spiritual nature, whereas all his imperfections and sinful actions are born of his material nature. If a man's Divine nature dominates his human nature, we have a saint.

Man has the power both to do good and to do evil; if his power for good predominates and his inclinations to do wrong are conquered, then man in truth may be called a saint. But if, on the contrary, he rejects the things of God and allows his evil passions to conquer him, then he is no better than an animal. Saints are men who have freed themselves from the world of matter and who have overcome sin. They live in the world but are not of it, their thoughts being continually in the world of the spirit. Their lives are spent in holiness, and their deeds show forth love, justice and godliness. They are illumined from on high; they are as bright and shining lamps in the dark places of the earth. These are the saints of God. The apostles, who were the disciples of Jesus Christ, were just as other men are; they, like their fellows, were attracted by the things of the world, and each thought only of his own advantage. They knew little of justice, nor were the Divine perfections found in their midst. But when they followed Christ and believed in Him, their ignorance gave place to understanding, cruelty was changed to justice, falsehood to truth, darkness into light. They had been worldly, they became spiritual and divine. They had been children of darkness, they became sons of God, they became saints! Strive therefore to follow in their steps, leaving all worldly things behind, and striving to attain to the spiritual Kingdom."[3]

The heart of man has been described by Bahá'u'lláh as *"His own, His exclusive possession."*[4]
He proclaims:

"He hath chosen out of the whole world the hearts of His servants, and made them each a seat for the revelation of His glory. Wherefore, sanctify them from every defilement, that the things for which they were created may be engraven upon them."[5]

Proofs of Life after Death
The human heart is the seat of the true life of man, which is the Love and Knowledge of God. Bahá'u'lláh says:

"The spirit that animateth the human heart is the knowledge of God."[6]

This being so, it is evident that the death of the body cannot destroy the life of the spirit. There are many logical proofs that life continues after the death of the body. 'Abdu'l-Bahá expounded six in an address given in Montreal, from which three are given here:

"Consider the world of dreams wherein the body of man is immovable, seemingly dead, not subject to sensation; the eyes do not see, the ears do not hear nor the tongue speak. But the spirit of man is not asleep; it sees, hears, moves, perceives and discovers realities. Therefore it is evident that the spirit of man is not affected by the change or condition of the body. Even though. the material body should die the spirit continues eternally alive, just as it exists and functions in the inert body in the realm of dreams. That is to say

the spirit is immortal and will continue its existence after the destruction of the body...

Consider another proof. Every cause is followed by an effect and vice versa there could be no effect without a cause preceding it. Sight is an effect; there is no doubt that behind that effect there is a cause. When we hear a discourse, there is a speaker. We could not hear words unless they proceeded from the tongue of a speaker. Motion without a mover or cause of motion is inconceivable. His Holiness Jesus Christ lived two thousand years ago. Today we behold his manifest signs; his light is shining, his sovereignty is established, his traces are apparent, his bounties are effulgent. Can we say that Christ did not exist? We can absolutely conclude that His Holiness Christ existed* and that from Him these traces proceeded.

"Still another proof: The body of man becomes lean or fat, it is afflicted with disease, suffers mutilation, perhaps the eyes become blind, the ears deaf, but none of these imperfections and failings afflict or affect the spirit. The spirit of man remains in the same conditions, unchanged. A man is blinded, but his spint continues the same. He loses his hearing, his hand is cut off, his foot amputated, but his spirit remains the same. He becomes lethargic, he is afflicted with apoplexy but there is no difference, change or alteration in his spirit. This is proof that death is only destruction of the body, while the spirit remains immortal, eternal."[7]

Preparation for the Life to Come
Bahá'í believe that the life of man on earth is only a prelude to his life in the spiritual world in which he will have his being when freed from the body. While here, he must seek Eternal Life, and to the extent that he acquires it he is ready for the life to come. Should he

---

* i.e. continued to exist after the crucifixion.

fail to acquire it, the fire of remorse will be his lot when he ultimately recognises what opportunities he has missed.

Bahá'u'lláh compares life on earth to the life of a baby in the womb before it is born; it acquires powers which have no apparent use in the womb, such as the powers of sight and hearing, which can be used only after birth. So in this world we acquire powers and qualities that we will be able to use only after the spirit has separated from the body: lack of them will then be a severe handicap.

Speaking in New York on how to acquire the qualities needed, 'Abdu'l-Bahá said:

> *"By what means can man acquire these things? How shall he obtain these merciful gifts and powers? First, through the knowledge of God. Second, through the love of God. Third, through faith. Fourth, through philanthropic deeds. Fifth, through self-sacrifice. Sixth, through severance from this world. Seventh, through sanctity and holiness. Unless he acquires these forces and attains to these requirements he will surely be deprived of the life that is eternal. But if he possesses the knowledge of God, becomes ignited through the fire of the love of God, witnesses the great and mighty signs of the kingdom, becomes the cause of love among mankind, and lives in the utmost state of sanctity and holiness, he shall surely attain to second birth, be baptised by the Holy Spirit and enjoy everlasting existence."*[8]

Erring souls continue to exist after leaving their bodies, but a lower kind of existence that is as death compared with the existence of those who acquired Eternal Life while on earth.

> *"...the rewards of the other world are the eternal life which is clearly mentioned in all the Holy Books, the divine perfections, the eternal bounties, and everlasting felicity.... In the same way the punishments of the other*

world, that is to say, the torments of the other world,
consist in being deprived of the special divine blessings
and the absolute bounties, and falling into the lowest
degrees of existence. He who is deprived of these divine
favours although he continues after death, is
considered as dead by the people of truth."[9]

Progress after Death

Progress is still possible in the world to come, although always on
the human plane. The soul cannot leave the Kingdom of creation to
enter the Kingdom of Divinity; a man can never become a
Manifestation of God. Nevertheless his progress is endless. However
nearly perfect a man may become, how ever great the spiritual
qualities he acquires, further improvement within the station of
humanity is always possible.

Progress in the spiritual world, according to Bahá'u'lláh, does
not come as in this world from choosing good and rejecting evil.
There it comes from the bounty of God, from prayer, from the
intercession of others, and from good works done on earth in the
name of the departed. Prayer for the departed is not only permitted,
but encouraged. 'Abdu'l-Bahá spoke of this in detail.

"As the spirit of man after putting off this material form
has an everlasting life, certainly any existing being is
capable of making progress; therefore it is permitted to
ask for advance ment, forgiveness, mercy, beneficence,
and blessings for a man after his death, because
existence is capable of progression. That is why in the
prayers of Bahá'u'lláh forgiveness and remission of
sins are asked for those who have died. Moreover, as
people in this world are in need of God, they will also
need Him in the other world. The creatures are always
in need, and God is absolutely independent, whether
in this world or in the world to come.... It is even
possible that the condition of those who have died in
sin and unbelief may become changed; that is to say,
they may become the object of pardon through the

bounty of God, not through His justice; for bounty is giving without desert, and justice is giving what is deserved. As we have power to pray for these souls here, so likewise we shall possess the same power in the other world, which is the Kingdom of God.... Through their own prayers and supplications they can also progress; more especially when they are the object of intercession of the Holy Manifestations."[10]

The State of Pure Souls
Pure souls progress until they reach a state of happiness and perfection beyond anything that can be imagined in this earthly world. Bahá'u'lláh speaks of it in moving terms:

"Know thou of a truth that the soul, after its separation from the body, will continue to progress until it attaineth the presence of God, in a state and condition which neither the revolution of ages and centuries, nor the changes and chances of this world, can alter. If will endure as long as the Kingdom of God, His sovereignty, His dominion and power will endure. It will manifest the signs of God and His attributes, and will reveal His loving kindness and bounty. The movement of My Pen is stilled when it attempteth to befittingly describe the loftiness and glory of so exalted a station. The honour with which the Hand of Mercy will invest the soul is such as no tongue can adequately reveal, nor any other earthly agency describe. Blessed is the soul which, at the hour of its separation from the body, is sanctified from the vain imaginings of the peoples of the world. Such a soul liveth and moveth in accordance with the Will of its creator, and entereth the all-highest Paradise. The Maids of Heaven, inmates of the loftiest mansions, will circle around it, and the Prophets of God and His chosen ones will seek its companionship. With them that soul will freely converse, and will recount unto them

that which it has been made to endure in the path of God, the Lord of all worlds. If any man be told that which hath been ordained for such a soul in the worlds of God, the Lord of the throne on high and of earth below, his whole being will instantly blaze out in his great longing to attain that most exalted, that sanctified and resplendent station."[11]

Our achievement of this station of 'the presence of God' is the purpose of our life on earth; in one sense it is the purpose of the whole creation. No man is barred from attaining it; those who do not reach it before leaving the earth may, by the bounty of God, attain it afterwards. Bahá'u'lláh says:

"The nature of the soul after death can never be described, nor is it meet and permissible to reveal its whole character to the eyes of men. The Prophets and Messengers of Gomd have been sent down for the sole purpose of guiding mankind to the straight Path of Truth. The purpose underlying their revelation hath been to educate all men, that they may, at the hour of death, ascend, in the utmost purity and sanctity and with absolute detachment, to the throne of the Most High. The light which these souls radiate is responsible for the progress of the world and the advancement of its peoples. They are like unto leaven which leaventh the world of being, and constitute the animating force through which the arts and wonders of the world are made manifest. Through them the clouds rain their bounty upon men, and the earth bringeth forth its fruits... These souls and symbols of detachment have provided, and will continue to provide, the supreme moving impulse in the world of being."[12]

Communication with the other world
These excerpts from the Bahá'í Holy Writings show that 'Abdu'l-Bahá taught there could be communication of a kind

between people who have passed on and those still on earth. We can help them by prayer and they us. Pure souls can inspire all the arts and wonders of the world. But this does not imply that 'Abdu'l-Bahá encourages belief in mediums or any other means of stimulating contact with the spiritual world. 'Abdu'l-Bahá said to a pilgrim, whose notes of His pronouncement He later revised:

> *"To tamper with psychic forces while in this world interferes with the conditions of the soul in the world to come. These forces are real, but, normally, are not active on this plane. The child in the womb has its eyes, ears, hands, feet, etc., but they are not in activity. The whole purpose of life in the material world is the coming forth into the world of Reality, where those forces will become active. They belong to that world."*[13]

He explained further that pure souls may have spiritual experiences resulting from communication with spirits. These are comparable to the experience of acquiring spiritual knowledge. The visions of the Prophets of old were of this kind; in reality they were spiritual experiences expressed in terms of the senses. They bear no relation to the control by spirits that mediums claim, to materialisations, Or to similar manifestations, about which 'Abdu'l-Bahá says:

> *"The other kind of spiritual discoveries is made up of pure imaginations; but these imaginations become embodied in such a way that many simple-hearted people believe they have a reality. That which proves it clearly is that from this controlling of spirits no result or fruit has ever been produced; no, they are but narratives and stories."*[14]

Thus Bahá'ís believe that communication with those who have passed on is possible, but must not be sought, and occurs rarely. Much that is claimed to be communication with spirits is in fact imagination.

Reincarnation

It should be clear from what has been said that Bahá'ís do not believe in reincarnation, about which 'Abdu'l-Bahá commented:

> *"No logical arguments and proofs of this question are brought forward; they are only suppositions and inferences from conjectures, and not conclusive arguments. Proofs must be asked for from the believers in reincarnation, and not conjectures, suppositions, and imaginations."*[15]

The attraction of the theory of reincarnation for some people seems to be that it is thought to explain apparent injustices; they claim that all souls are created equal, but differences arise through good and bad actions in the course of successive appearances on earth. Reflection reveals two objections to this theory. Firstly, God creates no two things equal; even two peas in a pod are riot alike; there seems no reason why God should make human beings an exception to this rule. Secondly, the theory does not really explain what it seeks to explain; for two equal souls must take the same decision in equal circumstances; differences between souls created equal can, therefore, arise only from differences in circumstance; the inequalities which now exist must all be traceable to chance differences of environment. If this were true, it would be the epitome of injustice.

Nevertheless, there is a sense in which 'return' may be said to take place. Jesus spoke of John the Baptist as being the return of Elias, although John himself had denied this. Bahá'u'lláh explains that Jesus was referring to the return of the spiritual qualities 'which Elias had manifested. It is as though the light shining from a lamp today were said to be the same as a light shining from the same lamp yesterday; the qualities of the light are the same, but yesterday's light has not returned to enter our eyes again. Similarly John showed the same heavenly qualities as Elias, but his soul was a different soul. Other Manifestations of God have spoken of their followers and opponents as the return of the followers and opponents of earlier Messengers. The same qualities were shown forth by the earlier and the later souls, who were therefore called one.

Suffering

Suffering is one of the mysteries of the universe. If God is good, why is suffering necessary? 'Abdu'l-Bahá explained:

> *"The mind and spirit of man advance when he is tried by suffering. The more the ground is ploughed, the better the seed will grow, the better the harvest will be. Just as the plough furrows the earth deeply, purifying it of weeds and thistles, so suffering and tribulation free man from the petty affairs of this worldly life until he arrives at a state of complete detachment. His attitude in this world will be that of divine happiness. Man is, so to speak, unripe: the heat of the fire of suffering will mature him. Look back to the times past and you will find that the greatest men have suffered most."*[16]

He points out that all suffering comes from the material world; the remedy is to turn to the spiritual world:

> *"The trials which beset our every step, all our sorrow, pain, shame and grief, are born of the world of matter; whereas the spiritual kingdom never causes sadness. A man living with his thoughts in this kingdom knows perpetual joy. The ills all flesh is heir to do not pass him by, but they only touch the surface of his life, the depths are calm and serene.*
>
> *Today, humanity is bowed clown with trouble, sorrow a grief, no one escapes; the world is wet with tears; but, thank God, the remedy is at our doors. Let us turn our hearts away from the world of matter and live in the spiritual world. It alone can give us freedom. If we are hemmed in by difficulties, we have only to call upon God, and by His great Mercy we shall be helped. . . . You see all round you proofs of the inadequacy of*

material things—how joy, comfort, peace and
consolation are not to be found in the transitory things
of the world. Is it not then foolishness to refuse to seek
these treasures where they may be found? The doors of
the spiritual kingdom are open to all, and without is
absolute darkness."[17]

These comments reveal the true purpose of suffering—O cause
man to progress spiritually. Suffering, 'Abdu'l-Bahá explains, is of
two kinds. It may be brought upon man by himself, as indigestion is
brought about by unwise eating; this kind of suffering may be
compared to the punishment a benevolent father gives his child to
persuade it to do what will benefit it. Or the suffering may be sent
by God as a test, to develop the inward virtues each man potentially
possesses. Of this suffering 'Abdu'l-Bahá says:

"Men who suffer not, attain no perfection. The plant
most pruned by the gardeners is that one which, when
the summer comes, will have the most beautiful blossoms
and the most abundant fruit."[18]

Hence Bahá'u'lláh says we should be thankful in adversity. In
one of the brilliant aphorisms called 'The Hidden Words' He sums
up the whole matter concisely and succinctly:

"O Son of man! My calamity is my providence, outwardly
it is fire and vengeance, but inwardly it is light and
mercy. Hasten thereunto that thou mayest become an
eternal light and an immortal spirit. This is my command
unto thee, do thou observe it."[19]

Evil
Bahá'u'lláh taught that evil has no real existence. As darkness is
only the absence of light, so evil is only the absence of good. Thus
ignorance is lack of knowledge, hatred lack of love.

Every created thing in its inmost essence is purely good and a
useful part of the universe. Even poison is useful, for example in

homoeopathic medicine. Moreover the appearance of evil has itself a purpose; just as we could not recognise the light if there were no darkness, so we could not recognise goodness if there were no evil.

These are deep philosophical principles that scholars of the future will no doubt elaborate; they are stated here solely to indicate the direction in which Bahá'u'lláh's solution to the problem lies.

The Science of Medicine

Part of the study of man is the study of healing. A great development of man's power of healing is to be expected in the Bahá'í Dispensation, of which the progress of medicine in the last hundred years is merely a foretaste.

Bahá'ís recognise two kinds of healing, spiritual and material. Although they believe doctors will in time acknowledge the truth of Bahá'u'lláh's medical teachings, they are aware that medicine is a specialised profession, to be entered only after long training. Bahá'u'lláh advises those who are ill to consult a good doctor.

So far as material healing is concerned, 'Abdu'l-Bahá says:

"The science of medicine is still in a condition of infancy: it has not reached maturity; but when it has reached this point, cures will be performed by things which are not repulsive to the smell and taste of man; that is to say, by aliments, fruits and vegetables which are agreeable to the taste and have an agreeable smell. For the provoking cause of disease—that is to say, the cause of the entrance of the disease into the human body—is either a physical one or is the effect of the excitement of the nerves.

But the principal causes of disease are physical; for the human body is composed of numerous elements, but in the measure of an especial equilibrium. As long as the equilibrium is maintained, man is preserved from disease; but if this essential balance, which is the pivot of the constitution, is disturbed, the constitution is disordered, and disease will supervene.

For instance, there is a decrease in one of the constituent ingredients of the body of man, and in another there is an increase, so the proportion of the equilibrium is disturbed, and disease occurs. . . . When by remedies and treatments the equilibrium is re-established, the disease is banished.... All the elements that are combined in man exist also in vegetables; therefore if one of the constituents which compose the body of man diminishes, and he partakes of foods in which there is much of that diminished constituent, then the equilibrium will be established, and a cure will be obtained. So long as the aim is the readjustment of the constituents of the body, it can be effected either by medicine or by food.... When the science of medicine reaches perfection, treatment will be given by foods, ailments, fragrant fruits, and vegetables, and by various waters, hot and cold in temperature."[20]

Spiritual Healing

The relation between material and spiritual healing is summed up by 'Abdu'l-Bahá in one of His Tablets:

"There are two ways of healing sickness, material means and spiritual means. The first is by the use of remedies, of medicines; the second consists of praying to God and in turning to Him. Both means should be used and practised.

Illness caused by physical accident should be treated with medical remedies; those which are due to spiritual causes disappear through spiritual means. Thus an illness caused by affliction, fear, nervous impressions, will be healed by spiritual rather than by physical treatment. Hence, both kinds of remedies should be considered. Moreover, they are not contradictory, and thou shouldst accept the physical remedies as coming from the mercy and favour of God, who hath revealed and made manifest medical science so that His servants may profit from this kind of treatment also. Thou shouldst give equal attention to spiritual treatments, for they produce marvellous effects. "[21]

Bahá'u'lláh has revealed a number of healing prayers to attract the healing power of the Holy Spirit, the power by which Christ healed. This is the greatest of all healing powers, the stuff of which apparent miracles are made. Of it 'Abdu'l-Bahá said:

"This does not depend on contact, nor on sight, nor upon presence; it is not dependent upon any condition. Whether the disease be light or severe, whether there be a contact of bodies or not, whether a personal connection be established between the sick person and the healer or not, this healing takes place through the power of the Holy Spirit." [22]

One of the healing prayers of Bahá'u'lláh is as follows:

"Thy name is my healing, O my God, and remembrance of Thee is my remedy. Nearness to Thee is my hope, and love for Thee is my companion. Thy mercy to me in my healing and my succour in both this world and the world to come. Thou, verily, art the All-Bountiful, the All-Knowing, the All-Wise." [23]

'Abdu'l-Bahá mentions three other kinds of healing without medicine, two of which He describes as material and one as spiritual. Of this lesser kind of spiritual healing He says:

"...the complete and perfect connection between the spiritual doctor and the sick person—that is, a connection of such a kind that the spiritual doctor entirely concentrates himself, and all the attention of the sick person is given to the spiritual doctor from whom he expects to realise health—causes an excitement of the nerves, and health is produced. But all this has

effect only to a certain extent, and that not always. For if someone is afflicted with a very violent disease, or is wounded, these means will not remove the disease nor close and heal the wound. That is to say, these means have no power in severe maladies, unless the constitution helps, because a strong constitution often overcomes disease. "[24]

The Human Spirit

Among the many explanations that flowed from Bahá'u'lláh and 'Abdu'l-Bahá to illuminate the nature of man, one is particularly suited to quotation in a book like this, because it contains in a short space the key to many mysteries. When asked to elucidate the difference between mind, spirit and soul, 'Abdu'l-Bahá said:

"It has been before explained that spirit is universally divided into five categories: the vegetable spirit, the animal spirit, the human spirit, the spirit of faith, and the Holy Spirit.

The vegetable spirit is the power of growth which is brought about in the seed through the influence of other existences.

The animal spirit is the power of all the senses, which is realised from the composition and mingling of elements; when this composition decomposes, the power also perishes and becomes annihilated. It may be likened to this lamp: when the oil, wick and fire are combined it is lighted, and when this combination is dissolved, that is to say when the combined parts are separated from one another, the lamp also is extinguished.

The human spirit which distinguishes man from the animal is the rational soul; and these two names—the human spirit and the rational soul—designate one thing. This spirit, which in the terminology of the philosophers is the rational soul, embraces all beings, and as far as human ability permits discovers the reality of things and becomes cognisant of their peculiarities and effects, and of the qualities and properties of beings.

But the human spirit, unless assisted by the spirit of faith, does not become acquainted with the divine secrets and the heavenly realities. It is like a mirror which, although clear, polished and brilliant, is still in need of light. Until a ray of the sun reflects upon it, it cannot discover the heavenly secrets.

But the mind is the power of the human spirit. Spirit is the lamp; mind is the light which shines from the lamp. Spirit is the tree, and the mind is the fruit. Mind is the perfection of the spirit, and is its essential quality, as the sun's rays are the essential necessity of the sun.

This explanation, though short, is complete; therefore reflect upon it, and if God wills, you may become acquainted with the details."[25]

Elsewhere, 'Abdu'l-Bahá explains more fully what is meant by the spirit of faith, the heavenly spirit by which man is led to Eternal Life:

"The fourth degree of spirit is the heavenly spirit; it is the spirit of faith and the bounty of God; it comes from the breath of the Holy Spirit, and by the divine power it becomes the cause of eternal life. It is the power which makes the earthly man heavenly, and the imperfect man perfect. It makes the impure to be pure, the silent eloquent: it purifies and sanctifies those made captive by carnal desires; it makes the ignorant wise."[26]

When 'Abdu'l-Bahá says that mind is the perfection of the spirit, He refers to the human spirit, not to the spirit of faith, still less to the Holy Spirit, which belongs to the Divine world and is possessed Only by Manifestations of God.

Man and the Animals

The human spirit comprises a spiritual kingdom of its own, quite distinct from the kingdom of the animal spirit. Whereas the animal spirit forms part of what we call 'nature,' the human spirit transcends nature. In Boston, 'Abdu'l-Bahá said:

"Just as the animal is more noble than the vegetable and mineral so man is superior to the animal. The animal is bereft of ideality,* that is to say, it is a captive of the world of nature and not in touch with what lies within and beyond nature, it is without spiritual susceptibilities, deprived of the attractions of consciousness, unconscious of the world of God and incapable of deviating from the law of nature. It is different with man. Man is possessed of the emanations of consciousness; he has perception, ideality* and is capable of discovering the mysteries of the universe. All the industries, inventions and facilities surrounding our daily life were at one time hidden secrets of nature, but the reality of man penetrated them and made them subject to his purposes. According to nature's laws they should have remained latent and hidden, but man having transcended those laws, discovered these mysteries and brought them out of the plane of the invisible into the realm of the known and visible. How wonderful is the spirit of man! One of the mysteries of natural phenomena is electricity. Man has discovered this illimitable power and made it captive to his uses. How many of nature's secrets have been penetrated and revealed! Columbus while in Spain discovered America. Man has accurately determined that the sun is stationary while the earth revolves about it. The animal cannot do this. Man perceives the mirage to be an illusion. This is beyond the power of the animal. The animal can only

---

* The Translator seems to mean 'the ability to form ideas'.

---

know through sense impressions and cannot grasp intellectual realities. The animal cannot conceive of the power of thought. This is an abstract intellectual matter and not limited to the senses. The animal is incapable of knowing that the earth is round. In brief, abstract intellectual phenomena are human powers. All creation below the kingdom of man is the captive of nature; it cannot deviate in the slightest degree from nature's laws. But man wrests the sword of dominion from nature's hand and uses it upon nature's head. For example, it is a natural exigency that man should be a dweller upon the earth, but the power of the human spirit transcends this limitation and he soars aloft in aeroplanes. This is contrary to the law and requirement of nature. He sails at high speed upon the ocean and dives beneath its surface in submarines. He imprisons the human voice in a phonograph and communicates in the twinkling of an eye from east to west. These are things we know to be contrary to the limitations of natural law. Man transcends nature, while the mineral, vegetable and animal are helplessly subject to it. "[27]

Evolution

Since the human spirit belongs to a different kingdom from the animal spirit, man can never have been limited to the animal kingdom; but this does not mean his body never had the shape of an animal.

Man contains within himself all the lower kingdoms. He has the mineral power of cohesion that makes possible the existence of solids; the vegetable power of growth, which separates the vegetable kingdom from the mineral kingdom; and also the power of sense perception, which is the essential quality of animals. Beyond all these, he has also the special powers of the human spirit that are denied to the lower kingdoms. Whatever the shape of his body, however far from full physical development he was at any stage of his evolution, he always possessed the human spirit. As compared with the animals of the age, man must always have shown signs of his inner glory. In early days, these were no doubt far, far from those shown in his present state of physical and spiritual development, just as the present signs are no doubt far, far from those that he will show in the distant future; but any being able to recognise the signs would have been able to see then as now that man differed from the animals.

This principle has often been stated by 'Abdu'l-Bahá, Who asserted that scientists would one day recognise its truth. In San Francisco He said:

> *"Let us suppose that the human anatomy was primordially different from its present form, that it was gradually transformed from one stage to another until it attained its present likeness, that at one time it was similar to a fish, later an invertebrate and finally human. This anatomical evolution or progression does not alter or affect the statement that the development of man was always human in type and biological in progression. For the human embryo when examined microscopically is at first a mere germ or worm. Gradually as it develops it shows certain divisions; rudiments of hands and feet appear; that is to say an upper and a lower part are distinguishable. Afterwards it undergoes certain distinct changes until it reaches its actual human form and is born into this world. But at all times even when the embryo resembled a worm, it was human in potentiality and character, not animal. The forms assumed by the human embryo in its successive changes do not prove that it is animal in its essential character. Throughout this progression there has been a transference of type, a conservation of species or kind. Realising this we may acknowledge the fact that at one time man was an inmate of the sea, at another period an invertebrate, then a vertebrate and finally a human being standing erect. Though we admit these changes, we cannot say man is an animal.*

In each one of these stages are signs and evidences of his human existence and destination."[28]

Maybe the scientists of the future will find that evolutionary development is governed by what the creature is destined to evolve into, as well as by ancestry and environment.

The Glory of Man

All the beautiful, complicated existences in creation culminate in man. He is as a soul to the body of the world and a fruit upon the tree of creation. He unites the world of nature with the heavenly world. Of this 'Abdu'l-Bahá says:

"If there were no man, the perfections of the spirit would not appear, and the light of the mind would not be resplendent in this world. This world would be like a body without a soul. This world is also in the condition of a fruit-tree, and man is like the fruit; without fruit the tree would be useless."[29]

For man is distinguished from the animals not only by the power of the human spirit, but also by the power this gives him to acquire the spirit of faith, which leads him to Eternal Life, that is, the Knowledge and the Love of God. Eternal Life is the bearer of all the attributes of God, and is the true glory of man. Potentially, he has this glory within him; it remains only for him to polish the mirror of his heart so that it can reveal the hidden glory. The mirror cannot clean itself from dross nor the lamp ignite itself, so God sends His Manifestations to enable man to rise to that station for which he was created. Bahá'u'lláh pronounces:

"In the kingdoms of earth and heaven there must needs be manifested a Being, an Essence Who shall act as a Manifestation and Vehicle for the transmission of the grace of the Divinity Itself, the Sovereign Lord of all. Through the Teachings of this Day Star of Truth every man will advance and develop until he attaineth the station at which he can manifest all the potential forces

with which his inmost true self hath been endowed. It is for this very purpose that in every age and dispensation the Prophets of God and His Chosen Ones have appeared amongst men, and have evinced such power as is born of God and such might as only the Eternal can reveal. "[30]

Creation

The whole of creation derives its life from the Grace of God transmitted by His Manifestations, which is also the Love and the Knowledge of God; for in their essence all the attributes of God are one. This is the Light of God, which is perpetually and unchangingly radiated by the Sun of Truth. It falls upon created beings and becomes the very cause of their existence. Were it to cease to shine for even an instant, they would all cease to exist.

"Whatever is in the heavens and whatever is on the earth is a direct evidence of the revelation within it of the attributes and names of God, inasmuch as within every atom are enshrined the signs that bear eloquent testimony to the revelation of that Most Great Light. Methinks, but for the potency of that revelation, no being could ever exist." [31]

This Grace has always shone and will always shine, for the created world has neither beginning nor end. Similarly the process of creation is also eternal. Bahá'u'lláh exclaims:

"A drop of the billowing ocean of His endless mercy hath adorned all creation with the ornament of existence, and a breath wafted from His peerless Paradise hath invested all beings with the robe of His sanctity and glory. A sprinkling from the unfathomed deep of His sovereign and all-pervasive Will hath, out of utter nothingness, called into being a creation which is infinite in its range and deathless in its duration. The wonders of His bounty can never cease, and the stream

of His merciful grace can never be arrested. The process of His creation hath had no beginning and can have no end. In every age and cycle He hath, through the splendrous light, shed by the Manifestations of His wondrous Essence, recreated all things, so that whatsoever reflecteth in the heavens and on the earth the signs of His glory may not be deprived of the outpourings of His mercy, nor despair of the showers of His favours."[32]

Pantheism

However, these teachings must not be confused with pantheism. Bahá'u'lláh says emphatically that the Essence of God cannot be divided; Bahá'ís regard as blasphemy any suggestion that God could partake of the nature of creation. Bahá'u'lláh states:

"To every discerning and illuminated heart it is evident that God, the unknowable Essence, the Divine Being, is immensely exalted beyond every human attribute, such as corporeal existence, ascent and descent, egress and regress. Far be it from His glory that human tongue should adequately recount His praise, or that human heart comprehend His fathomless mystery. He is, and hath ever been, veiled in the ancient eternity of His Essence, and will remain in His Reality ever lastingly hidden from the sight of men."[33]

Only the Knowledge of God is revealed in creation; the Essence of God remains for ever beyond man's reach.

CHAPTER X

Relation of the Bahá'í
Faith to Other Religions

Misunderstanding of Prophecy

The Bahá'í Faith does not deny the older religions; it fulfils them.* They all look forward to a time when the appearance of a Great One Who shall usher in a period unique in human history shall complete the purpose of the Founder of the religion. That time has now come; the advent of Bahá'u'lláh fulfils prophecies in all the Holy Books. Therefore He says:

> *"The revelation which, from time immemorial, hath been acclaimed as the Purpose and Promise of all the Prophets of God, and the most cherished Desire of His Messengers, hath now, by virtue of the pervasive Will of the Almighty and at His irresistible bidding, been revealed unto men, The advent of such a Revelation hath been heralded in all the sacred Scriptures. Behold how, notwithstanding such an announcement, mankind hath strayed from its path and shut out itself from its glory."* [1]

It should cause no surprise that most people have failed to recognise the 'Purpose and Promise of all the Prophets' as the One promised by the Founder of their own religion. The Holy Books themselves warn us to expect it. In Isaiah it is written:

> *"Make the heart of this people fat and make their ears heavy, and shut their eyes; lest they see with their eyes,*

---

* Many other passages in this book deal with this theme. For example, Chapters II, XIV, XVII.

*and hear with their ears, and understand with their
heart, and convert, and be healed."*[2]

And in Matthew:

*"But as the days of Noe were, so shall also the coming
of the Son of man be. For as in the days that were
before the flood they were eating and drinking,
marrying and giving in marriage, until the day that Noe
entered into the ark, and knew not until the flood came,
and took them all away; so shall also the coming of the
Son of man be."*[3]

The difficulty of recognising the Manifestation of God for this
age is as great as that former generations experienced in recognising
former Manifestations of God. Although all the Holy Books prophesy
His coming, traditional interpretation of the prophecies has obscured
their meaning. When Jesus came, the Jews were expecting a
Messiah; but having utterly failed to comprehend the signs by which
He was to be recognised, they rejected Him. 'Abdu'l-Bahá describes
what happened:

*"When Christ came, they denounced and slew Him,
saying This is not the One for whom we wait. Behold
when the Messiah shall come, signs and wonders shall
testify that He is in truth the Christ. We know the signs
and conditions, and they have not appeared. The
Messiah will arise out of an unknown City. He shall sit
upon the throne of David, and behold, He shall come
with a sword of steel, and with a sceptre of iron shall
He rule! He shall fulfil the Law of the Prophets, He
shall conquer the East and the West, and shall glorify
His chosen people the Jews. He shall bring with Him a
reign of peace, during which even the animals shall
cease to be at enmity with man. For behold the wolf
and the lamb shall drink from the same spring, and the
lion and the doe shall lie down in the same pasture, the*

*serpent and the mouse shall share the same nest, and
all God's creatures shall be at rest."*

*According to the Jews, Jesus the Christ fulfilled none
of these conditions, for their eyes were holden and they
could not see. He came from Nazareth, no unknown
place. He carried no sword in His hand, nor even a
sticks He did not sit upon the Throne of David, He was
a poor man. He reformed the Law of Moses, and broke
the Sabbath Day. He did not conquer the East and the
West, but was Himself subject to the Roman Law. He
did not exalt the Jews, but taught equality and
brotherhood, and rebuked the Scribes and Pharisees.
He brought in no reign of peace, for during His lifetime
injustice and cruelty reached such a height that even
He Himself fell victim to it, and died a shameful death
upon the Cross.*

*Thus the Jews thought and spoke, for they did not
understand the Scriptures nor the glorious truths that
were contained in them. The letter they knew by heart,
but of the life-giving spirit they understood not a word.*

*Hearken, and I will show you the meaning thereof.
Although He came from Nazareth, which was a known
place, He also came from heaven. His body was born
of Mary, but His Spirit came from heaven. The sword
He carried was the sword of His tongue, with which He
divided the good from the evil, the true from the false,
the faithful from the unfaithful, and the light from
darkness. His Word was indeed a sharp sword! The
throne upon which He sat is the Eternal Throne from
which Christ reigns for ever, a heavenly throne, not an
earthly one, for the things of the earth pass away but
heavenly things pass not away. He re-interpreted and
completed the Law of Moses and fulfilled the Law of*

the Prophets. His Word conquered the East and the West. His Kingdom is everlasting. He exalted those Jews who recognised Him. They were men and women of humble birth, but contact with Him made them great and gave them everlasting dignity. The animals who were to live with one another signified the different sects and races, who, once having been at war, were now to dwell in love and charity, drinking together the Water of Life from Christ the Eternal Spring.

Thus all the spiritual prophecies concerning the coming of Christ vere fulfilled, but the Jews shut their eyes that they should not see, and their ears that they should not hear, and the Divine Reality of Christ passed through their midst unheard, unloved and unrecognised."[4]

The particular prophecies that foretell the coming of another Manifestation of God may differ from these in detail, and their source may be some other Messenger than Moses or the Jewish Prophets, but the error that leads to the rejection of each is the same: he is said not to fulfil the prophecies of the previous Dispensation because these have been interpreted wrongly.

Old Testament Prophecies

Consider the prophecies of the Old Testament. Christians believe them all to point to the coming of Jesus; those which were not fulfilled at His first coming, they say, will be fulfilled when He comes again. If, then, Bahá'u'lláh fulfils the Old Testament prophecies not already fulfilled by Jesus, both Christians and Jews should accept Him as their Promised One. Among the prophecies is this, from Joel:

"The earth shall quake before them; the heavens shall tremble: the sun and the moon shall be dark, and the stars shall withdraw their shining."[5]

This prophecy was fulfilled at the coming of Jesus and has

been fulfilled again at the coming of Bahá'u'lláh. It is not, of course, to be taken literally. The earth of the human spirit has quaked and the heaven of faith has trembled; the sun and the moon of religion have been darkened. The stars of the previous Dispensation have ceased to shine.

These terms may be interpreted in several equally right ways, for the Word of God has many meanings; those interested in the interpretation of Scripture should read the *Kitáb-i-Íqán*, in which Bahá'u'lláh explains a number of these terms.

Typical of the prophecies not fulfilled at the first coming of Jesus is this from Isaiah:

> *"For unto us a child is born, unto us a son is given: and the government shall be upon his shoulder: and his name shall be called Wonderful, Counsellor, The mighty God, The everlasting Father, The Prince of Peace."*[6]

So far from the government being upon the shoulder of Jesus, His Message is addressed especially to the individual, more so than that of most Manifestations of God; He did not claim to be the Prince of Peace, but said, *"Think not that I am come to send peace on earth: I came not to send peace, but a sword."*[7] Moreover, 'The everlasting Father' would be a strange name for the Son of man, which no reference to an imperfectly understood Trinity can justify.

Among other prophecies unfulfilled in the time of Jesus is that the Jews will return to the Holy Land. So far from its being fulfilled then, Jerusalem was destroyed and the Jews were more widely scattered than ever before; but in our day they are returning to Israel.

Another such prophecy is the one introduced in the following words:

> *"And there shall come forth a rod out of the stem of Jesse, and a Branch shall grow out of His roots."*[8]

Although orthodox Christians believe this to refer to the first coming of Jesus, the opinion is most extraordinarily based on two inconsistent genealogies showing the descent from Jesse of Joseph, who was not Jesus' father; the opinion must therefore be regarded as biased.

Many passages in the Old Testament prophesy an era of peace, which Jesus did not introduce. For example:

"And he shall judge among the nations, and shall rebuke many people: and they shall beat their swords into ploughshares and their spears into pruning hooks: nation shall not lift up sword against nation, neither shall they learn war any more."[9]

When the Most Great Peace dawns upon the world, this prophecy will be clearly seen to have been fulfilled in the Dispensation of Bahá'u'lláh.

The Old Testament even mentions the name of Bahá'u'lláh, the Glory of God, and the place of His Manifestation, Carmel:

"The wilderness and the solitary place shall be glad for them; and the desert shall rejoice, and blossom as the rose. It shall blossom abundantly, and rejoice even with joy and singing: the glory of Lebanon shall be given unto it, the excellency of Carmel and Sharon, they shall see the glory of the Lord and the excellency of our God."[10]

Quite a large part of the Old Testament is about the coming of the Messiah and the Lord of Hosts. It will be found that although some of the prophecies refer to Jesus and a few to Muḥammad, many of them can refer only to Bahá'u'lláh.

New Testament Prophecies
A large number of the prophecies about the second coming of Christ, including some from the Old Testament, are collected in Chapters 24 and 25 of the Gospel of St. Matthew. Several of these, such as

the one about the sun being darkened and the moon not giving her light, are fulfilled at the appearance of each Manifestation of God; others refer specifically to the Second Coming of Christ. They are fulfilled in this age by Bahá'u'lláh.

One such prophecy is:

"And this gospel of the kingdom shall be preached in all the world for a witness unto all nations; and then shall the end come."[11]

The Gospel of Jesus is now preached in all the world. Another prophecy is:

"Wherefore if they shall say unto you, Behold, he is in the desert; go not forth: behold, he is in the secret chambers; believe it not. For as the lightning cometh out of the east, and shineth even unto the west; so shall also the coming of the Son of man be."[12]

The Bahá'í Faith is not esoteric its teachings are pen to all. Having been founded in the East, its light now shines most brightly in the United States of America in the West.

Many false prophets have arisen, but Jesus Himself told how to distinguish them:

"Beware of false prophets, which come to you in sheep's clothing, but inwardly they are ravening wolves. Ye shalt know them by their fruits. Do men gather grapes of thorns or figs of thisties? Even so every good tree bringeth forth good fruit; but a corrupt tree bringeth forth evil fruit. A good tree cannot bring forth evil fruit, neither can a corrupt tree bring forth good fruit. Every tree that bringeth not forth good fruit is hewn down and cast into the fire. Wherefore by their fruit ye shall know them."[13]

Any unprejudiced investigation will reveal that the fruit of the tree of those who attack the Bahá'í Faith is evil. Jesus Himself prophesied that trees bringing forth evil fruit will be hewn down; many such trees have already fallen.

The general picture Jesus painted of the world at the time of His Second Coming is of prevalent materialism and iniquity, causing widespread irreligion; of the darkening of the sun of faith and the moon of religious laws; of hatred and conflict; of idle fancy and heedlessness. When these signs appeared, as they had done by the nineteenth century, men would know that the time of His coming was near.

Although many of the prophecies were fulfilled at the coming of Muḥammad, this was not their final fulfilment; the heaven of Revelation and the earth of the human spirit passed away and were renewed then, as at the coming of each Manifestation of God, but in accordance with the prophecy of Jesus,* His words remained. They have remained until now, when His prophecies have been finally fulfilled by His coming in the clouds of heaven about which Bahá'u'lláh said:

"...regarding His words, that the Son of man shall 'come in the clouds of heaven.' By the term 'clouds' is meant those things that are contrary to the ways and desires of men.... These "clouds" signify, in one sense, the annulment of laws, the abrogation of former Dispensations, the repeal of rituals and customs current amongst men, the exalting of the illiterate faithful above the learned opposers of the Faith. In another sense, they mean the appearance of that immortal Beauty in the image of mortal man, with such human limitations as eating and drinking, poverty and riches, glory and abasement, sleeping and waking, and such other things as cast doubt in the minds of men, and cause them to turn away. All such veils are. symbolically referred to as 'clouds.'"[14]

Since Christ has come *"in such an hour as ye think not the*

* Matt. xxiv:35.

Son of man cometh"[15] and veiled such clouds as these, how can anyone wonder that more people have not yet recognised Him?

Prophecies in the Qur'án

It has been said that the most potent part of the Qur'án consists of prophecies about the 'Last Day,' the time of the resurrection of mankind. These prophecies are similar to the ones in the Bible and have a similar meaning. For example:

> *"On that day we will roll up the heaven as one rolleth up written scrolls. As we made the first creation, so will we bring it forth again. This promise bindeth us; verily, we will perform it."*[16]

In each religious cycle creation is recreated and all is made new. The heaven of the previous Revelation, of faith in the previous Manifestation of God, is rolled up and a new heaven laid out in its stead; belief in the new Manifestation of God becomes the criterion of true faith.

Muḥammad also says:

> *"But if ye lapse after that our clear signs have come to you, know that God is Mighty, Wise. What can such expect but that God should come down to them overshadowed with clouds, and the angels also, and their doom be sealed? And to God shall all things return."*[17]

Not only do the erring fail to recognise the Manifestation of God when He comes, but they also fail to recognise the saintly souls who are His immediate followers. They torment and martyr them as they torment the Manifestation of God Himself. Such persecutors prepare for themselves their own punishment in the worlds of God:

> *"On the resurrection day the whole earth shall be but His handful and in His right hand shall the heavens be folded together. And there shall be a blast on the trumpet,*

*and all who are in the Heavens and all who are in the
earth shall expire, save those whom God shall vouchsafe
to live. Then shall there be another blast on it, and lo!
arising they shall gaze around them:*

*And the earth, shall shine with the light of her Lord,
and the Book shall be set, and the prophets shall be
brought up, and the witnesses; and judgment shall be
given between them with equity; and none shall be
wronged: And every soul shall receive as it shall have
wrought, for well knoweth He men's actions."*[18]

Elsewhere in the Qur'án Muḥammad says:

*"One day, the disturbing-trumpet blast shall disturb it,
which the second blast shall follow.... Verily, it will be
but a single blast."*[19]

This signifies that the Revelation of Bahá'u'lláh would follow
so quickly after the Revelation of the Báb that they could be regarded
as Founders of one religion.

There is no space here to detail the multitudinous sayings of
Muḥammad about the Last Day. Modern Muslims take them as
literally as the Jews took the prophecies about Jesus. Enough have
been quoted to show their similarity both to those and to the
prophecies Jesus made—a likely resemblance, since all refer to the
same events.

Prophecies in Other Religions
The records of the Jewish, the Christian, and particularly the Muslim
Scriptures are much more reliable than are those of other religions.
It is almost impossible to know which of the teachings given in
Zoroastrian, Buddhist and Hindu Scriptures were given by Zoroaster,
Krishna* and Buddha; and even the name of the Manifestation of
God on whose teachings Taoism and Confucianism are ultimately
based is uncertain.

---

* Bahá'ís regard Krishna as the Central Figure of the Hindu Faith.

References in the Scriptures of these religions to the coming of a Great Being do not prove that the Founder of the Faith made the comments attributed to Him, but it is of great interest that again and again such comments are found. One example each from Hinduism, Buddhism and Zoroastrianism must suffice.

In the Bhagavad-Gita, the most widely honoured book of Hindu Scripture, which records the supposed teachings of Krishna, He is reported to have said:

"Whenever there is decay of righteousness, O Bharata, and there is exaltation of unrighteousness, then I Myself come forth; for the protection of the good, for the destruction of evil-doers, for the sake of firmly establishing righteousness, I am born from age to age."[20]

There is no need to accept the doctrine of reincarnation to accept as valid this statement in which Krishna speaks with the voice of the Holy Spirit.

Buddha is reported in the Digha Nikaya, one of the earliest collections of Buddhist teachings, to have said:

"At this period, brethren, there will arise in the world an Exalted One named Maitreye, Arahant, Fully Awakened, abounding in wisdom and goodness, happy with knowledge of the worlds, unsurpassed as a guide to mortals willing to be led, a teacher for gods and men, an Exalted One, a Buddha, even as I am now..... The truth, lovely in its origin, lovely in its progress, lovely in its consummation, will he proclaim, both in the spirit and in the letter, the higher life will he make known, in all its fulness and in all its purity, even as I do now."[21]

In the Dinkird, a late collection of traditional Zoroastrian Scripture, the following is attributed to Zoroaster:

"When a thousand two hundred and some years have passed from the inception of the religion of the Arabian and the over throw of the Kingdom of Írán and the degradation of the followers of My religion, a descendant of the Íránian kings will be raised up as a Prophet."[22]

Bahá'u'lláh was a descendant of the SásánIyán kings of Írán and lived twelve hundred-old years after the time of Muḥammad.

Validity of the Text of the Bible and the Qur'án

Of the validity of the text of the Qu'rán, there is little doubt. Most, perhaps all, of it was committed to writing during the life time of the Prophet, Who seems Himself to have distinguished in some way between sayings that were to be included and those that were not. Within twenty years of His passing all extant versions were collected, one was chosen as the most authoritative, and the others were destroyed. Thus the Qu'rán is substantially a record of the actual words of Muḥammad, without addition or amendment.

The New Testament is a less valid record. The Epistles, which make up a large part of it, represent what early Christians understood Jesus to have taught without pretence of giving these teachings in His own words. They were written at varying times during the hundred years or so following the Crucifixion, and according to modern Christian scholars few were written by the one to whom tradition attributes them. Some of the letters of Paul are probably the most authentic.

The four Gospels also were written during the hundred years or so after the Crucifixion. Whether any of them was written by its supposed author is doubtful although St. Luke may well have been. St. Mark, the earliest Gospel, probably written about fifty years after the Crucifixion, provides with an unknown source called 'Q' by scholars most of the matter in St. Matthew and St. Luke, which cannot therefore be regarded as independent records. Since 'Q' consisted primarily of sayings of Jesus, the chief authority for the story of Jesus is St. Mark. This Gospel seems to be a compilation of anecdotes from different sources, put together without knowledge of their correct sequence, and probably edited before it became the version we now have.

The fourth Gospel, St. John, is thought to have been written at Ephesus early in the second century A.D. Its author was concerned more with the Teaching than the life of Jesus. It has been suggested that he sometimes deliberately exaggerated the miracles he related in order to show the stories had some other than their obvious meaning; for example, Lazarus was raised from the dead after four days when decomposition must have set in, over a hundred gallons of wine were provided to supplement the exhausted supply at a village wedding, and so on.

Regarding the actual Teaching of Jesus, it is likely that when a small number of interpolated passages have been put aside, the Gospels provide a tolerably accurate, although very incomplete, record. Regarding the story of Jesus, however, there can be no doubt that much legend has been. incorporated. Discrepancies between the Gospels confirm this: the record of the teachings of Jesus is fairly consistent, but the legends frequently differ. Anyone who doubts this should compare the genealogies of Jesus in St. Matthew (i.1-16) and St. Luke (iii. 23-28), or the accounts in these two Gospels of His birth.

The Old Testament is still more legendary than the New. For instance, the so-called 'Five Books of Moses' were probably compiled by Jewish priests about the sixth century before Christ from early traditions. Some of the Prophetic Books were written before this, some after, and some, like Isaiah, are compilations of writings of various periods. Although there is much authentic material embedded in the Old Testament, there is also much that is not authentic, and the two cannot easily be distinguished.

The Growth of Doctrine and Legend

The growth of doctrine and legend round the central core of the Teaching of the Manifestation of God is most easily traced in Christianity. Early Christians had a very different attitude to miracles from our own. They were credulous and mostly uneducated people with no scientific knowledge, who yearned to be told of miracles, and were not only ready, but even eager, to believe what they were told. Many spurious gospels, of which 3, several survive, were written to satisfy this yearning; the miracles in them are so fantastic as to proclaim these gospels unauthentic; the early Church rightly rejected them from the Canon of Scripture.

That some of the less fantastic mythical stories current in the early days of Christianity, however, have been incorporated in the Gospels of the New Testament is more than likely; likelier still is it that stories that were told and retold before being recorded grew in the telling. Their emphasis may easily have changed from the didactic to the sensational; the thirst for miracles was not to be gainsaid.

All this does not imply that Jesus performed no deeds we would regard as miracles; it implies only that His actions and achievements never contravened spiritual law. The Manifestations of God achieve many things beyond the reach of men, which may be termed miracles; for example, they heal spiritual sickness and raise the spiritually dead to spiritual life. Some signs remain even in the recorded Gospels that these were the kind of miracles Jesus performed; when He said to the disciple whose father had just died *"Follow me; and let the dead bury their dead,"*[23] clearly He referred to spiritual death. If Jesus and the Apostles spoke in this way of bringing to life the spiritually dead, the stories of the miracles would quickly follow.

No doubt He also performed 'miracles' of healing; the author has himself met people who were healed miraculously by 'Abdu'l-Bahá, and others. who were healed miraculously by prayer, in defiance of the opinion of their doctors; but such miracles are in a different category from raising to life a man who has been four days dead. They constitute no proof that the one who performed them was other than a man, whereas the true miracles of Jesus, the giving of spiritual life, could be performed only by a Manifestation of God.

The same circumstances that induced the early Christians to accept impossible legends also influenced the development of doctrine in the early Church. At first, Christianity was one among many religions competing with the state religion of Rome that was so grossly incapable of fulfilling man's most elementary religious need. The others were known as 'mystery religions.' These were esoteric; their more sophisticated initiates believed that by the performance of certain rites, such as eating food consecrated to the god, they could become one with the god and be assured of life after death. To eat the flesh and drink the blood of a sacrificial animal thus secured the devotee salvation.

During the first two centuries of the Christian era, the popularity and prestige of such mystery religions was greater than that of the persecuted sect of Christ. Naturally the early Church did all it could to win the often sincere devotees of these religions from their false beliefs; to this end, they adopted certain of the customs of the religions. For example, the early Church knew as Festivals only Easter and Pentecost; the other Festivals and Commemorations now celebrated were either taken over from paganism and the mystery religions, or instituted by the Church later. Christmas was not celebrated at all by the early Church; the date ultimately adopted was that of the chief festival of the popular cult Mithraism.

Inevitably, doctrine too was affected by competitive beliefs. The concept of the risen God was prevalent in the mystery religions—salvation through rites instead of through good deeds was typical of them. Dimly, without certainty of detail, it is possible to see the early Church interpreting the Teaching of Jesus in the context of current pagan beliefs, and in doing so, blurring the clear outline of the Teaching Jesus gave.

Much of the doctrine of the Churches, for example the doctrine of the Trinity, was determined even later, at oecumenical Councils in the fourth and fifth centuries after Christ. If the criterion of Jesus, 'By their fruits ye shall know them,' is applied to those who attended these Councils, and to the proceedings of the Councils and the circumstances surrounding them, the conclusion is inescapable that the Councils were not divinely guided. *The Cambridge Medieval History* says of them: 'Questions of dogmatic theology and ecclesiastical authority are intermingled with the conflict of national ideals and the lower strife of personal rivalries.' On at least one occasion, two Councils sat at the same time, each excommunicating the leaders of the other. As Jesus asked, 'Do men gather grapes of thorns, or figs of thistles?'

Christian Doctrines accepted by Bahá'ís

Nevertheless, although Bahá'ís recognise the fallible human origin of many of the doctrines of the Christian Churches, they believe fully in the essential doctrines of the Christian Faith. Shoghi Effendi has written: *"As to the position of Christianity, let it be stated without any hesitation or equivocation that its divine, origin is unconditionally acknowledged, that the Sonship and Divinity of Jesus Christ are fearlessly asserted, that the divine inspiration of the Gospel is fully recognised, that the reality of the mystery of the Immaculacy of the Virgin Mary is confessed, and the primacy of Peter, the Prince of the Apostles, is upheld and defended."*[24]

The Churches' interpretation of these doctrines, on the other hand, is not necessarily upheld. Jesus is regarded as a Manifestation of God, one with other Manifestations of God; the inspired Gospels are valid spiritual records, but do not necessarily record material happenings accurately; the Immaculacy of the Virgin Mary is a mystery that does not imply original sin in others, except insofar as imperfection is sin. Study of the following eulogy by Bahá'u'lláh will reveal the spirit in which Bahá'í regard both Jesus and the doctrines of the Churches:

"Know thou that when the Son of Man yielded up His breath to God, the whole creation wept with a great weeping. By sacrificing Himself, however, a fresh capacity was infused into all created things. Its evidences, as witnessed in all the peoples of the earth, are now manifest before thee. The deepest wisdom which the sages have uttered, the profoundest learning which any mind bath unfolded, the arts which the ablest hands

*have produced, the influence exerted by the most potent
of rulers, are but manifestations of the quickening
power released by His transcendent, His all-pervasive,
and resplendent Spirit.*

*We testify that when He came into the world, He shed
the splendour of His glory upon all created things.
Through Him the leper recovered from the leprosy of
perversity and ignorance. Through Him, the unchaste
and wayward were healed. Through His power, born
of Almighty God, the eyes of the blind were opened,
and the soul of the sinner sanctified.*

*Leprosy may be interpreted as any veil that interveneth
between man and the recognition of the Lord, his God.
Whoso alloweth himself to be shut out from Him is
indeed a leper, who shall not be remembered in the
Kingdom of God, the Mighty, the All- Praised. We bear
witness that, through the power of the Word of God
every leper was cleansed, every sickness was healed,
every human infirmity was banished. He it is Who
purified the world. Blessed is the man who, with a face
beaming with light, hath turned towards Him."*[25]

Baptism

The manner in which rites deteriorate with time is illustrated by the
rite of baptism. The rite is an old one, adopted by John the Baptist,
and confirmed by Jesus when He insisted that John baptise Him. It
was used by early Christians as a symbol of repentance; when an
enquirer, after a suitable period of attendance at Christian meetings,
was accepted into the Church, baptism symbolised his entry into a
new way of life.

True baptism, however, Jesus Himself declared on one occasion
to be with spirit and with water, and elsewhere it is said to be with
spirit and with fire. Both water and fire are used allegorically.
'Abdu'l-Bahá comments:

"Therefore the spirit is the bounty of God, the water is knowledge and life, and the fire is the love of God. For material water does not purify the heart of man; no, it cleanses his body; but the heavenly water and spirit, which are knowledge and life, make the human heart good and pure; the heart which receives a portion of the bounty of the Spirit becomes sanctified, good and pure. . . . Man cannot free himself from the rage of carnal passions except by the help of the Holy Spirit. That is why he says baptism with the spirit, with water and with fire is necessary, and that it is essential."[26]

Since this is the true meaning of baptism, to baptise newly born children is pointless. 'Abdu'l-Bahá comments pungently:

"Other peoples are amazed, and wonder why the infant is plunged into the water, since this is neither the cause of the spiritual awakening of the child, nor of its faith or conversion, but it is only a custom which is followed."[27]

In the days of the mystery religions, when initiation ceremonies were a commonplace, baptism had a point and a purpose as a symbol of repentance for adults. However, as it is used now, in a different way and in changed conditions, it has become no more than a meaningless anachronism.

The Eucharisty
Throughout the New Testament appear allegorical statements whose true meaning has been forgotten. The ideas of the time disposed early Christians, immersed in a world of mystery religions and superstitions, to take literally what should be taken figuratively. The episode of the Last Supper was particularly suited to such misinterpretation. No doubt Jesus foresaw the temptation and therefore made such comments as:

"Ye seek me, not because ye saw the miracles, but

because ye did eat of the loaves and were filled.... The bread of God is he which cometh down from heaven, and giveth life to the world....I am the bread of life: he that cometh to me shall never hunger; and he that believeth in me shall never thirst ... it is the spirit that quickeneth, the flesh profiteth nothing."[28]

Clearly the loaves of which the disciples ate and were filled were spiritual bounties; the bread of God that came down from heaven was the spirit of Jesus, not the body born of Mary; coming to Him is described as eating and believing in Him as drinking; it is the celestial spirit that quickeneth, not the flesh of the body.

Moreover, at the time Christ is supposed to have said 'This is my body,' His body was visible to the disciples; He cannot have intended His words to be taken literally. The bread and wine are symbols by means of which the Gospel conveys that Jesus gave to the disciples at the Last Supper Eternal Life and the Bounty of God. 'Abdu'l-Bahá says:

"The disciples had taken many meals from the hand of Christ; why was the Last Supper distinguished from others? It is evident that the heavenly bread did not signify this material bread, but rather the divine nourishment of the spiritual body of Christ, the divine graces and heavenly perfections of which His disciples partook, and with which they became filled....

Then it is clear that the bread and wine were symbols which signified: I have given you my bounties and perfections, and when you have received this bounty, you have gained eternal life and have partaken of your share and your portion of the heavenly nourishment."[29]

An early Church Manual known as the 'Didache' shows that this was the way in which Christians of the first century A.D. understood the sacrament of bread and wine.

The Resurrection

A Bishop of the Church of England has written of the resurrection stories in the synoptic Gospels:

"From the summaries which we have given it is difficult to avoid the conclusion that we are in the domain of religious romance, not of religious history. The early Christians were convinced that the Spirit of the Lord Jesus was with them. To their great joy His peace rested upon them. His continual guidance was their fundamental certainty. They received such guidance when critical decisions had to be made. The Lord Himself was felt to be present at their gatherings and particularly at 'the breaking of the bread.' How came it that He was thus present and active? He obviously must be alive. But, if alive, He must have risen from the dead. The stories of the empty tomb and of the resurrection appearances are attempts to explain how He thus rose to eternal life, attempts to buttress spiritual certainty by material fact. Religious conviction began the story: the activity of faith with impressive seriousness added details."[30]

'Abdu'l-Bahá explains the meaning of the resurrection as follows:

"The disciples were troubled and agitated after the martyrdom of Christ. The Reality of Christ, which signifies His teachings, His bounties, His perfections and His spiritual power, was hidden and concealed for two or three days after His martyrdom, and was not resplendent and manifest. No, rather it was lost; for the believers were few in number and were troubled and agitated. The Cause of Christ was like a lifeless body; and, when after three days the disciples became assured and steadfast, and began to serve the Cause

198

of Christ, and resolved to spread the divine teachings,
putting His counsels into practice, and arising to serve
Him, the Reality of Christ became resplendent and His
bounty appeared; His religion found life, His teachings
and His admonitions became evident and visible. In
other words, the Cause of Christ was like a lifeless body,
until the life and the bounty of the Holy Spirit
surrounded it. "[31]

Mary Magdalen, 'Abdu'l-Bahá tells us was the first to understand that Christ, the Spirit of God, was still with them; when she informed the disciples of her discovery, they also realised it. Their despondency turned to joy and they set out to give the glad tidings of the living Christ to the world.

Jewish and Muslim Doctrines

Although only Christian doctrines have so far been discussed in this chapter, the doctrines of other religions are no more free than the Christian from misunderstandings. The growth of Jewish doctrine is less easily traced, since Moses' original teaching and the early history of His followers are lost, except for the traditions handed down and recorded nearly a thousand years later in the Pentateuch. That so much should have remained after so long without authoritative record is another of God's miracles; but these Books do not constitute accurate history.

The formation of Muslim doctrine is more easily traced; it has been derived under the influence of political factions, partly from the Qur'án, partly from the misinterpretation of the Qur'án, and partly from inferences from supposed sayings and doings of the Prophet. One example must suffice.

Muslims believe that when Muḥammad said He was the 'Seal of the Prophets' He was denying that any religion would succeed His. This is inference only, and mistaken inference. For Muḥammad Himself said 'I am all the Prophets,' and He also said 'I am Adam, Noah, Moses, and Jesus.' Bahá'u'lláh comments:

*"Why should Muḥammad, that immortal Beauty, Who
hath said: 'I am the first Adam' be incapable of saying
also: 'I am the last Adam'? For even as He regarded
Himself to be the 'First of the Prophets' —that is Adam—
in like manner, the 'Seal of the Prophets' is also
applicable unto that Divine Beauty. It is admittedly
obvious that being the 'First of the Prophets', he
likewise is their Seal."*[32]

The Prophetic cycle that started with Adam ended with
Muḥammad; after Him came the Báb as Herald of the Cycle of
fulfilment Muḥammad was therefore the Seal of the Prophets in
the Adamic cycle.

The Need for a new Manifestation of God

Studying the errors, the misinterpretations, the idle fancies that have
masked the Word of God as given through the ages, how can we
doubt the need for a new Manifestation of God? The pure stream
of Divine Teaching emitted by the Founders of the old religions has
been defiled; earthy obstructions dam its powerful flow; men wander
as lost in a desert from which the water of the spirit has gone; the
blackness of winter encompasses the world.

Yet the desert is not quite arid and the winter not quite at its
most severe. Signs can be detected that spring may be on the way
and that the desert may yet blossom as a rose. Already the blind
adherence of former generations to indefensible rites and doctrines
is being questioned; superstition is losing its grip on the sincere; a
longing for a faith that satisfies at the same time mind, soul, and
spirit is producing a new attitude among the followers of all religions.

As this tendency grows and people recognise that much they
have been taught is a corruption of the true Teaching of the Founder
of their religion, more and more will find in the Faith of Bahá'u'lláh
the fulfilment of the essential spirit of their own Faith. They will
distinguish between the divine truth their Faith contains and the
transitory forms, suited to a former age, in which it is expressed;
they will cast out the debris of superstition obstructing its flow and

turn from the human concepts that have for so long misguided those who seek it.

Then they will see that their own Faith leads them straight to Bahá'u'lláh, the Source in this age of the stream of Truth they are seeking—a stream whose water is the same in all Dispensations, whatever the name of the Manifestation of God emitting it. They will understand that by quaffing this water they can be born again as the earlier followers of their own religion were born again by quaffing it before. They will learn that rebirth depends on the nature of the water, not on the name of the Fountain from which it comes, and learning this, they will understand that in the Bahá'í Faith they have discovered 'the changeless Faith of God, eternal in the past, eternal in the future.' Then they will rejoice for they will know with an unshakabie knowledge that creation has indeed been recreated; with heart and tongue they will praise the Glory of God and joyfully bear witness that in this age once more all things have been made new.

PART TWO

THE CENTRAL FIGURES
OF THE FAITH

CHAPTER XI

The Báb

The Forerunners

The first stirring of the new age in the East occurred at the beginning of the nineteenth century when an eminent divine of Shí'ih Islám,* Shaykh Aḥmad-i-Aḥsá'í of Aḥsá, became aware that the Promised One of Islám would soon appear. This respected and learned man founded a sect, named Shaykhí in his honour, whose members he sought to prepare for the advent of the Qá'im, the Promised One of the Shí'ihs. In like manner, God has sent one or more wise men at the end of each Dispensation to prepare people for the advent of His next Messenger.

When Shaykh Aḥmad died in 1826 he was succeeded as leader of the Shaykhís by Siyyid Kázim-i-Rashtí who he is reported to have said was the only man properly to understand his teaching. Knowing the Promised One to be already on earth, Siyyid Kázim urged the Shaykhís to scatter after his own death in search of the Goal of their Desire. 'Persevere till the time when He, who is your true Guide and Master, will graciously aid you and enable you to recognise Him. Be firm till the day when He will choose you as the companions and the heroic supporters of the promised Qá'im. Well is it with every one of you who will quaff the cup of martyrdom in His path.' He warned them that some might outlive their Lord and that these must remain assured and steadfast, since the first trumpet

---

* The two principal sects of Islám are the Shi'ihs and the Sunnis. The Shi'ihs believe that after the passing of Muḥammad, His son-in-law 'Alí was the rightful leader of Islám, and trace a line of twelve successive leaders, called Imáms, whom they consider to have been under the special guidance of God. Persia is the chief stronghold of the Shi'ihs who disapprove of Sunuís as much as Roman Catholics disapprove of Protestants.

205

blast (by which he meant the Báb) would be succeeded by a second (Bahá'u'lláh).

On the death of Siyyid Kázim 1843, some of his disciples wanted to acknowledge one of their number as the Qá'im, a young man named Mullá Ḥusayn-i-Bushrú'í whom Siyyid Kázim had praised very highly. Mullá Ḥusayn, however, vigorously denied being the One they were looking for. He first urged his fellow disciples to follow Siyyid Kázim often repeated instruction to scatter in search of the Qá'im and then himself became the most energetic and persevering of the seekers. Thus it happened that he was blessed by being the first to whom the Báb revealed Himself.

Declaration of the Báb

It was on the night of May 22, 1844. Irresistibly attracted to Shíráz, he was met on the day of his arrival by a young man who invited him home to refresh himself after his journey. After plying him with many kindnesses, the young man asked about his quest and the signs by which the Qá'im would be recognised. These having been enumerated, the strange young man exclaimed in a vibrant voice: 'Behold! All these signs are manifest in Me.'

Mullá Ḥusayn was at first reluctant to believe his host could be the One for Whom he searched. He resolved as a test to demand an explanation of certain difficult passages he had himself written and then the composition of a commentary on a chapter of the Qur'án called the Súrih of Joseph. The Báb told him afterwards that had he not been a guest at the time his position would have been grievous, since it was for God to test His servants, not His servants the Messenger of God.

As it was, the Báb consented to explain the passages queried, then revealed fresh truths unasked; before the second request had even been voiced. He began a commentary on the Súrih of Joseph that came to be considered the most important of all His Writings. Mullá Ḥusayn was so enthralled by the sweetness of the revelation that he lost all sense of time: describing the event afterwards, he said: 'All the delights, all the ineffable glories, which the Almighty

The Báb's House in Shiraz where He Declared His Mission.

His Bedchamber.

has recounted in His book, as the priceless possessions of the people of Paradise—these 1 seemed to be experiencing that night.' The Báb at one time forbade his departure, saying: 'If you leave in such a state, whoever sees you will assuredly say: "This poor youth has lost his mind."' The Bayán* records that the Báb declared Himself at two hours and eleven minutes after sunset, at which hour the Bahá'ís now commemorate His Declaration annually.

The Báb instructed Mullá Ḥusayn not to tell his fellows of the success of his search. Eighteen people had spontaneously to recognise God's Messenger before the news of His coming could be spread. This number was quickly reached, as though Mullá Ḥusayn's recognition had broken a seal, unleashing some force that attracted holy souls to the Object of their quest. The Báb called these first eighteen people to believe in Him 'The Letters of the Living.'

Last to come, but first in rank, was Quddús, then only twenty-two years old. On arriving in Shíráz, he found Mullá Ḥusayn following the Báb home. When Mullá Ḥusayn turned aside a query whether he had found the One they sought, Quddús exclaimed: 'Why seek you to hide Him from Me? I can recognise Him by His gait.' Later he was accepted by the Bábí as the one upon whom the Báb had bestowed primacy.

Last before Quddús, the only woman among the Letters of the Living had declared her recognition of the Báb's station. This was the beautiful, talented Ṭáhirih, who wrote great poetry and worsted eminent divines in theological argument. After dreaming that she met the Báb, she conveyed her confession of faith to Him in the following beautiful manner through her brother-in-law, who also became a Letter of the Living: "Say to Him from me: 'The effulgence of Thy face flashed forth, and the rays of Thy visage rose on high. Then speak the word, "Am I not your Lord?" and "Thou art, Thou art!" we will all reply."

The eighteen Letters of the Living, are the chosen ones of the Bábí Dispensation, described by the Báb as a 'company of angels

* See pages 221-22.

arrayed before God on the day of His coming' and the 'repositories of His mystery' who 'enjoy nearest access to God.' Each religion acknowledges a few people to have been especially close to the spirit of the Manifestation of note, like the twelve Imáms of Shí'ih Islám, the twelve Disciples of Jesus, the twelve leaders of the tribes of Israel in the Day of Moses, and so on. The greatness of the Revelation of the Báb was signified by there being eighteen such chosen ones and in the Dispensation of Bahá'u'lláh there are to be twenty-four.

Childhood a Youth of the Báb

The Báb, whose name was Siyyid 'Alí-Muḥammad, was born on October 20, 1819, of a father and mother descended from the Prophet Muḥammad. While He was still very young, His father died and a maternal uncle, named Ḥájí Mírzá Siyyid 'Alí, later to become a Bábí martyr, assumed responsibility for the child. He placed his charge under a schoolmaster, who, on becoming a Bábí, said that he had found the boy so wise he considered it beyond his power to inculcate further knowledge and had tried to get the uncle to stop sending the boy to school.

Eventually Ḥájí Mírzá Siyyid 'Alí was induced to take his nephew to work as a merchant in his business. The young man soon gained a reputation for piety, integrity and generosity. One who met him several times in those days recounted: 'His downcast eyes, his extreme courtesy, and the serene expression on his face made an indelible impression upon my soul. I often heard those who were closely associated with him testify to the purity of his character, to the charm of his manners, to his self-effacement, to his high integrity and to his extreme devotion to God.'

The Báb had only one child, who died in infancy. He spoke of this as a sacrifice made on the altar of the Love of God, which was a prelude to the sacrifice of His entire being on the same altar.

The First Two Years

The Báb sent the Letters of the Living to spread news of His coming throughout Persia, but Quddús He took with Him on a pilgrimage to Mecca and Medina. There He announced Himself to the Sherif of Mecca, who was, however, too pre-occupied at the time to attend to the document the Báb handed him. When later he heard of the Báb's martyrdom, he spoke censoriously of the oppressors.

Mullá Husayn was sent on a special mission to Ṭihrán, which the Báb told him enshrined a Mystery of transcendental holiness. There he conveyed to Bahá'u'lláh a Tablet written by the Báb, upon receipt of which Bahá'u'lláh commented to His brother: 'Verily I say, whoso believes in the Qur'án a recognises its divine origin, and yet hesitates, though it be for a moment, to admit that these soul-stirring words are endowed with the same regenerative power, has most assuredly erred in his judgment and has strayed far from the path of justice.

The Letters of the Living soon met opposition. The new message was both startling and challenging. Although some who met with it caught flame at once and others recognised that the Báb's audacious claims deserved careful investigation, most, including nearly all the eminent divines, condemned Him unheard. Already while the Báb was on pilgrimage a few believers suffered ignominy, beating, or martyrdom for His sake. On His return, excitement and controversy spread throughout Shiráz, making apparent the momentous character of the spiritual convulsion that was overtaking the people of Persia.

The Báb had sent Quddús ahead to Shiráz while He Himself remained for a time in Búshihr the excitement grew so quickly that the alarmed Governor sent soldiers to Búshihr to arrest Him. This first arrest did not last long, however, for the leading divine of Shiráz, a just man, intervened to secure His quick release to the custody of His uncle.

A year of comparative tranquillity followed; during which the fame of the Báb grew rapidly. A number of well-known divines became Bábís during this period, amongst them Siyyid Yahyáy-i-Dárábi, named Vahid, by the Báb, whom the Sháh had sent to investigate and report on the new Teaching, and Mullá Muhammad-'Alíy-i-Zanjáni, named Hujjat by the Báb, who was

almost as eminent in rank as Vaḥíd. So many and important were
the visitors who flocked to the Báb's home that the Governor
became alarmed again and resolved to arrest Him, this time with a
view to having Him executed. There followed events which Shoghi
Effendi has graphically described:

"By order of the governor the chief constable,
'Abdu'l-Ḥamíd Khán, scaled, in the dead of night, the wall
and entered the house of Ḥájí Mírjá Siyyid 'Alí, where the
Báb was confined, arrested Him, and confiscated all His
books and documents. That very night, however, took place
an event which, in its dramatic suddenness, was no doubt
providentially designed to confound the schemes of the
plotters, and enable the Object of their hatred to prolong
His ministry and consummate His Revelation. An outbreak
of cholera, devastating in its virulence, had, since midnight,
already smitten above a hundred people. The dread of the
plague had entered every heart, and the inhabitants of the
stricken city were, amid shrieks of pain and grief, fleeing in
confusion. Three of the governor's domestics had already
died. Members of his family were lying dangerously ill. In
his despair, he, leaving the dead unburied, had fled to a
garden in the outskirts of the city. 'Abdu'l-Ḥamíd Khán,
confronted by this unexpected development, decided to
conduct the Báb to his own home. He was appalled, upon
his arrival, to learn that his son lay in the death-throes of
the plague. In his despair he threw himself at the feet of
the Báb, begged to be forgiven, adjured Him not to visit
upon the son the sins of the father, and pledged his word to
resign his post, and never again to accept such a position.
Finding that his prayer had been answered, he addressed a
plea to the governor begging him to release his Captive,
and thereby deflect the fatal course of this dire visitation.
Ḥusayn Khán acceded to his request, and released his
Prisoner on condition of His quitting the city."[1]

The Báb in Iṣfáhán

From Shlráz, the Báb went to Iṣfáhán, where He at first lived in the house of the chief Muslim dignitary, known as the Imám-Jum'ih. Soon, like iron filings attracted by a magnet, innumerable visitors flocked to this house to meet Him. Manúchihr Khán, the Governor, himself came and was convinced that the Báb was superhumanly endowed. So greatly did the people of the city honour the Báb that on one occasion a crowd clamoured for the water He had bathed in, which they believed to have power to heal.

As signs of His influence increased, the growing plaints of the divines of Iṣfáhán found a ready listener in Ḥáji Mirzá Áqásí, the Sháh's Chief Minister. Manúchihr Khán became fearful for the Báb and had Him live in the Governor's Palace for protection. When the local divines condemned Him to death as a heretic. Manúchihr Khán pretended to send Him out of the city, but had Him secretly brought back to live in the private part of the Palace. This noble Governor would have intervened personally with the Sháh to secure royal approval of the Báb's Cause, had not the Báb explained that God willed otherwise.

Not long afterwards, Manúchihr Khán died suddenly, leaving the Báb all his vast possessions. However, his successor found the will, destroyed it, and arranged for the Báb to be summoned to Ṭihrán. Ḥáji Mirzá Áqásí, fearing that the Young Man's charm might ensnare the Sháh if they met, managed to have Him diverted without an audience to exile in Adhirbáyján in the remote north-west of Persia. Here He was imprisoned in the fortress of Máh-Kú with only one of His followers to keep Him company.

Máh-Kú and Chihríq

The inhabitants of that part of Persia are Kurds belonging to the Sunní sect of Islám, who hate all Shí'ihs, especially Siyyids, the descendants of Muḥammad, of whom the Báb was one. They speak a different language from other Persians and were then known as a wild and turbulent people. Moreover, Ḥáji Mirzá Áqásí, who had been born in the vicinity of Máh-Kú, had treated its inhabitants well. Not realising that the Báb wielded superhuman power, he fondly imagined these circumstances would be sufficient to ensure the severance of the life-vein of the Bábí Community, which would then languish into ultimate extinction through lack of communication with the Source of its life.

To make more certain of this, he instructed the warden of the fortress to guard his Prisoner with the utmost rigour, a command that was at first faithfully obeyed. The Báb Himself has testified that the inmates of the fortress were limited to two guards and four dogs, that His room had no door, and that He was granted no lamp for use after dark

Little did these precautions avail! The turbulent inhabitants were soon subdued by the gentle Báb; they grew so to love Him that each day from outside the fortress, in spite of repeated attempts by the warden to stop them, they would invoke His blessing on their daily work. They would even meet there in cases of dispute to adjure each other by His name to speak the truth. Presently a radical change came over the attitude of the warden himself, following a strange vision, which rendered him so lenient that thenceforth he admitted a constant stream of pilgrims to the presence of the Báb, whom, according to his enemies, he be sought to marry a daughter he had refused to the Heir Apparent. A few months after the Báb's arrival in Máh-Kú, virtually nothing remained of the restrictions that had at first been imposed so rigidly.

That Ḥáji Mirzá Áqásí would have the Báb removed to another fortress was certain. He chose the castle of Chihríq, whose warden was the Sháh's brother-in-law. Here the story was repeated; the villagers sought the Báb's blessing each day to the extent that a European observer reported the courtyard would not hold all who came; the Sháh's brother-in-law became His devoted servant; divines and officials of the neighbouring town of Khuy flocked to see Him and became firm believers in His Cause.

In spite of His imprisonment, the influence of the Báb was growing daily. To find ways of counteracting it, a convocation was called in Ṭabríz, to which He was summoned; but far from achieving its purpose, this merely provided Him with an opportunity to make the following momentous declaration of His station: *"I am, I am, I am, the Promised One! I am the One Whose name you have for a thousand years invoked, at Whose mention you have risen. Whose advent you have longed to witness, and the hour of Whose Revelation you have prayed to God to hasten. Verily, I say, it is incumbent upon the peoples of both the East and the West to obey My word, and to pledge allegiance to My person."*

From beginning to end, the Báb dominated the proceedings. Finding on His entry to the hall that the only vacant seat was one reserved for the heir to the throne. He occupied it, and such was His presence, none dared object. After His declaration, the divines attempted to reprimand Him, but succeeded only in providing fresh opportunities for Him to demonstrate His ascendancy. Eventually He closed the hearing Himself by suddenly rising and quitting the room after brushing aside a frivolous question.

To cover their discomfiture, the divines prevailed upon the civil authorities to order the Báb to be bastinadoed, but even in this they were only partly successful. The Governor's body guard asserted that the matter was one for the divines alone and refused to act. Eventually a Muslim dignitary carried out the sentence personally in his own home.

In the teeth of this fiasco. Ḥáji Mirzá Áqásí was left with no alternative but to return the Báb to Chihríq.

The Conference of Badasht

Meanwhile events of the utmost significance for the Bábí Faith were taking place far from Ṭabríz and Chihríq. The whole of Persia was aflame with the new Revelation, but as yet the Bábí Community was bound in the fetters of ecclesiastical tradition. The break with the past came as a sudden dramatic cleavage at the Conference of Badasht where eighty-one leading Bábís met in three gardens Bahá'u'lláh had rented. Nabíl comments on this Conference: 'Each day of that memorable gathering witnessed the abrogation of a new law and the repudiation of a long-established tradition. The veils that guarded the sanctity of the ordinances of Islm were sternly rent asunder.'

Bahá'u'lláh unobtrusively guided the course of the Conference from start to finish. As a symbol of its importance. He gave each attendant a new title, whose origin was, however, concealed from the recipient. He Himself was thereafter designated Bahá, and from then the names Quddús and Ṭáhirih also date.

To soften the impact of the blow that the abrogation of old laws and customs, must comprise, a mock quarrel was staged between the impetuous Ṭáhirih and Quddús representing the conservative element. This and the Conference both culminated one day when Bahá'u'lláh was confined to bed, indisposed. On that day, Ṭáhirih, the pure, so reverenced that even to gaze at her shadow was deemed improper, appeared unveiled before the friends gathered in His bedroom. Consternation and dismay forthwith seized the assembled company. One severely shaken witness cut his own throat and fled bleeding from her presence. A few others also abandoned both their companions and the Faith. Quddús meanwhile remained seated, his face apparently betraying inexpressible anger and his whole demeanour giving the impression that he might at any moment strike the exultant Ṭáhirih with his sword.

Ṭáhirih rose confidently from her seat, illumined by triumphant joy. In language markedly reminiscent of the Qur'án, she delivered a most moving address to the residue, ending with the resonant declaration: 'I am the Word which the Qá'im is to utter, the Word which shall put to flight the chief and nobles of the earth!' Thus was a prophecy almost literally, as well as symbolically, fulfilled.

On that memorable day the purpose of the Conference was achieved, so the mock feud between Ṭáhirih and Quddús could soon be ended. The 'stunning trumpet-blast' mentioned in the Qur'án had been sounded, initiating that liberation from Muslim tradition which was so important a function of the Bábí Dispensation. Revolutionary changes took place in the outlook, habits and manner of worship of the assembled friends. After the Conference of Badasht, realisation grew among the Bábís that the laws of the

Báb, not those of Muḥammad mad, now held sway, a realisation that opened the path to the eventual introduction of the laws of Bahá'u'lláh.

Upheavals

The Báb's audacious behaviour before the Tabríz Convocation fanned the fire that was enveloping Persia to still fiercer flame. It raised the zeal of the Bábís to white heat, provoked violent controversy among both laymen and divines, and led to the masses being openly incited from the pulpits to attack and maltreat the Bábís, their women, and their children.

With controversy reaching alarming proportions, the Sháh died and the cruel Mírzá Taqí Khán took the place of Ḥájí Mírzá Áqásí as Chief Minister. He quickly let loose upon the helpless Bábís a systematic campaign of persecution in which civil and ecolesiastical powers combined. The Bábís were struck down by mobs, by civil and military authorities, and even by the divines themselves. When they defended themselves, as they did in a few places where a large number of Bábís had congregated, their enemies misrepresented them as rebelling. A brief reference to the most famous of these defences will serve both to illustrate the exalted spirit that inspired the defenders and to show how absurd such tales of rebellion are.

The epic of Shaykh Ṭabarsi began when the Báb instructed Mullá Ḥusayn to raise the black standard that Muḥammad had said would announce the coming of the Qá'im, and to journey to help Qudddús in Mázindarán. He came with his companions to Bárfurúsh where the divines caused the populace to issue forth from the city to attack them. Only when seven of his companions had been shot would Mullá Ḥusayn permit the Bábís to fight back; then he himself, although untrained in fighting, led the charge and with a scarcely credible stroke of his sword severed the body of a man, his musket, and the tree behind which he sheltered—a stroke so extraordinary that the townsmen fled in terror.

That night Mullá Ḥusayn and his companions spent in a

caravanserai. Three of them in succession mounted to the roof to sound the traditional call to prayer, each of whom in turn was shot at the very beginning of the holy chant. Thereupon the Bábís charged their assailants and decimated them. This time the local notables proffered an escort to conduct the formidable band safely away from Bárfurúsh but a Muslim dignitary prevailed on the leader of the escort to slaughter the Bábís en route. Some had already been slaughtered when one succeeded by means of a stratagem in killing the leader; after the struggle that followed it was the escort who were left dead.

Space forbids any detailed account of the heroism and suffering which followed. At no time were there as many as four hundred Bábís in the fortress they erected, yet for eleven months they withstood the assault of thousands of trained soldiers, both infantry and cavalry, backed by artillery, and under eminent command. From time to time Qudddús, who had joined the besieged, would raise the call 'Mount your steeds. O heroes of God,' upon which a party of Bábís would sally forth to the cry of 'Yá Ṣáḥibu'z-Zamán' (O Lord of the Age) and rout the frightened enemy. One of these sallies led to the opposing Commander-in-Chief's jumping barefooted into the moat from a back window of his private apartment. Another, executed by only nineteen Bábís, scattered two regiments in terror and caused their general, after falling frightened from his horse leaving one boot in the stirrup, to limp half-shod to his commander with news of yet another rout.

The siege brought great suffering to the defenders. Their shortage of food was such that at times their only nourishment was grass, or the bark of trees, or even leather, 'Abdu'l-Bahá says in *Memorials of the Faithful:*

"*For eighteen days they remained without food. They lived on the leather of their shoes. This too was soon consumed and they had nothing left but water. They drank a mouthful every morning, and lay famished and exhausted in their fort. When attacked, however, they*

*would instantly spring to their feet and manifest in the
face of the enemy a magnificent courage and
astonishing resistance.... Under such circumstances to
maintain an unwavering faith and patience is extremely
difficult, and to endure such dire afflictions a rare
phenomenon.*"[2]

Eventually, unable to conquer by fair means, the opposing
general resorted to foul. He induced surrender by means of a
guarantee of safe conduct written in a copy of the Qur'án, upon
which Holy Book he then brought shame by having some of his
surrendered opponents killed, others tortured, and the rest sold into
slavery. Mullá Ḥusayn had already fallen in battle, but Quddús was
handed over to the divines, who incited a mob to execrate him and
hack him to pieces. Thus ended in triumphant death the most
remarkable siege in recorded history.

Nor was the siege of Shaykh Ṭabarsi the only example of
prolonged Bábí resistance to the attacks of vastly superior forces.
Vaḥíd and Ḥujjat, eminent divines with no experience of fighting,
each led a heroic defence characterised by great contrast between
the devout, courageous defenders, who had neither military training
nor adequate equipment, and the degraded, cowardly, but well-trained
and continually reinforced attackers. Both Vaḥíd and Ḥujjat lost
their lives as a result of these struggles, the second of which was
still in progress when the Báb was martyred.

The Martyrdom of the Báb
Mírzá Taqí Khán's campaign to exterminate the Bábís by brutal
repressive measures had dismally failed. It had served only to
intensify the zeal and devotion of the suffering Bábís. Moreover,
the determination and ability they had shown when resisting attacks
sent a chill of fear into ministerial hearts.

Mírzá Taqí Khán decided to try to stem the torrent at its source
by executing the Báb. The Báb was therefore taken to Ṭabríz and
the Governor, a royal prince, was ordered to have Him publicly shot
in the courtyard of the barracks in the centre of the city. The prince

flatly refused to comply, where upon Mírzá Taqí Khán instructed his own brother, who had carried the orders, to arrange the execution himself.

As the Báb was led to the place of His Martyrdom. Tabríz experienced turmoil worse than any it had known. Crowds thronged the route in frenzied excitement. Suddenly a youth burst from the throng to throw himself at the feet of the Báb, fervently imploring to be allowed to remain with Him always. The Báb replied: "Rest assured that you will be with Me. Tomorrow you shall witness what God has decreed."

The next day, July 9, 1850, saw one of the most extraordinary episodes the world has known. It began with the arrival of a messenger sent to conduct the Báb to the leading divines of the city for them to authorise the execution. When the messenger arrived, the Báb was talking confidentially to His secretary; the messenger interrupted the conversation, whereupon the Báb exclaimed: "Not until I have said to him all those things that I wish to say can any earthly power silence Me. Though all the world be armed against Me, yet shall they be powerless to deter Me from fulfilling, to the last word, my intention."

Now the courtyard is prepared for the execution. Two ropes are made fast to a nail driven into a pillar adjoining the room of the Báb's secretary. From these the Báb and the youth who had begged to accompany Him are suspended. Sám Khán regiment of seven hundred and fifty men take aim and fire, while ten thousand people watch expectantly from neighbouring roofs and houses to see the victims die.

As the smoke of the seven hundred and fifty rifles clears, a shout of bewildered surprise bursts from the throng. There, standing alive and unhurt is the Báb's companion; the Báb Himself is nowhere to be seen. Hurried investigation showed that although the bullets had cut the ropes to pieces, not one had touched either of the human targets. The Báb was eventually found in His secretary's room tranquilly finishing His interrupted discourse, "I have finished my conversation." He commented when the messenger who had interrupted Him appeared, "Now you may proceed to fulfil your intention." But the man was too much shaken; he left the scene without performing his duty and resigned his post.

Sám Khán also refused to proceed further with the execution. He ordered his men to quit the barracks and swore never to resume the task of shooting the Báb, even though his refusal should cost him his life.

However, the Colonel of a Muslim regiment volunteered to have his men execute the sentence. This time the victims were shattered by the bullets, except their faces which were little marred; they could not afterwards be separated and thus the Báb's prophecy to the ardent youth was literally fulfilled. His last words as He gazed on the watching crowds were: "O wayward generation! Had you believed in Me, every one of you would have followed the example of this youth, who stood in rank above most of you, and willingly would have sacrificed himself in My path. The day will come when you will have recognised Me; that day I shall have ceased to be with you."

The Martyrdom of the Báb took place at noon. The very moment the fatal shots were fired, a gale of exceptional severity arose, causing a whirlwind of dust to obscure the sun for the rest of that momentous day. Some years later, one-third of the firing squad that shot the Báb were killed in an earthquake and the remainder were themselves shot after mutinying. Both Mírzá Taqí Khán and his brother were disgraced and put to death within two years. The Báb's arch-enemy, Hájí Mirzá Áqásí, was also disgraced, to become in exile a victim of disease and poverty. In varying degrees, all others who opposed the Báb experienced misfortune or early death.

It may be that some who read this book will think the story of the Báb's Martyrdom too much like legend to be believed. Such doubters are referred to document F.O. 60/152/88 in the archives of the Foreign Office at the Public Records Office in London. This document is an official letter dated July 22, 1850, from Sir Justin Sheil. Queen Victoria's Envoy Extraordinary and Minister Plenipotentiary in Ṭihrán, to the Secretary of State for Foreign Affairs,

Lord Palmerston. It reads: 'The founder of the sect has been executed at Tabreez. He was killed by a volley of musketry, and his death was on the point of giving his religion a lustre which would have largely increased his proselytes. When the smoke and dust cleared away after the volley. Báb was not to be seen, and the populace proclaimed that he had ascended to the skies. The balls had broken the ropes by which he was bound but he was dragged* from the recess where after some search he was discovered and shot. His death, according to the belief of his disciples, will make no difference as Báb must always exist.'

The bodies of the Báb and His companion were put on the edge of the moat outside the city in the hope that they would, contrary to prophecies about the body of the Promised One, be eaten by wild animals. The Bábís succeeded, however, in removing the bodies, which were thereafter transferred from one place to another as each hiding-place became insecure. Fifty years later they were finally brought to the Holy Land by instruction of 'Abdu'l-Bahá and laid to rest on Mt. Carmel in a specially erected Shrine.**

The Writings of the Báb

The core of the Báb's Teaching is contained in the Persian Bayán, written in Máh-Kú and not to be confused with the less weighty Arabic Bayán. Its theme is the coming of 'Him Whom God shall make manifest,' the Great One to Whom the Báb was the Gate.

"The whole of the Bayán is only a leaf amongst the leaves of His paradise,"[3] He exclaims, and elsewhere: *"To-day the Bayán is in the stage of seed; at the beginning of the manifestation of him Whom God shall make manifest its ultimate perfection will become apparent."*[4] Moreover, He affirms: *"All that hath been revealed in the Bayán is but a ring upon My hand, and I Myself am, verily, but a ring upon the hand of Him Whom God shall make manifest. . . . He turneth it as He pleaseth. ... He, verily, is the Help in Peril, the Most High,"*[5] The Báb

---

* Not literally, of course.
** See pages 252-53.

specifically asserts:

"Better is it for thee to recite but one of the verses of Him Whom God shall make manifest than to set down the whole of the Bayán, for on that Day that one verse can save thee, whereas the entire Bayán cannot save thee," Such passages from the Báb's own Writings fully explain why the Bahá'ís turn to the Writings of Bahá'u'lláh for guidance rather than to those of the Báb.

The Persian Bayán abrogated the Laws of the Muḥammadan Dispensation and was thus the authority for the actions taken at the Conference of Badasht. Shoghi Effendi tells us that one of its objects was *"to administer a sudden and fatal blow to obsolete and corrupt institutions,"*[7] to which end its own Laws were both revolutionary and severe. The Báb knew that before these Laws were fully established they would be abrogated by Bahá'u'lláh; meanwhile their severity and revolutionary character would help wean the Bábís from the past.

Among the teachings of the Báb is that certain terms in Scripture are to be taken allegorically rather than literally; the meaning of some of these He explains. He was the first to expound the theme of progressive revelation and the oneness of the Manifestations of God. Although few of His Laws survived, certain of His social teachings have been confirmed by Bahá'u'lláh as appropriate to our own age. Among these are that all should receive education, that Women should be more free, that begging should be forbidden and the poor provided for from public funds, that useful arts and crafts should be cultivated, and that drinking alcohol should be prohibited.

Although the Bayán contains the core of the Báb's Teaching. Bahá'u'lláh has described the commentary on the Súrih of Joseph, entitled the Qayyúmu'l-Asmá and revealed in answer to the unspoken request of Mullá Ḥusayn, as *'the first, the greatest and mightiest of all books'* of the Bábí Dispensation. This contains an announcement of the Báb's advent and warnings both to people generally and to particular groups, as well as to the Sháh and His Ministers. With the warnings are mingled prophecies, most of which have already been fulfilled. Even in this first Book, the coming of Bahá'u'lláh is foreshadowed.

Another important work is *The Seven Proofs*, in which the Báb lucidly authenticates His Mission. He also revealed innumerable Tablets, including several to the Sháh of Persia and one to the Sultán of Turkey. A Tablet was addressed to the divines of every city in Persia, in which He detailed the errors committed by each of them.

Unfortunately many of the Báb's Tablets and Commentaries have been lost and many others have been maliciously interpolated, or corrupted. What survives, however, is a lasting treasure for future generations.

The Station of the Báb

That the Báb is both an independent Manifestation of God and the Forerunner of Bahá'u'lláh is proclaimed by 'Abdu'l Bahá in His Will to be part of the foundation of Bahá'í belief. The Guardian explains in *'The Dispensation of Bahá'u'lláh'* that the intensity of the Báb's Revelation was greater than that of any previous Manifestation. Bahá'u'lláh Himself affirmed:

"No eye hath beheld so great an outpouring of bounty, nor hath any ear heard of such a Revelation of loving-kindness."[9]

The Báb proclaimed His station thus in a Tablet to Muḥammad Sháh:

"I am the Primal Point from which have been generated all created things.... I am the Countenance of God Whose splendour can never be obscured, the light of God Whose radiance can never fade... All the keys of heaven God hath chosen to place on my right hand, and all the keys of hell on My left I am one of the sustaining pillars of the Primal Word of God. Whosoever hath recognised Me, hath known all that is true and right, and hath attained all that is good and seemly.... The substance wherewith God hat created Me is not

the clay out of which others have been formed. He hath
conferred upon Me that which the worldly-wise can
never comprehend nor the faithful discover."[10]

This is no mere claim to be the gate to a hidden Imám, which some of the Muslims of the time thought the title 'Báb' signified. That designation had long been used of four men supposed to have acted as intermediaries between the twelfth Imám, who disappeared, and the faithful. Some imagined the Báb was claiming to be a fifth such gate; but His own words clearly define His station as something far more exalted than that. He was no less than the Promised One, known as the Qá'im by the Shí'ih sect of Islm and the Mihdí by the rival Sunní sect. He was indeed a Gate, but not to a hidden Imám; He was the Gate to the new age, to the Bahá'í era, the Gate to the Promise of All Ages, the Gate to the Glory of God, Bahá'u'lláh.

It is one of the signs of the greatness of this age that the Forerunner of Bahá'u'lláh was Himself a Manifestation of God with a Revelation so intense. The magnitude of the outpouring of grace may be gauged from a traditional utterance of Muḥammad quoted by Bahá'u'lláh:

"Knowledge is twenty and seven letters. All that the
Prophets have revealed are two letters thereof. No man
thus far hath known more than these two letters. But
when the Qá'im shall arise. He will cause the remaining
twenty and five letters to be made manifest."

Upon this Bahá'u'lláh comments:

"Consider; He hath declared Knowledge to consist of
twenty and seven letters, and regarded all the Prophets,
from Adam even unto the "Seal," as Expounders of
only two letters thereof and of having been sent down
with these two letters. He also saith that the Qá'im will
reveal all the remaining twenty and five letters. Behold
from this utterance how great and lofty is His station!
His rank excelleth that of all the Prophets, and His

Revelation transcendeth the comprehension and understanding of all their chosen ones."

How much greater, then, must be the station of 'Him Whom God shall make manifest,' of Whom the Báb wrote:

"Were He to appear this very moment. I would be the first to adore Him, and the first to bow down before Him."[12]

CHAPTER XII

Bahá'u'lláh

Early Life

Bahá'u'lláh was born on November 12, 1817, of a noble family, descendants of the ancient Sassanid kings of Persia. Although He attended no school. He displayed great knowledge and wisdom at an early age. 'Abdu'l-Bahá gave J. E. Esslemont the following particulars about the childhood and youth of His Father:

> "From childhood He was extremely kind and generous. He was a, great lover of outdoor life, most of His time being spent in the garden or the fields. He had an extraordinary power of attraction, which was felt by all. People always crowded round Him. Ministers and people of the Court would surround Him, and the children also were devoted to Him. When He was only thirteen or fourteen years old He became renowned for His learning. He would converse on any subject and solve any problem presented to Him. In large gatherings He would discuss matters with the 'Ulamá (divines) and would explain intricate religious questions. All of them used to listen to Him with the greatest interest."

When Bahá'u'lláh was twenty-two years old, His father died, and the Government wished Him to succeed to His father's position in the Ministry, as was customary in Írán, but Bahá'u'lláh did not accept the offer. Then the Prime Minister said: *"Leave Him to Himself. Such a position is unworthy of Him. He has some higher aim in view. I cannot understand Him, but I am convinced that He is destined for some lofty career. His thoughts are not like ours. Let Him alone."* [1]

Bahá'u'lláh during the Ministry of the Báb

On being informed of the Báb's declaration, Bahá'u'lláh at once arose to support the Bábí Cause. He quickly won for it a large number of notables and officials of Núr, His birthplace, including members of His own family; soon thereafter ecclesiastical dignitaries, traders and peasants followed them into the Cause. Through His intimate association with the most distinguished of the Bábís, He was able to guide and foster the growth of the infant community, in a way that the Báb Himself, being a prisoner, could not. At the same time, He exerted His influence as a noble to protect individual Bábís, so far as protection was possible; both Quddús and Táhirih were helped thus.

Inevitably such active support of the Bábí Cause attracted its own measure of persecution. In the course of helping Táhirih, Bahá'u'lláh suffered imprisonment at the hands of a local official, which lasted a few days. Later, mischief-makers induced the Sháh to order His arrest, but the execution of the order was permanently stayed by the Sháh's sudden death. He was again imprisoned when on His way to join the defenders of Shaykh Tabarsi an occurrence no doubt ordained by God to prevent His reaching the fort and being slaughtered in the final massacre there. On this occasion He was stoned, bastinadoed until His feet bled, and insulted.

After the martyrdom of the Báb, Bahá'u'lláh was the real leader of the stricken Community. The Báb, before leaving for Chihríq, had shown Whom He most trusted by despatching His pen-case, seals and agate rings to Bahá'u'lláh for safe-keeping, together with a scroll on which He had written three hundred and sixty derivatives of the word Bahá, in the form of a pentacle. However, to divert attention from Bahá'u'lláh and permit Him to promote the Cause without interference, people were allowed to think that His brother Mirzá Yahyá had become its leader.

The Attempt on the Life of the Sháh

In the years immediately following the Báb's martyrdom, the Bábí Community laboured in great difficulty. Most of its *élite* had been killed. The Writings of the Báb were dispersed, unclassified and badly preserved. Powerful enemies, encouraged by the reverses the Faith had sustained, were constantly abusing and slandering it. To make matters worse, Mirzá Taqí Khán the Chief Minister, who still opposed the Faith relentlessly, indicated to Bahá'u'lláh that it would be preferable for Him to go to Karbilá, outside Persia, for a time. Bahá'u'lláh complied with this wish, and continued there to attract people to the Báb's Cause until 1852, when Mirzá Taqí Khán fall from favour decided Him to return to Ṭihrán.

The next year an event occurred that brought crushing calamity upon both Bahá'u'lláh and the Bábís. A confectioner's assistant, a Bábí, overcome by grief and rage at the execution of the Báb, tried with the help of a friend to murder the Sháh. The attempt provided its own evidence that Bábí leaders had not organised it, for the misguided youth's pistol was loaded only with shot, which no man with competent advisers would have used for such a purpose. In spite of this and although the Sháh was only slightly wounded, the deed unleashed a reign of terror surpassing in malevolence and unrestrained bestiality any persecution of historical times. The shadow of its horror may be seen in the following account by an Austrian officer who resigned his employment because of what he then witnessed:

"Follow me, my friend, you who lay claim to a heart and European ethics, follow me to the unhappy ones who, with gouged-out eyes, must eat, on the scene of the deed, without any sauce, their own amputated ears; or whose teeth are torn out with inhuman violence by the hand of the executioner; or whose bare skulls are simply crushed by blows from a hammer; or where the bazaar is illuminated with unhappy victims, because on right and left the people dig deep holes in their breasts and shoulders, and insert burning wicks in the

wounds. I saw some dragged in chains through the bazaar, preceded by a military band, in whom these wicks had burned so deep that now the fat flickered convulsively in the wound like a newly extinguished lamp. Not seldom it happens that the unwearying ingenuity of the Oriental leads to fresh tortures. They will skin the soles of the Bábís' feet, soak the wounds in boiling oil, shoe the foot like the hoof of a horse, and compel the victim to run. No cry escaped from the victim's breast; the torment is endured in dark silence by the numbed sensation of the fanatic; now he must run; the body cannot endure what the soul has endured; he falls. Give him the coup de grace! Put him out of his pain! No! The executioner swings the whip, and—I myself have had to witness it—the unhappy victim of a hundredfold tortures runs."[2]

With the exception of Bahá'u'lláh this holocaust took the lives of all the remaining Bábí leaders including Ṭáhirih, whose death by strangling was comparatively merciful. Bahá'u'lláh Himself suffered grievous imprisonment. At the time of the attempt. He was a guest of the Chief Minister; disregarding advice to remain where He was for safety. He immediately rode to the headquarters of the Imperial army. There He was arrested and was conducted 'on foot, in chains, and with bare head and feet' to the underground dungeon in Ṭihrán known as the Síyáh-Chál, a disused reservoir for one of the public baths.

Bahá'u'lláh describes the place graphically: *"As to the dungeon in which this Wronged One and others similarly wronged were confined, a dark and narrow pit were preferable. Upon our arrival We were first conducted along a pitch-black corridor, from whence We descended three steep flights of stairs to the place of confinement assigned to Us. The dungeon was wrapped in thick darkness, and our fellow-prisoners numbered nearly a hundred and fifty souls: thieves, assassins and highwaymen. Though crowded, it had no other outlet than the passage by which We entered. No pen can depict thd place, nor any tongue describe its loathsome smell."*[3]

Here He spent four months, chained by chains of notorious weight, which permanently marked Him. For three days and nights He received no food. Sleep was almost impossible in that chill, damp, vermin infested hole. Later, His guards sought favour from those in authority by poisoning His food, an act which, although it failed to kill Him, impaired His health for many years.

In these unprepossessing surroundings, when His life seemed forfeit, Bahá'u'lláh was called by God to His glorious Mission. Without the knowledge even of His companions in suffering, that dark pit became the scene of the most momentous event of historical times. Silently and unspectacularly, the Bahá'í Revelation was there born.

Birth of the Bahá'í Revelation

To each of the Manifestations of God has come a time when He was made aware of His Mission. The experience of each has been described in symbolic terms that picture for man an event beyond human comprehension. Bahá'u'lláh commented in His Tablet to the Sháh of Persia: *"I was but a man like others, asleep upon My couch, when lo, the breezes of the All-Glorious were wafted over Me and taught Me the knowledge of all that hath been,"*[4] Jesus told of the heavens opening when He was baptised and the Holy Ghost descending on Him like a dove; Moses related the allegory of the Burning Bush; Muḥammad spoke of the voice of Gabriel telling Him to cry in the name of the Lord.

Bahá'u'lláh has given us several accounts of the experience. The first stirrings of God's Revelation He describes as follows: *"One night in a dream these exalted words, were heard on every side: 'Verily, We shall render Thee victorious by Thyself and by Thy pen. Grieve Thou not for that which hath befallen Thee, neither be Thou afraid, for Thou art in safety. Erelong will God raise up the treasures of the earth—men who will aid Thee through Thyself and through Thy Name, wherewith God hath revived the hearts of such as have recognised Him'."* In another passage

He relates: *"During the days I lay in the prison of Ṭihran, though the galling weight of the chains and the stench-filled air allowed Me but little sleep, still in those infrequent moments of slumber I felt as if something flowed from the crown of My head over My breast, even as a mighty torrent that precipitateth itself upon the earth from the summit of a lofty mountain. Every limb of My body would, as a result, be set afire. At such moments My tongue recited what no man could bear to hear."*[6]

By this experience, the soul of Bahá'u'lláh was fully awakened; what had always been latent within Him became manifest; but He did not reveal Himself to men yet. Another ten years were to pass before He made His true station known to the Bábís—ten years during which He transformed the Bábí Community.

With the birth of Bahá'u'lláh's Mission, the Dispensation of the Báb ended and that of Bahá'u'lláh began. Even its date had been given by the Báb, who had repeatedly stressed the years nine and nineteen in His references to *"Him Whom God shall make manifest."* The birth of Bahá'u'lláh's Mission took place in the year nine of the new era and His Declaration in the year nineteen.

Bahá'u'lláh's Banishment to Baghdád

It was not the will of Providence that Bahá'u'lláh should lose His life during the persecution of 1853. The Russian Minister, whose secretary was Bahá'u'lláh's brother-in-law, exerted every effort to obtain His release; the instigator of the attempt on the Sháh publicly confessed and insisted Bahá'u'lláh had had no part in it; His relatives worked unceasingly to help Him; the appetite of the monster crying for Bábí blood became gradually sated. In the end, Bahá'u'lláh was released from the Síyáh-Chál and ordered to leave Persia within one month. Refusing an offer from the Russian Minister of sanctuary in Russia. He decided to go with His family to Baghdád Thus began a period of exile lasting the rest of His life, reminiscent of Abraham's banishment from Ur of the Chaldees,* whose effect on world history has been more extensive than that of any other exile before

---

* Mentioned in the Qur'án.

Bahá'u'lláh's.

Although on arriving at Baghdád Bahá'u'lláh did not disclose His newly realised station, the power and might emanating from Him could not be wholly concealed. Officials, including the governor of the city, felt it and became His friends; divines who had been companions of Siyyid Kázim felt it and showed their admiration; the Bábís felt it and manifested an ever-deepening veneration for Him; in various ways He began to take His rightful place before men as Bábí leader.

A lull in the persecution of the Bábís followed His banishment, but now the first signs of a crisis of a different kind became evident. Mírzá Yahyá the nominal head of the Cause, had passed most of the period following the Martyrdom of the Báb in hiding. When Bahá'u'lláh went to Baghdád, he followed and became there the prey of one Siyyid Muhammad, who developed an intense jealousy of Bahá'u'lláh. This unscrupulous schemer organised a clandestine opposition among the demoralised Bábís, which sought to frustrate every move Bahá'u'lláh took to rehabilitate the Community; it presented Him as a subverter of the laws of the Báb and a usurper, criticised His interpretation and misrepresented His Teaching.

This attack from within the Cause affected Bahá'u'lláh far more than any from without. *"In these days,"* He exclaimed, *"such odours of jealousy are diffused, that... from the beginning of the foundation of the world ...until the present day, such malice, envy and hate have in no wise appeared, nor will they ever be witnessed in the future."* Eventually, without warning even the members of His own family. He left Baghdád for the wastes of Kurdistán. *"Our withdrawal,"* He comments, *"contemplated no return, and our separation hoped for no reunion. The one object of our retirement was to avoid becoming a subject of discord among the faithful, a source of disturbance unto our companions, the means of injury to any soul, or the cause of sorrow to any heart."*[8]

Bahá'u'lláh in the Wilderness
Bahá'u'lláh dwelt in the wilderness under an assumed name as

a dervish.* Of His sojourn there He says: *"From Our eyes there rained tears of anguish, and in Our bleeding heart there surged an ocean of agonising pain. Many a night We had no food for sustenance, and many a day Our body found no rest. By Him Who hath My being between His hands! Notwithstanding these showers of afflictions and unceasing calamities. Our soul was wrapt in blissful joy, and Our whole being evinced an ineffable gladness. For in Our solitude We were unaware of the harm or benefit, the health or ailment, of any soul. Alone, We communed with Our spirit, oblivious of the world and all that is therein."*[9]

A large part of His time in Kurdistán was spent on a mountain so secluded that peasants visited it only twice a year, for sowing and harvest. He dwelt in a crude stone structure erected to shelter the peasants, or in a cave. Odes revealed at this time are among the first fruits of His Revelation.

Later He was persuaded to reside in the town of Sulaymáníyyih, famous as a seat of learning. Although at first He maintained silence, the curiosity of eminent divines and their students was aroused by a specimen of His exquisite penmanship they accidentally saw. Realising that so unusual a dervish might have exceptional knowledge, a delegation went to question Him and were amazed at the fluency and profundity of His answers.

Now more and more of the religious leaders of Sulaymáníyyih turned to Him for elucidation of their problems. They were amply requited; He opened new doors of understanding that led them far along the path of knowledge. They grew to regard Him with such reverence and affection that the envoy who eventually came from the Bábís of Bag to implore Bahá'u'lláh to return felt that had they known the purpose of his visit they would have killed him. Among the eminent divines who became devoted to Bahá'u'lláh were the heads of three important Muslim orders, men themselves profoundly venerated by their many followers.

While Bahá'u'lláh was in Kurdistán, the standing of the Bábí Community sank under the misdirected leadership of Mirzá Yaḥyá

---

* A dervish is a Muslim dedicated to a holy life of poverty.

to its lowest point. Timorously closeted in his own house, he enbarked upon a campaign of derogation of Bahá'u'lláh, backed by assassination. Siyyid Muḥammad was permitted to encourage ruffians to filch from wealthy pilgrims and pilfer the Shrine of Imám Ḥusayn. So low was the reputation of the Bábís that they hardly dared to show themselves in public. 'Abdu'l-Bahá has recorded that as many as twenty-five of them had the effrontery to declare themselves to be 'He Whom God shall make manifest.'

When news of a dervish in Sulaymániyyih, of unsurpassed knowledge and a Persian, began to trickle to Baghdád, the handful of faithful Bábís realised at once that this must be Bahá'u'lláh. They immediately sent one of their number to beg Him to return. Mírá Yaḥyá, who recognised what his unrestrained leadership had accomplished, reinforced their plea in writing.

Bahá'u'lláh acceded to these urgent requests. He came with the envoy, slowly and with many halts, because as He told His fellow traveller, these were 'the only days of peace and tranquillity' remaining to Him. He arrived back in Baghdád in March 1856, just two years after leaving for Kurdistán.

Triumph in Baghdád

With the return of Bahá'u'lláh, the prestige of the Bábí Community rose rapidly from the lowest depth to a height surpassing even that reached when the Báb was in Iṣfáhán. Immediately after Bahá'u'lláh's return. Kurdish divines and mystics from Sulaymániyyih began to flock to Baghdád to visit Him. This caused the local divines to follow suit, then government officials and eminent Persians living in Baghdád or visiting the nearby Shrines as pilgrims. Towards the end of Bahá'u'lláh's sojourn there, even the Governor demonstrated respect by a formal call.

Concurrently, Persian Bábís began to flow to Baghdád to visit Him; these carried back to Persia stories of His rising glory and something of the spirit He was instilling into the Bábí Community. By personal example, oral statements, and written exhortations. He was leading its members to behaviour consistent with the high standard demanded by the Báb. Through Bahá'u'lláh's efforts the

Bábí Faith was dissociated from all political activity; non-violence and obedience to those in authority were emphasised, back-biting and revenge banned, the virtues described in this book under the heading 'Personal Conduct'* extolled. 'Bahá'u'lláh's, after His return,' 'Abdu'l-Bahá tells us, *"made such strenuous efforts in educating and training this community, in reforming its manners, in regulating its affairs and in rehabilitating its fortunes, that in a short while all these troubles and mischiefs were quenched and the utmost peace and tranquillity reigned in men's hearts."*[10] Such was His influence on the Bábís that Shoghi Effendi asserts the Bábí Community truly became a Bahá'í Community in these years.

The state of exaltation reached by its Baghdád members at that time may be discerned in the words of Nabil, who was one of them: "So intoxicated were those who had quaffed from the cup of Bahá'u'lláh's presence that in their eyes the palaces of kings appeared more ephemeral than a spider's web ... I, myself, with two others lived in a room which was devoid of furniture.... Many a night no less than ten persons subsisted on no more than a pennyworth of dates. No one knew to whom actually belonged the shoes, the cloaks, or the robes that were to be found in their houses.... Their own names they had forgotten, their hearts were emptied of aught else except adoration for their Beloved.... Each one had entered into a pact with one of his fellow-disciples, in which they agreed to admonish one another, and, if necessary, chastise one another with a number of blows on the soles of the feet, proportioning the number of strokes to the gravity of the offence against the lofty standards they had sworn to observe."[11]

The same exalted spirit was felt by all who entered the presence of Bahá'u'lláh at this time. One royal prince commented: 'I know not how to explain it. Were all the sorrows of the world to be crowded into my heart they would. I feel, all vanish when in the presence of Bahá'u'lláh. It is as if I had entered Paradise itself.' Another confused the feeling he obtained with the impression given by the

---

* See Chapter VII.

simple room in which visitors assembled, and declared his intention of building a duplicate of it in his own home. Bahá'u'lláh, when told of the plan, remarked smilingly. 'He may well succeed in reproducing outwardly the exact counterpart of this low-roofed room made of mud and straw with its diminutive garden. What of his ability to open on to it the spiritual doors leading to the hidden worlds of God?'

Bahá'u'lláh has ordained the house in which He lived in Baghdád to be a place of pilgrimage, the most important out side the Holy Land.

That enemies of the Faith would be frightened by His expanding popularity and influence was certain. A crafty divine, working with the Persian Consul General, tried innumerable devices to neutralise this influence, for many years without success. Neither the Governor nor the populace would listen to their calumny. A ruffian they hired to murder Bahá'u'lláh found his resolution unequal to the task; on one occasion, after lying in ambush, he dropped his pistol from fear, to have it handed back to him by his intended victim, and on another, after forcing his way into Bahá'u'lláh's presence, he found he lacked courage to shoot. A convocation of local Shí'ih divines, summoned to declare a holy war against the exiles, failed to do so because the most eminent of them all refused to lend his name for such a purpose.

Finally, an emissary of the divines, having had all his questions satisfactorily answered by Bahá'u'lláh, requested a miracle as decisive proof of His station. Bahá'u'lláh offered to perform any one upon which the divines agreed, providing they signed a statement saying they would admit the truth of His Cause if He performed it. Their failure to agree upon a miracle and their decision to drop the matter was widely publicised in Persia by the emissary himself.

However, in due course the term God had set for Bahá'u'lláh's stay in Baghdád was completed and the crafty divines' unremitting efforts were successful. Persistent misrepresentation of the facts at last induced the Sultan to transfer Bahá'u'lláh to Constantinople. The friendly Governor of Baghdád withheld the order for three months, during which he received five successive commands from the Chief Minister of Turkey, but at last he could delay no longer. Bahá'u'lláh was notified, the Bábí colony was in formed, and on April 21, 1863. Bahá'u'lláh moved to a garden outside the city, preparatory to beginning His journey.

The Declaration of Bahá'u'lláh

He remained in this garden for twelve days, during which He declared to His followers that He was the One foretold by the Báb. The Bábís, known after this Declaration as Bahá'ís poured into the garden to express their intense sorrow at His leaving. A multitude of distinguished visitors also came, including the Governor, who gave to Bahá'u'lláh's escort a written order requesting the governors of the provinces through which the exiles would pass to show them the utmost consideration. When the cortege ultimately left for Constantinople, crowds assembled to do homage to Bahá'u'lláh as He went by. He Himself declared later that *"God enabled Me to depart out of the city, clothed with such majesty as none, except the denier and the malicious, can fail to acknowledge."*[12]

No record exists of the exact circumstances attending Bahá'u'lláh's Declaration. In the days immediately preceding His departure from His Baghdád House, signs of the impending assumption of prophetic office were many. The fervour of His devoted followers, as well as His own demeanour and allusions, foreshadowed the approaching hour. When the declaration was made to a selected group of His followers, none objected. He was already established in their hearts as their true leader, so that to hear Him affirm He was the One they longed for must have seemed to them no more than confirmation of what in their inmost being they already knew.

The twelve days Bahá'u'lláh remained in the garden, called by Bahá'í the Riḍván Garden, are celebrated annually as the Riḍván Festival; the first, ninth and twelfth days are specially commemorated as Holy Days. Writing of His Declaration, Bahá'u'lláh has said: *"Rejoice, with exceeding gladness, O people of Bahá! as ye call to remembrance the Day of supreme felicity, the Day whereon the Tongue of the Ancient of Days hath spoken, as He departed from His House proceeding to the Spot from which He shed upon the whole creation the splendours of His Name, the All-Merciful.... Were We to reveal the hidden secrets of that Day, all that dwell on earth and in the heavens would swoon away and die, except such as will be preserved by God, the Almighty, the All-Knowing, the All-Wise."*[13]

Constantinople and Adrianople

The journey to Constantinople was rendered a triumphal march by the letter the Governor of Baghdád had given the escort; it caused every town and village on the road to honour the party, a reception Bahá'u'lláh encouraged by acting like a magnate. Nabíl affirms that: "According to the unanimous testimony of those we met in the course of that journey, never before had they witnessed along this route, over which governors and mushírs continually passed back and forth between Constantinople and Baghdád, anyone travel in such state, dispense such hospitality to all, and accord to each so great a share of His bounty."[14] This memorable journey created goodwill for the Faith of inestimable value to the many pilgrims who travelled the road in peril later.

Bahá'u'lláh remained only four months in Constantinople. The Persian Ambassador there constantly sought a chance to strike at the exiles, in which he was helped by Bahá'u'lláh's refusal to pay the customary calls on Ministers and leading divines—behaviour contrasting commendably with that usual among Persian nobles arriving in Constantinople, who were wont to seek favours everywhere.

The Ambassador's intrigue soon resulted in the Sultán's issuing an edict for the immediate further banishment of the party to Adrianople—an edict tantamount to an alliance of the Turkish and Persian Governments against the Glory of God. The resulting twelve-day journey to Adrianople took place in the coldest spell within living memory. It brought great hardship to the party, whose clothes were suited to the warmth of Baghdád; such suffering, however, was as oil to the fire of love with which they were aflame.

In Adrianople, fresh evidence of Bahá'u'lláh's sovereignty appeared. He began to reveal the momentous Tablets to kings, ministers, religious leaders and others that constituted the formal proclamation of His Mission. Here began, also, the influx of pilgrims to the Centre of the Cause, which has continued with only brief interruptions until now, drawing its members from an ever more varied and widely dispersed community. In Adrianople, it became increasingly evident that the Bábí Community had become a Bahá'í Community centred in Bahá'u'lláh.

Recognising that the Faith still progressed in spite of all it had suffered, its enemies in various countries began to persecute it afresh. In Egypt, 'Iráq, and various parts of Persia, Bahá'ís were vilified, imprisoned and martyred. But of more fundamental and far-reaching importance than these attacks from outside was the opposition of Mírzá Yahyá, and his evil genius Siyyid Muḥammad. For half a century this crisis left its mark upon the infant Faith, damaged its prestige, emboldened its external enemies, and confused its supporters.

The Rebellion of Mírzá Yaḥyá

Mírzá Yaḥyá had spent most of the time since Bahá'u'lláh returned from the wilderness closeted in his own house. Disregarding Bahá'u'lláh's advice that he should go to Persia to disseminate the Writings of the Báb, he joined the exiles on the way to Constantinople and was sent with them to Adrianople.

His offences at this time already included corrupting the text of the Báb's writings to make it appear that the Báb had named him as successor, adding to the call to prayer a formula identifying himself with the Godhead, commissioning several murders, and violating the honour of the Báb in a way Shoghi Effendi could not bring himself to specify when referring to it in God Passes By.

About a year after the transfer to Adrianople, Mírzá Yaḥyá initiated a series of attempts to murder Bahá'u'lláh. The first resulted in Bahá'u'lláh's being so severely poisoned as to be ill for a month. That He did not die was miraculous; for the rest of His life His hand shook from the effect of the poison.

Bahá'u'lláh now brought the hidden discord into the open by formally acquainting His unsatisfactory half-brother with the character of His Mission. Mírzá Yaḥyá replied with a counter-declaration, in which he averred he had received an independent Revelation from God. Thereupon Bahá'u'lláh ensured that Mírzá Yaḥyá got more than a fair share of all income and possessions to which he had any claim and Himself withdrew from intercourse with the friends. However, the infamous behaviour of Mírzá Yaḥyá, who spread baseless slander about Him in every direction, impelled Him to emerge from retirement after two months. One of the Bahá'ís later induced Siyyid Muḥammad to get Mírzá Yaḥyá to agree to meet Bahá'u'lláh so that the truth could be publicly established, but Mírzá Yaḥyá evaded the meeting, thereby acknowledging his inability to make his case good.

So deeply was Bahá'u'lláh affected by this episode that He wrote: *"The cruelties inflicted by My oppressors have bowed Me down, and turned My hair while, Shouldst thou present thyself before My throne, thou wouldst fail to recognise the Ancient Beauty, for the freshness of His countenance is alter and its brightness hath faded, by reason of the oppression of the infidels."*[15]

Temporarily, there was a breach in the ranks of the Faith, which delayed its development and tarnished its glory; but the irresistible power that protected it healed the breach by causing all except a negligible handful of its followers to eventually attain to recognition of Bahá'u'lláh. Throughout its history, such crises have occurred, whose spiritual purpose has been to cleanse the Community from pollution. Freed from the impurity represented by Mírzá Yaḥyá and Siyyid Muḥammad, who were no longer able to distract the souls of Bahá'ís from within the Community, the Cause surged forward. The immediate outcome of the discomfiture of Mírzá Yaḥyá was the public and widespread proclamation of Bahá'u'lláh's Message already referred to.[*]

---

[*] See Chapter III.

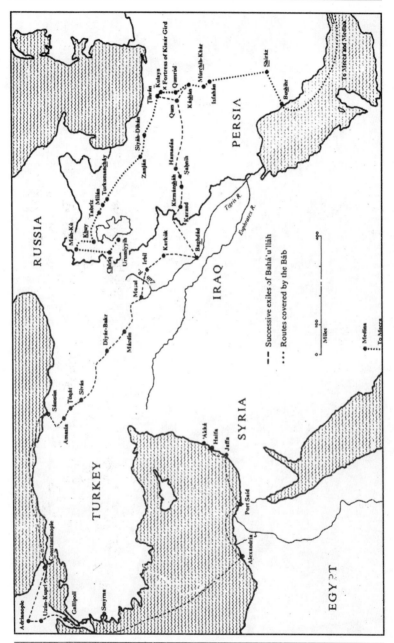

The Journeys of the Báb and Bahá'u'lláh.

The Prison City of 'Akká.

'Akká

These dissensions strengthened the hands of those at Constantinople opposed to Bahá'u'lláh. From Adrianople, Siyyid Muhammad and Mírzá Yahyá worked ardently but injudiciously against Him. Their machinations included perversion of His Writings, anonymous accusatory letters, and petitions to the Sultan; these reinforced a growing fear of Bahá'u'lláh's influence on all He met, causing the Sultan to ban Him and His companions to the notorious prison city of 'Akká. Mírzá Yahyá and his associates, caught in the trap they had themselves baited, were sent to Famagusta in Cyprus, except Siyyid Muhammad and two others who were sent to 'Akká.

Bahá'u'lláh arrived in 'Akká in August 1868, thereby fulfilling prophecies about the importance of the city made both by Muhammad and the Jewish Prophets. It was then a mass of filthy and tortuous lanes, flea-infested, damp, and with no source of water inside the gates. Proverbially, the air was so putrid that a bird flying over 'Akká would drop dead.

The decree of banishment specified that the exiles should be strictly imprisoned and should associate neither with each other nor with the local inhabitants. Moreover, the Persian Ambassador to Constantinople had arranged for representatives to report whether the decree was being obeyed. At first the exiles' only food was black bread of poor quality, later replaced by a small sum of money with which to buy provisions. The water in the courtyard of the army barracks where they were imprisoned was undrinkable. All except two of the party fell ill shortly after arrival; when three of them died. Bahá'u'lláh sold His carpet to pay for their burial, but nevertheless they were buried without coffins, unwashed and unshrouded. Pilgrims arriving at this time were unable to visit Bahá'u'lláh, so they stood for hours beyond the second moat of the fortress in hope of seeing Him wave His arm from His prison window.

To all these tribulations was added soon the tragic death of a much-loved son He had entitled 'The Purest Branch,' who died after falling through a skylight on to a wooden crate, which pierced his ribs. Bahá'u'lláh spoke of the event as an act of atonement like the crucifixion of Jesus, a sacrifice like Abraham's attempted sacrifice of his son: *"I have, O my Lord, offered up that which Thou hast given Me, that Thy servants may be quickened, and all that dwell on earth be united."*[16]

After two years, the exiles were taken from the barracks to make room for more troops; for a year they were moved from house to house, ending in one much too small for their need; Their difficulties were intensified when a group of Bahá'ís, defying Bahá'u'lláh's specific command, murdered Siyyid Muḥammad and the two other Azalís* who had been sent to 'Akká. The animosity and slander against the exiles after this incident reached such a pitch that they were stoned on sight, and their neighbour reinforced from fear the party wall between the two houses.

Gradually the situation changed, Bahá'u'lláh's utter innocence was recognised by the populace; 'Abdu'l-Bahá's constant efforts brought Him personal popularity and enabled Him to shield His Father; the spirit of Bahá'u'lláh's Revelation impressed itself more and more on the inhabitants of 'Akká, both high and low.

Marks of esteem for Bahá'u'lláh increased. The flow of pilgrims swelled and people of note began to visit Him to pay their respects. One governor intimated that He might leave the prison city whenever He wished, but He declined to do so, saying that He was a prisoner. Later, 'Abdu'l-Bahá encouraged the Mufti of 'Akká, who greatly respected Bahá'u'lláh, to beg Him to leave the city and at last, nine years after His arrival, He consented. For two years He lived at Mazri'ih, then moved to a resplendent mansion at Bahjí, on the plain of 'Akká, whose owner had hastily abandoned it because of an outbreak of disease.

The Sulṭán order that Bahá'u'lláh should be stringently confined had never been repealed, but the might of the King of Kings had rendered it a dead letter. Now, in the words of 'Abdu'l-Bahá, *"the doors of majesty and true sovereignty were flung wide open."* *"The rulers of Palestine,"* He has written, *"envied His influence*

---

* Followers of Mírzá Yaḥyá are sometimes called Azalís after Mírza Yaḥyá's title 'Ṣubḥ-i-Azal' (Morning of Eternity).

and power. Governors and mutisarrifs, generals and local officials, would humbly request the honour of attaining His presence—a request to which He seldom acceded."[17] Never before has the world witnessed so remarkable a triumph of a prisoner over His oppressors.

From the Holy Land Bahá'u'lláh, condemned to strict confinement with the might of both Sultán and Sháh arrayed against Him, managed the affairs of His Cause with conspicuous success. A Bahá'í agency was established in Alexandria for the despatch to Persia of His enormous correspondence; another agency in Beirut safeguarded the interests of the many pilgrims passing through that city; Bahá'í centres in Persia and neighbouring territories multiplied; the Bahá'í Community became more diverse; and inevitably its progress called forth fresh outbreaks of persecution.

It soon became clear to the enemies of the Faith in Persia that the 'Akká banishment would no more arrest its progress than had previous banishments. Incensed by the glowing reports about Bahá'u'lláh brought back by returning pilgrims, both clergy and laity committed barbarities that eternally shamed their country. Although these were on a smaller scale than the ones following the attempt on the life of the Sháh, they were no less fierce and extended over a far longer period. As persecution always does, they released unseen forces, which promoted the rapid spread of the Faith and greatly increased the size of the Bahá'í Community.

The life of Bahá'u'lláh on earth was now drawing to a close. On May 29, 1892, His spirit ascended, leaving His followers overwhelmed with grief.

His Ministry had consisted throughout of a series of alternate crises and triumphs, a pattern of development the Faith has experienced since its inception. The crises, and the suffering attending them, release spiritual power that ensures the subsequent triumph. Thus the bloodbath resulting from the attempt on the life of the Sháh was followed by the Birth of Bahá'u'lláh's Mission; His first banishment and the events succeeding it led to His Baghdád triumph and the Declaration of His Mission; His further banishment to Constantinople and Adrianople was followed by the general proclamation of His Message; and finally the banishment to 'Akká released the spiritual force represented by the revelation of His laws and ordinances, and the promulgation of the Covenant to be described later.

The effect that rejection of His Message had upon kings and religious institutions has already been described.* Both the Sulṭán and the S͟háh who persecuted Him were assassinated; their dynasties eventually disappeared in shame. Those Ministers and dignitaries who had worked against the Faith almost all died suddenly, or were dismissed from their posts to languish miserably as outcasts. Mírzá Yaḥyá saw eleven of the eighteen 'Witnesses' he had appointed forsake him to turn repentantly to Bahá'u'lláh, and the one he had named as his successor publicly repudiate both him and the Bábí Faith. So, from the beginning of time, have those who oppose a Manifestation of God experienced Divine retribution.

Portrait of Bahá'u'lláh
Pilgrims to the Holy Land see portraits of Bahá'u'lláh in the International Bahá'í Archives, but these are not reproduced for general circulation. Westerners who want to visualise His external appearance may read a wonderful description of Him by Professor E. G. Browne of Cambridge, which conveys an idea of His imposing presence more effectively than could any detailed description. Professor Browne saw Him in 1890, two years before His Ascension, and wrote: "Though I dimly suspected whither I was going and whom I was to behold (for no distinct intimation had been given me), a second or two elapsed ere, with a throb of wonder and awe. I became definitely conscious that the room was not untenanted. In the corner where the divan met the wall sat a wondrous and venerable figure, crowned with a felt head-dress of the kind called *táj* by dervishes (but of unusual height and make), round the base of which was wound a small white turban. The face of him on whom I gazed I can never forget, though I cannot describe it. Those

---

* See Chapter III.

piercing eyes seemed to read one's very soul; power and authority sat on that ample brow; while the deep lines on the forehead and face implied an age which the jet-black hair and beard flowing down in undistinguishable luxuriance almost to the waist seemed to belie. No need to ask in whose presence I stood, as I bowed myself before one who is the object of a devotion and love which kings might envy and emperors sigh for in vain!"[18]

Writings of Bahá'u'lláh

The Writings of Bahá'u'lláh are too multitudinous to be fully discussed here, but a few of the principal ones will be briefly mentioned. Most of His laws and ordinances are contained in the *Kitáb-i-Aqdas* (The Most Holy Book), revealed in 'Akká. Already in Adrianople He had begun revealing a series of Tablets that prepared the Bahá'ís for this great work. After its revelation, He requested several Bahá'í scholars to put questions about anything in it they found unclear; His replies to these questions form a kind of explanatory appendix to the Book.*

His weightiest work, the *Kitáb-i-Íqán* (The Book of Certitude) was revealed in Baghdád before His Declaration. It expounds teachings of the Báb about God, His Manifestations and the interpretation of various terms appearing in the Qu'rán and the Bible. In Baghdád too, He revealed *'The Hidden Words,'* the greatest of His ethical Writings and *'The Seven Valleys,'* His greatest mystical work.

Other important Writings include the Tablets proclaiming His Message to kings, ministers, leaders of religion, and various special groups, which were revealed in Adrianople and 'Akká.** His many Tablets to individual Bahá'ís, not all of which have yet been collected, constitute a rich and varied fund of Bahá'í Scripture. Moreover, prayers and meditations flowed from Him throughout His Ministry.

---

* The full text of the *Kitáb-i-Aqdas* is not yet available in English, but it will be made available when all the explanatory and interpretive passages have been codified.
** See Chapter III.

No other religion has ever possessed so much in written form of the Teaching of its Founder. The extent of these voluminous Writings constitutes one of the bounties of this great age.

Station of Bahá'u'lláh

The greatness of the age has been extolled in this book in various places.* Its splendour consists wholly in its having been blessed by the Revelation of Bahá'u'lláh, but the glory of His Revelation must not obscure His essential oneness with the Founders of other religions. Although as a Manifestation of God He reflects the Divine Light, disclosing whatever of God man can know, to regard Him as partaking of the Essence of God, would be blasphemy.** He Himself says: *"I swear by Thy glory, O Thou Who art the one alone Beloved! I find myself to be only nothing before the habitation of Thy great glory. Every time I attempt to extol anyone of Thy virtues, my heart restraineth me, for naught but Thee is able to soar into the atmosphere of the kingdom oj. Thy nearness, or reach up to the heaven of Thy presence."*[19] He is one with all other Manifestations of God, neither greater nor less than they.

His Revelation, however, is more intense than theirs. It so surpasses all former Revelations that Bahá'u'lláh has proclaimed: *"That which hath been made manifest in this pre-eminent, this most exalted Revelation, stands unparalleled in the annals of the past, nor will future ages witness its like." "In this most mighty Revelation,"* He announces, *"all the Dispensations of the past have attained their highest, their final consummation."*[20]

God has ordained its immensity to supply the need of the present stage in the development of mankind. Its incomparable power has been repeatedly stressed by Bahá'u'lláh in terms, such as these: *"Every single letter proceeding from Our mouth is endowed with such regenerative power as to enable it to bring into existence a new creation—a creation the magnitude of which is inscrutable to all save God."*[21]

---

* See especially Chapter XVII.
**See pages 35-36.

Bahá'u'lláh is the Promise of All Ages. Shoghi Effendi says: "To Israel He was neither more nor less than the incarnation of the 'Everlasting Father,' the 'Lord of Hosts' come down with 'thousands of saints'; to Christendom. Christ returned 'in the glory of the Father'; to Shí'ih Islm the return of the Imám Ḥusayn; to Sunní Islm the descent of the 'Spirit of God' (Jesus Christ); to the Zoroastrians the promised Sháh Bahrám; to the Hindus the reincarnation of Krishna; to the Buddhists the fifth Buddha."[22] Bahá'u'lláh Himself asserts: *"All the Divine Books and Scriptures have predicted and announced unto men the advent of the Most Great Revelation. None can adequately recount the verses recorded in the Books of former ages which forecast this supreme Bounty, this most mighty Bestowal."*

Nor is this all, Bahá'u'lláh ushers in a new cycle of Revelation that will continue into the distant future. Shoghi Effendi has said that "to strive to obtain a more adequate understanding of the significance of Bahá'u'lláh's stupendous Revelation must, it is my unalterable conviction, remain the first obligation and the object of the constant endeavour of each one of its loyal adherents."[23] We will therefore return to this subject, of unsurpassed importance, at the end of this book in the part intended more specially for Bahá'ís and close students of the Faith.

CHAPTER XIII

'Abdu'l-Bahá

The Station of 'Abdu'l-Bahá

Bahá'u'lláh specified in His Will that after His ascension Bahá'ís should turn to His eldest Son, 'Abdu'l-Bahá. This was an expression of His Covenant, whose significance is explained in Chapter XIV; Bahá'u'lláh's Covenant, and the appointment of 'Abdu'l-Bahá as its Centre, are among the most distinctive and important features of His Revelation.

'Abdu'l-Bahá fulfils a function different from that of any other figure in religious history. Bahá'u'lláh emphasised this fact by calling Him *"The Mystery of God,"* a designation that Shoghi Effendi has said is particularly appropriate "to One Who, though essentially human and holding a station radically and fundamentally different from that occupied by Bahá'u'lláh and His Forerunner, could still claim to be the perfect Exemplar of His Faith, to be endowed with superhuman knowledge, and to be regarded as the stainless mirror reflecting His light."[1]

'Abdu'l-Bahá has been endowed with a contingent infallibility that is beyond the understanding of man. All His words, His actions, His judgments and His interpretations are infallibly right, but only because Bahá'u'lláh has willed it so. 'Abdu'l-Bahá revealed nothing new; He had not the direct intercourse with God of a Divine Manifestation; nevertheless. His every act reflected the Light of God and His every word bore witness to His superhuman knowledge.

Bahá'u'lláh praised Him in many Tablets. One ran: *"We have made Thee a shelter for all mankind, a shield unto all who are in heaven and on earth, a stronghold for whosoever hath believed in God, the Incomparable, the All-Knowing, God grant that through Thee He may protect them, may enrich and sustain them, that He may inspire Thee with that which shall be a wellspring of wealth unto all created things, an ocean of bounty unto all men, and the dayspring of mercy unto all peoples.*"[2]

In the Tablet of the Branch, Bahá'u'lláh describes 'Abdu'l-Bahá station as follows: *"Render thanks unto God, O people, for His appearance; for verily He is the most great Favour unto you, the most perfect bounty upon you; and through Him every mouldering bone is quickened... Whoso turneth away from Him hath turned away from My Beauty, hath repudiated My Proof, and transgressed against Me. He is the Trust of God amongst you, His charge within you, His manifestation unto you, and His appearance among His favoured servants.*"[3]

Shoghi Effendi has commented: "Wide as is the gulf that separates 'Abdu'l-Bahá from Him Who is the Source of an independent Revelation [Bahá'u'lláh], it can never be regarded as commensurate with the greater distance that stands between Him Who is the Centre of the Covenant ['Abdu'l-Bahá] and His ministers who are to carryon His work, whatever be their name, their rank, their functions or their future achievements."[4]

While 'Abdu'l-Bahá was on earth, some of the Bahá'ís wanted to honour Him as the equal, or even the superior, of Bahá'u'lláh and the Báb, but He would have none of such mistaken glorification. He repeatedly warned His followers against it in such words as: *"This is my firm, my unshakable conviction, the essence of my unconcealed and explicit belief-a conviction and belief which the denizens of the Abhá Kingdom fully share. The Etehed Beauty is the Sun of Truth, and His light the light of truth. The Báb is likewise the Sun of Truth, and His light the light of truth... My station is the station of servitude—a servitude which is complete, pure and real, firmly established, enduring, obvious, explicitly revealed and subject to no interpretation whatever.... I am the Interpreter of the Word of God; such is my interpretation.*"[5]

'Abdu'l-Bahá was the Servant of the Glory, the Centre of the Covenant, the Exemplar and Interpreter of the Teaching of

Bahá'u'lláh. Those who tried to make something else of Him were playing into the hands of His enemies, who defied the Will of Bahá'u'lláh and alleged maliciously and unfoundedly that 'Abdu'l-Bahá was claiming to be a Manifestation of God.

Before the Ascension of Bahá'u'lláh

'Abdu'l-Bahá was born on the very day that the Báb declared Himself to Mulla Husayn. While still a young child; He recognised the glory of His Father's as yet unrevealed station. First in Baghdád and then in Adrianople, His knowledge and character earned Him the respect of officials and leading divines. In 'Akká, as He grew to maturity, He was able to increasingly relieve Bahá'u'lláh of the less vital responsibilities of the Cause, such as 'interviewing officials and purchasing property. The respect He received from civil and ecclesiastical leaders contributed much to the prestige of the Cause in Bahá'u'lláh later years.

One of 'Abdu'l-Bahá's daughters has described His life in 'Akká after Bahá'u'lláh had gone to Bahjí: "The Master, by making all arrangements, doing all the business, seeing applicants and pilgrims, planning interviews at stated hours, protected His Father from every troublesome detail, and made it possible for Him to lead a peaceful life, with leisure in which to write His Tablets and to formulate laws and instructions for the world of the future. The Master occupied Himself with the affairs and interests of the people of the place, all outside news being brought to Him by the Governor and the Muftí. Every week the Master went to Bahjí, carrying all the news which would be of interest to Bahá'u'lláh....

'The life of the Master in 'Akká was full of work for others' good. He would rise very early, take tea, then go forth to His self-imposed labours of love. Often He would return very late in the evening, having had no rest and no food.... The Arabs called Him the 'Lord of Generosity'... It would be impossible to write even a small part of the many compassionate acts of love and charity wrought by the Master; all His life was spent in ministering service to every unhappy creature who came to Him, and in being the devoted son to His Father."[6]

'Abdu'l-Bahá, the centre of the covenant and perfect exemplar of his Father's teachings.

Rebellion of Mírzá Muhammad-'Alí

Although Bahá'u'lláh had quite distinctly decreed in His Will that after His Ascension all must turn to 'Abdu'l-Bahá, the Cause was not to be spared attempts to promote schism.

One of His sons, a half-brother of 'Abdu'l-Bahá named Muhammad-'Alí, had already in Bahá'u'lláh's lifetime boasted that he felt capable of usurping the leadership when his Father ascended. Bahá'u'lláh's Will placed him next in rank to 'Abdu'l-Bahá, Whom he could have succeeded, but this was not enough for Muhammad-'Alí. His jealousy continually deepened as he witnessed daily proof of his brother's indubitable superiority. Others of Bahá'u'lláh's family, similarly jealous, were easily induced to join him in a campaign of calumny against the Centre of Bahá'u'lláh's Covenant. Gradually, by lying and misrepresentation, they won to their infamous cause almost the whole family and several of the Bahá'ís who had been closely associated with Bahá'u'lláh. An unmarried sister of 'Abdu'l-Bahá, His wife, His daughters, and an uncle were the only members of the family to remain loyal.

Again there was an appearance of schism in the Cause, but again the forces protecting it ensured no permanent breach was made. Temporarily, Muhammad-'Alí's accusation that 'Abdu'l-Bahá was an ambitious, unprincipled usurper who defied His Father's Will by claiming to be a Manifestation of God disturbed the hearts of the Bahá'ís; but after a few years the truth was gradually recognised. Although Muhammad-'Alí and his associates continued long thereafter to promote opposition and confuse the minds of Westerners visiting Palestine, their true standing as a small, malicious group of troublemakers became apparent to all who investigated carefully. One of their number, Bahá'u'lláh, a brother of Muhammad-'Alí, realising for a time that his true interest lay in supporting 'Abdu'l-Bahá, published a full confession of their misdeeds, which remains as perpetual witness to the truth.

The Turkish authorities, however, were not interested in careful investigation. When Muhammad-'Alí saw he had failed to split the Bahá'í Community, he turned his attention to making Turkish officials suspicious of 'Abdu'l-Bahá, and in this he succeeded. For a while, not only 'Abdu'l-Bahá, but also the brothers who had deliberately induced the suspicion, were again strictly confined within the walls of the city, 'Abdu'l-Bahá managed to persuade the authorities to remove the restrictions from them, but He Himself remained restricted.

In spite of this noble intervention on their behalf, His brothers' operations against Him continued. They accused Him to various notables and officials of various misdeeds, adapting their accusations to the interests and prejudices of those they approached. Among their slanders were that He had hoisted the ensign of revolt in distant villages of Palestine and Syria; that He had raised an army of thirty thousand men; that He was building a fortress on Mount Carmel; that He had exalted to Godhead Bahá'u'lláh. Whom they alleged in making this accusation to have been no more than a retired dervish; and that He contemplated making a new Mecca and Medina of 'Akká and Haifa.

The Commissions of Enquiry

It was natural that such grave charges should disturb the Sultán, who appointed a Commission to enquire into the matter. There followed a period of extreme peril for 'Abdu'l-Bahá. Rumour had it that He was to be exiled to the desert of Tripolitania, or hanged, or cast into the sea. Such evidence of disfavour increased the aggressiveness of His enemies, and even His friends ceased to call on Him for fear of incurring suspicion.

'Abdu'l-Bahá reduced the number of pilgrims coming to 'Akká and encouraged Bahá'ís living there to migrate; He arranged for His mail to be handled through an agent in Egypt instead of Haifa and for all Bahá'í Writings to be removed to a safe place. However, He did not interrupt work on the mausoleum for the Báb's remains He was constructing on Mount Carmel, which lent colour to the accusation that He was building a fortress there; nor did He arrest for a moment the vast flow of His Tablets to followers and admirers of the Faith. He is reported to have written at this time no less than ninety Tablets in one day with His own hand.

Throughout these years, 'Abdu'l-Bahá remained imperturbably confident. He continued to minister to the sick and the destitute, dispensing alms regularly and generously and visiting those who could not or would not come to Him. When the Spanish Consul proffered an Italian freighter for His escape. He declined to leave, Shoghi Effendi writes: "To the amazement of His friends and the amusement of His enemies. He was to be seen planting trees and vines in the garden of His house, whose fruits when the storm had blown over. He would bid His faithful gardener... pluck and present to those same friends and enemies on the occasion of their visits to Him."[7]

Moreover, during these troubled times He initiated many important enterprises. The construction of the first Mashríqu'l-Adhkár* was started at 'Ishqábád in Turkistan; the House of the Báb in Shiraz, the second holiest Bahá'í Shrine outside the Holy Land, was restored; the project of building the Mother Temple of the West was conceived; the table talks recorded as *"Some Answered Questions"* were given; His Will and Testament, the Charter of the New World Order** was written; and the first institutions of the Faith began to develop.

In the winter of 1907, another Commission of Enquiry, with unrestricted powers, arrived in 'Akká. They immediately assumed control of the telegraph and postal services, dismissed officials suspected of being friendly to 'Abdu'l-Bahá (including the Governor of the city), took up residence in the home of intimate associates of the Covenant-breakers, and proceeded to call as witnesses the very people who had made the charges they had come to investigate.

The Covenant-breakers were jubilant. Victory seemed to dangle within their reach and excitedly they intensified their activity. Interviews with people they hoped to influence filled gaps between entertainment designed to win favour. Scoundrels were encouraged to believe that the property of the exiles would soon be ripe for plunder. The attitude of the populace to 'Abdu'l-Bahá deteriorated.

* See page 308.
**See pages 281-82.

Rumours, calumnies and insults markedly increased.

Serenely unperturbed and blandly ignoring veiled threats conveyed through a messenger, 'Abdu'l-Bahá refused to meet the Commission or deal with it in any way. A few days before its arrival, He had narrated to the believers a dream wherein a ship had cast anchor off 'Akká. Birds like sticks of dynamite had flown from it to circle round His head as He stood among the frightened inhabitants, but eventually they had returned to the ship without exploding. 'The meaning of the dream I dreamt is now clear and evident,' He said, 'Please God, this dynamite will not explode.'

One day, the ship in which the members of the Commission had come and in which they were expected to take 'Abdu'l-Bahá away was seen to be sailing across the bay from Haifa. News spread quickly that the members of the Commission had embarked; the inhabitants of 'Akká waited, some joyfully, some fearfully, for it to call to collect 'Abdu'l-Bahá. Anguish mastered His family and the few Bahá'ís who remained in 'Akká, who wept as they waited for the boat to take their beloved Master away for ever. Meanwhile, 'Abdu'l-Bahá paced the courtyard of His house, silent and alone.

Suddenly it was noticed that the ship had changed its course and was now heading for Constantinople. The dynamite birds, their circling finished, were returning unexploded whence they came. It was learnt later that the precipitate and unexpected departure of the Commission had been brought about by news of an attempt on the Sultan's life. When they reached Constantinople, the government was too preoccupied to deal with their report. It was again brought forward some months later, only to be rendered conclusively ineffective by the success of the Young Turk Revolution of 1908, which led to the release of all political and religious prisoners in the Turkish Empire.

Thus was 'Abdu'l-Bahá's confidence vindicated and the scheming of the Covenant-breakers balked.

The Shrine of the Báb

In the year following these events; 'Abdu'l-Bahá achieved another of the great tasks He had set Himself by the entombment of the

Báb's remains on Mount Carmel. These had reached the Holy Land in 1899, and that same year 'Abdu'l-Bahá had laid the foundation-stone of a mausoleum for them at a spot on Mount Carmel Bahá'u'lláh had indicated. Shoghi Effendi writes of its construction: 'The long drawn out negotiations with the shrewd and calculating owner of the building-site of the holy Edifice, who, under the influence of the Covenant-breakers, refused for a long time to sell; the exorbitant price at first demanded for the opening of a road leading to that site and indispensable to the work of construction; the interminable objections raised by officials, high and low, whose easily aroused suspicions had to be allayed by repeated explanations and assurances given by 'Abdu'l-Bahá Himself; the dangerous situation created by the monstrous accusations brought by Mírzá Muhammad-'Alí and his associates regarding the character and purpose of that building; the delays and complications caused by 'Abdu'l-Bahá's prolonged and enforced absence from Haifa, and His consequent inability to supervise in person the vast undertaking He had initiated—all these were among the principal obstacles which He, at so critical a period in His ministry, had to face and surmount ere He could execute in its entirety the Plan, the outline of which Bahá'u'lláh had communicated to Him on the occasion of one of His visits to Mount Carmel. "Every stone of that building, every stone of the road leading to it," He, many a time was heard to remark, "I have with infinite tears and at tremendous cost, raised and placed in position."[8]

The entombment of the remains of the Báb in the completed mausoleum established on Mount Carmel a focal centre of Divine illumination and power. Since then, the original building has been extended and a magnificent canopy erected over it having a dome covered with gold-glazed tiles, which can be seen from most parts of Haifa. Around the Shrine, beautiful gardens have been laid out, where there are several fine monuments and where other Bahá'í buildings are being erected. With the erection of this Shrine, the visible emergence of the World Centre of the Bahá'í Faith began.[*]

---

[*] See pages 314-15.

Rise of the Faith in the West

While all this was going on in Palestine, events of the greatest significance for the development of the Faith were taking place in America. Its first mention there was in 1893 at the World Parliament of Religion held in Chicago. A paper written by Rev. Henry H. Jessup, a Presbyterian Missionary in Syria, closedby quoting words Bahá'u'lláh had uttered to the Cambridge Orientalist, Edward G. Browne. The next year; Ibrahim Khayru'lláh, a Bahá'í from Syria, who had arrived in New York in 1892, moved to Chicago where he began to teach the Cause systematically.

He met with remarkable success. The first American believer, Thornton Chase, accepted the Faith in 1894. By 1895 there were flourishing Bahá'í Communities in Chicago and in nearby Kenosha. In 1868, the first Western pilgrims arrived in 'Akká to establish personal contact between the Centre of the Covenant and the Western Bahá'ís.

The spiritual forces released by this contact resulted not only in the diffusion of the Faith through more of the United States, but also in the formation of a Bahá'í Group in Paris (the first in Europe), another in London, and later one in Montreal Nor did the defection of Ibrahim Khayru'lláh, who joined the Covenant-breakers and published attacks on 'Abdu'l-Bahá, succeed in splitting the Western Bahá'í Community. Successive teachers despatched by 'Abdu'l-Bahá overcame the doubts and deepened the understanding of the American believers.

Bahá'í teachers began to take the Faith to new countries and to multiply the number of centres of Bahá'í activity in America. Rudimentary institutions arose, forerunners of the institutions of the Administrative Order to be established later. The project of building a Temple outside Chicago, which required the co-operation of all the American Bahá'í Communities, was initiated, thereby inaugurating Bahá'í activity on a national scale.

Such evidence of the vitality of the Faith in the West prompted 'Abdu'l-Bahá, now no longer a prisoner, to journey to Europe and America to participate Himself in the momentous work of spreading the Faith there.

Travels of 'Abdu'l-Bahá

Already before being freed He had decided to travel in the West when opportunity came, but the crisis induced by the Covenant-breakers had postponed His departure for a long time.

At His release in 1908, He had been a prisoner just forty years. He had never addressed a public audience and was unfamiliar both with Western customs and with Western languages. His health was poor and His age nearly seventy. Yet He arose to spend some three years travelling to Western countries, addressing Western audiences, and sowing the seeds of future growth in Western Bahá'í Communities.

His travels began with a visit to Egypt in the autumn of 1910. Thence He embarked for Europe, but He had to land again in Egypt on account of ill-health and did not reach Europe until the following autumn. After spending a few days at Thonon-les-Bains. He visited London for a month and Paris for nine weeks before returning to Egypt. In the spring of 1912, He sailed for the United States, where He remained nine months; on His return journey. He spent seven weeks in Britain, sixteen weeks in Paris (in two visits), sixteen days in Stuttgart (also in two visits), nine days in Budapest and seven days in Vienna.

During these years He proclaimed His Father's Message to audiences ranging from Churchmen to Freethinkers, from University graduates to men in charitable shelters, on social occasions and formally in churches and synagogues. Lady Blomfield, in whose home He stayed when in London, has recorded the following impression of those who came to visit 'Abdu'l-Bahá: "Remembering those days, our ears are filled with the sound of their footsteps—as they came from every country in the world. Every day, all day long, a constant stream, an intenninable procession! Ministers and missionaries. Oriental scholars and occult students, practical men of affairs and mystics, Anglicans, Catholics and Nonconformists, Theosophists and Hindus, Christian Scientists and doctors of medicine, Muslims, Buddhists, Zoroastrians. There also called politicians, Salvation Army soldiers, and other workers for human good, women suffragists, journalists, writers, poets and healers, dressmakers and great ladies, artists and artisans, poor workless people and prosperous merchants, members of the dramatic and musical world, these all came; and none were too lowly, nor too great, to receive the sympathetic consideration of this holy Messenger, Who was ever giving His life for others good."[9]

Stories of 'Abdu'l-Bahá during these travels are among the treasured possessions of the Western Bahá'ís. A few only can be related here. The first, retold from *The Chosen Highway* by Lady Blomfield, is typical of the selfless loving spirit of 'Abdu'l-Bahá...

A poor Bahá'í workman of Iṣfáhán heard that a traveller passing through his town was on the way to London to join 'Abdu'l-Bahá. Yearning to send a gift to his beloved Master and having nothing else to send, he tied up his dinner in a cotton handkerchief, which he begged the traveller to convey as a token of his love.

Weeks later the traveller reached London. He came to 'Abdu'l-Bahá at lunch among guests and faithfully presented the workman's gift with an account of the circumstances of its giving. 'Abdu'l-Bahá untied the handkerchief to expose to the gaze of the assembly a piece of very dry black bread and a shrivelled apple. Thereupon He left His own lunch untasted, ate the workman's meagre dinner and, breaking pieces from the dried bread, urged the guests to join Him saying "Eat with me of this gift of humble love' No doubt the poor workman later received a full account of the gracious way in which his gift had been received."[10]

In sharp contrast with this episode is one that occurred in America. His hostess, eager for her rich and cultured friends to meet 'Abdu'l-Bahá, invited some fifteen of them to lunch. She wondered how He, used neither to Western social functions nor Western indifference to religion; would handle the situation. Howard Colby Ives records: "As the meal progressed and no more than the usual commonplaces of polite society were mentioned, the hostess made an opening, as she thought, for, 'Abdu'l-Bahá to speak on spiritual things. His response to this was to ask if He might tell them a story, and He related one of the Oriental tales of which He had a great store and at its conclusion all laughed heartily. The ice was broken. Others added stories of which the Master's anecdote had reminded them. Then 'Abdu'l-Bahá, His face beaming with happiness, told another story and another. His laughter rang through the room; He said that the Orientals had many such stories illustrating different phases of life. Many of them were extremely humorous. It is good to laugh, Laughter is a spiritual relaxation. When They were in prison, He said, and under the utmost deprivation and difficulties, each of them at the close of the day would relate the most ludicrous event that had happened.... Happiness... is never dependent upon material surroundings, otherwise how sad these years would have been.... That was the nearest approach He came to any reference to Himself or to the Divine Teachings. But over that group before the gathering dispersed hovered a hush and reverence which no learned dissertation would have caused in them."[11]

It was not only, or even chiefly, what 'Abdu'l-Bahá said that was so remarkable. He emanated an aura of spiritual understanding which affected the very hearts of those He met. Some were acutely conscious of it; others who felt little at the time may, perhaps, in their innermost souls have been no less affected. Another extract from Howard Colby Ives' book illustrates the point: "There is a story told of an illiterate miner who made a long journey on foot to meet 'Abdu'l-Bahá when He was in San Francisco.... This man, though uneducated, had great spiritual capacity. He attended a meeting at which 'Abdu'l-Bahá spoke. He seemed enthralled as the measured, bell-like tones fell from the Master's lips. When the interpreter took up the passage in English, this miner started as if awakening, 'Why does that man interrupt?' he whispered. Then again 'Abdu'l-Bahá spoke, and again the visitor was lost in attention. Again the translator interpreted as the speaker paused. At this the miner's indignation was roused. 'Why do they let that man interrupt? He should be put out.' 'He is the official interpreter,' one sitting beside him explained. 'He translates the Persian into English.' 'Was

He speaking in Persian?' was the naive answer, 'Why, anyone could understand that'."[12]

Similar understanding sometimes reached people who had not even met 'Abdu'l-Bahá. Lady Blomfield relates that an American woman came to Him in Paris one day and explained her presence there as follows: "Oh, how glad I am to be in time! I must tell you the amazing reason of my hurried journey from America. One day, my little girl astonished me by saying: 'Mummy, if dear Lord Jesus was in the world now, what would you do?' 'Darling baby, I would feel like getting on to the first train and going to Him as fast as I could!' 'Well, Mummy, He is in the world!' I felt a sudden great awe come over me as my tiny one spoke. 'What do you mean, my precious? How do you know?' I said. 'He told me Himself, so of course He is in the world!' Full of wonder, I thought: Is this a sacred message which is being given to me out of the mouth of my babe? And I prayed that it might be made clear to me.

"The next day she said, insistently, and as though she could not understand: 'Mummy, darling, why isn't you gone to see Lord Jesus? He's told me two times that He is really here, in the world.' 'Tiny love, Mummy doesn't know where He is, how could she find Him?' 'We see, Mummy, we see.'

"I was naturally perturbed. The same afternoon, being out for a walk with my child, she suddenly stood still and cried out, 'There He is! There He is!' She was trembling with excitement and pointing at the windows of a magazine store where there was a picture of 'Abdu'l-Bahá. I bought the paper, found the address, caught a boat that same night, and here I am."[13]

One last sketch must complete the album. On Christmas night, 1912, 'Abdu'l-Bahá visited a Salvation Army Shelter in London where a thousand homeless men ate a special Christmas dinner. He spoke to them while they ate, reminding them that Jesus had been poor and that it was easier for the poor than the rich to enter the Kingdom of Heaven. The men sat enthralled. Some were so impressed that in spite of hunger and the special dinner before them they forgot to eat. When, on leaving, 'Abdu'l-Bahá gave the warden

of the Shelter money with which to buy a similar dinner on New
Year's night, the men rose to their feet to cheer Him as He went,
waving their knives and forks in the air. They little realised that He
had experienced trials, hardship and suffering far greater than any
they had known."[14]

Such was 'Abdu'l-Bahá. Truly, as the head of an American
University once said, He trod the mystic way with practical feet.

Last Years

'Abdu'l-Bahá returned to Palestine a year before the First World
War broke out. He was able to alleviate considerably the privation
that the incompetence, neglect and cruelty of the Turkish authorities,
reinforced by a strict Allied blockade, brought upon the inhabitants
of Palestine during the war. For several years before the war started.
He had been hinting at its coming; He had advised the Bahá'ís in
Palestine how to grow more food and had told them to store their
produce in pits. This food now ameliorated the suffering of the
inhabitants of that part of Palestine. Many women and children
whose menfolk had been called to the army leaving them destitute
were kept from starving by the food of 'Abdu'l-Bahá.

Throughout the war 'Abdu'l-Bahá was in peril. Danger that
the Allies would bombard Haifa was constant and for a time so
great that He removed to an inland village. Even the final Allied
conquest of Palestine brought a special peril; the Turkish Commander
asserted that if he had to leave Haifa, he would on leaving crucify
'Abdu'l-Bahá. Fortunately this threat became known to the British
Bahá'ís, who were able to ensure that the British army protected
Him when it entered Haifa.

Now, for the first time since the foundation of the Faith, the
Centre of the Cause lived under a liberal regime. Its senior officers
quickly developed a sincere, enduring respect for 'Abdu'l-Bahá. In
1920 the British Government knighted Him for what He had done
to alleviate suffering during the war, but He never used the title.

Among 'Abdu'l-Bahá's wartime activities had been the
revelation of a series of Tablets addressed to the American believers
collectively, known as the Tablets of the Divine Plan. These rank in

importance next to His Will among His Writings and now guide all work done to propagate the Faith of Bahá'u'lláh, whether by American Bahá'ís or others.

The Passing of 'Abdu'l-Bahá

Until the very last day of His earthly life, 'Abdu'l-Bahá continued to shower His love upon all and to minister to the poor and the unfortunate. On the afternoon before His passing. He received the Mufti of Haifa, its Mayor, and its Chief of Police. His last words were spoken soon after 1.0 a.m. that night, November 28, 1921, when He remarked on being offered food: 'You wish Me to take some food, and I am going?' A minute later. He had joined His beloved Father in the Abhá Kingdom.

Palestine had never seen a funeral like His. The High Commissioner, the Governor of Jerusalem, the Governor of Phoenicia and many other dignitaries walked behind the coffin, while ten thousand people, of every class, religion and race in Palestine crowded to witness what they could of the funeral. A procession headed by the City Police, after whom came Muslim and Christian Boy Scouts, and Muslim and Christian divines, wended its way to the Shrine of the Bib, where 'Abdu'l-Bahá also was to be interred. Near its entrance, nine speakers representing the Muslim, Jewish and Christian Communities gave funeral orations. For a week afterwards, the poor were fed daily in His memory, and corn was distributed to a thousand of them on the seventh day.

During His Ministry, the Bahá'í Community had developed from a persecuted Persian sect into a Movement active in four continents. Although Bahá'ís were still severely persecuted in Persia and martyrdoms were common there, the Persian Bahá'í Community began to emerge from the underground existence that had been forced upon it. Its numbers multiplied rapidly and rudimentary institutions were formed.

'Abdu'l-Bahá's influence on the development of the Faith is immeasurable; but His greatest contribution was undoubtedly to proclaim and vindicate the Covenant of Bahá'u'lláh, through which its unity was maintained and its enemies were disappointed. By virtue of the power of the Covenant, the leading Covenant-breakers, as well as people who persecuted the Faith, suffered similar fates to those that had overtaken the opponents of Bahá'u'lláh.

Although the passing of 'Abdu'l-Bahá deprived the Bahá'í Community of the earthly presence of the Centre of Bahá'u'lláh's Covenant, the power of that Covenant became greater rather than less. Some of its hidden gems were now disclosed in the Will of 'Abdu'l-Bahá. His greatest legacy to mankind, outweighing in importance even the multitudinous Writings in which He explained and applied the principles of His Father's Revelation. The Covenant of Bahá'u'lláh, as expressed in this momentous document, has ever since continued to guide and inspire the actions of the Bahá'ís. It will continue to do so until the World Order of Bahá'u'lláh has reached its ultimate perfection in the period of the Most Great Peace.

PART THREE

THE BAHÁ'Í COMMUNITY

CHAPTER XIV

The Covenant of Bahá'u'lláh

Bahá'u'lláh's Covenant is one of the distinguishing features of His Dispensation, 'Abdu'l-Bahá says of it:

> *"So firm and mighty is this Covenant that from the beginning of time until the present day no religious Dispensation hath produced its like."*[1]

Understanding its meaning is very important to all who study the Bahá'í Faith.

First the spiritual truth expressed by the word 'Covenant' must be understood. It is a truth long known to religion; 'Testament' in the Bible means 'Covenant,' so the Bible consists of the Old Mosaic Covenant and the New Christian Covenant. Before explaining the significance of the Covenant of Bahá'u'lláh, we will discuss some of the Covenants mentioned in the Holy Books of fonner Dispensations.

The Covenant of God with Man

The several kinds of religious Covenant have in cornman that spiritual blessings are released when the requisite actions are performed. The most general Covenant is that granted by God to mankind upon the appearance of each of His Manifestations. Should a man obey the commands of the Manifestation of God, follow the path laid down by the Manifestation's Teaching, lead a godly life, and turn his whole heart towards God, then God will bless him and cause him to grow in spiritual stature. Speaking of His own commandments, Bahá'u'lláh says:

> *"O ye peoples of the world! Know assuredly that My commandments are the lamps of My loving providence*

among My servants, and the keys of My mercy for My creatures. Thus hath it been sent down from the heaven of the Will of your Lord, the Lord of Revelation. Were any man to taste of the sweetness of the words which the lips of the All-Merciful have willed to utter, he would, though the treasuries of the earth be in his possession, renounce them one and all, that he might vindicate the truth of even one of His commandments shining above the dayspring of His bountiful care and loving-kindness."[2]

In the Dispensation of Moses, spiritual bounties flowed from obedience to the Old Testament and Covenant of God, in the Dispensation of Jesus from obedience to His New Testament and Covenant. In this age, obedience to His Covenant means following the teaching of Bahá'u'lláh, which embodies the newest Covenant and Testament of all. Everything consistent with it finds favour with God and prospers; everything contrary to it is abhorred by God and must in the end fail, wither, and die. It is the spirit of the Age, by whose standard all things are measured, through which they are invigorated and obtain life. Hence 'Abdu'l-Bahá says:

"The spirit of this age is the Covenant and Testament of God. It is like the pulsating artery in the body of the world."[3]

All men participate in and are subject to the Covenant of God for the age in which they live. Each time one performs an action in accordance with it, his heart is purified, his soul is filled with joy, and his spirit is drawn nearer to God. Each time he performs an action contrary to it, his conscience is troubled and the mirror of his soul is tarnished so that it reflects the light of truth less clearly. Even a man who has never heard the name Bahá'u'lláh is subject thus to the current Covenant of God, but since Bahá'u'lláh reaffirms the fundamental truths common to all Revelations, those who comply with earlier. Covenants comply also with much of the newest one, and likewise, those who turn away from the older Covenants turn away from the newest Covenant too. On the other hand, new truths arising from the new Covenant carry conviction to the hearts and minds of men who do not realise from what source their conviction comes, so that many of Bahá'u'lláh's teachings are accepted by people who have never read His Writings, nor heard them explained. The Covenant of God is the spirit of the age, and all who are influenced by the spirit of the age are influenced by the Covenant of God.

The Eternal Covenant

The age of Bahá'u'lláh differs from other ages, however, in comprising the fulfilment of a cycle. Every Messenger of God, from Adam to the Báb, has proclaimed its greatness. All that past ages witnessed, all that past Dispensations achieved, has been preparation for this supreme Day of God when He manifested Himself in unveiled glory. In this age all former ages culminate, and in this Day all former days mature.

God has covenanted about this Day in an Eternal Covenant that has permeated every Dispensation. The prophecies of all the Messengers of God about Bahá'u'lláh have been products of the Eternal Covenant. Every Revelation has contributed towards its fulfilment. It has been the guiding principle that harmonised the various Dispensations and the power that co-ordinated development of the various peoples of the world. And now, in this King of Days, it has culminated in the appearance of Bahá'u'lláh, Who introduces the cycle of fulfilment.

The greatness of the age of Bahá'u'lláh does not lie in His superiority to other Manifestations of God, for His inmost essence is identical with theirs; it does not even lie solely in the intensity of His Revelation, undeniably great though this may be. Its true significance is that it stands at the focal-point of all previous Revelations; here their rays converge here is the ultimate object of their existence; here, in our own age, the Eternal Covenant, from which all other Covenants have sprung, has been fulfilled.

The Covenant of God with His Manifestations

All other kinds of Covenant are adjuncts to the one Eternal Covenant of God. Among these is God's Covenant with His Manifestations, to which reference is made in the Bible and the Qur'án. In the Old Testament, for example, we read of the Covenant of God with Abraham; since this was made with a 249

Manifestation of God, no doubt could exist that both parties would fulfil it. Men may be liable to disobey God's Covenant, but the Messengers of God are not; so the Covenant of God with Abraham amounted to a promise to the Children of Israel and was accounted by them as such. The allotted measure of the Revelation of each Manifestation of God is a product of the Covenant of God with His Manifestation.

The Covenants of the Manifestations of God with Man

The Manifestations of God themselves make Covenants of two kinds with men: about the next Manifestation of God and about their own successor. An example of the former is the Covenant Moses made to help men recognise Jesus. That Jesus was rejected by the Jews and that each Manifestation of God has been rejected by the people among whom He lived demonstrates the need for such Covenants; even with their help, most men deny the long-awaited Promised One; without them, these Messengers sent by God to bring new life to creation would be rejected by all.

The power of the Covenant of each Manifestation of God prepares the way for the next Manifestation. For example, John the Baptist appeared as an expression of the Covenant of Moses; those who accepted him benefited spiritually by virtue of its power. Whenever the appointed time for the appearance of another Messenger of God draws near, things concealed in the Revelation of the earlier Messenger are manifested. Its inner potency finds expression in religious ferment and expectation of some great religious event, in the appearance of one who warns of the coming of God's Messenger, and finally in the coming of the Messenger Himself. Thus Moses prepared the way for Jesus. Jesus for

Muḥammad, and Muḥammad for the Báb. The Báb's own Revelation centred so definitely in His covenant about the appearance of 'Him Whom God shall make manifest,' that He Himself said:

> *"Glorified art Thou, O my God! Bear Thou witness that, through this Book, I have covenanted with all created things concerning the Mission of Him Whom Thou shalt make manifest, ere the Covenant concerning Mine own Mission had been established."*[4]

The Covenants of the Manifestations of God are also an adjunct to the Eternal Covenant. Acts conforming to the one conform to the other, and acts contrary to the one are contrary to the other. Obedience to the Eternal Covenant of God requires obedience to all His Covenants, by whatever name they are known; they will continue to do so in the Cycle of fulfilment.

The Covenant of Bahá'u'lláh

The second kind of Covenant made by each Manifestation of God centres in His successor. When the Covenant of Bahá'u'lláh is spoken of, the Covenant centring in 'Abdu'l-Bahá is usually meant; this is the one that so much excels earlier Covenants. In former ages, the Manifestation of God did not always name His successor clearly enough for His nominee to be certain of recognition. Jesus obliquely indicated the primacy of Peter, but the comment recorded leaves room for doubt about its significance; He did not say that Peter was the Centre of His Covenant or the sole interpreter of His teaching. Nor was the guidance given by Muḥammad about His successor enough to prevent Islám splitting into many sects, each recognising a different line of succession after Muḥammad. On the other hand, Bahá'u'lláh named His successor clearly, definitely, and in writing.

In the *Kitáb-i-Aqdas* (the Most Holy Book) Bahá'u'lláh reveals:

> *"When the ocean of My presence hath ebbed and the Book of My Revelation is ended, turn your faces towards Him Whom God hath purposed, Who hath*

branched from this Ancient Root.... When the Mystic Dove will have winged its flight from its Sanctuary of Praise and sought its far-off goal, its hidden habitation, refer ye whatsoever ye understand not in the Book to Him Who hath branched from this mighty Stock."[5]

In His last Will and Testament, known as the Book of the Covenant, Bahá'u'lláh says of this passage:

"The object of this sacred verse is none other except the Most Mighty Branch."[6]

'The Most Mighty Branch' is one of the titles of 'Abdu'l-Bahá that no one else could claim. Thus the Covenant of Bahá'u'lláh about His successor was established upon a firm basis from its inception.

'Abdu'l-Bahá, acting in accordance with what Bahá'u'lláh had revealed, in His turn ensured that the Cause would still have a visible centre after His passing, by providing in His Will and Testament for the possibility of a succession of Guardians of the Cause of God and by explaining Bahá'u'lláh's instructions regarding the formation of a world body for the Faith, the Universal House of Justice. Both these institutions were to be, as 'Abdu'l-Bahá in His Will assured us, specially and infallibly guided by God, *"under the care and protection of the Abhá Beauty, under the shelter and unerring guidance of His Holiness, the Exalted One (may my life be offered up for them both). Whatsoever they decide is of God."*[7]

The Guardian, Shoghi Effendi, was 'Abdu'l-Bahá's grandson and descended on his father's side from the family of the Báb. 'Abdu'l-Bahá says in His Will:

"He is the expounder of the words of God... the beloved of the Lord must turn unto him. He that obeyeth him not, hath not obeyed God; he that turneth away from him, hath turned away from God and he that denieth him hath denied the True One."[8]

Although there could have been a series of Guardians, there is nowhere in the writings any promise or guarantee that the line of Guardians would not be broken but would endure forever. When Shoghi Effendi passed on, the conditions laid down by 'Abdu'l-Bahá in His Will and Testament for further succession could not be fulfilled.

In His Will and Testament, 'Abdu'l-Bahá clarifies the unique station of the Universal House of Justice, its powers to legislate on all matters which are not covered in the Holy Scriptures themselves, and the promise contained in Bahá'u'lláh's Revelation that its decisions will be infallibly guided, saying... *"That which this body, whether unanimously or by a majority doth carry, that is verily the truth and the purpose of God Himself."*[9]

Thus the Covenant of Bahá'u'lláh gave to mankind 'Abdu'l-Bahá, the Centre of the Covenant, and to succeed Him it provided for the Guardian of the Cause of God. Shoghi Effendi, and, the Universal House of Justice. These are the initial effects of a Covenant so mighty that mankind has never seen its like. Indeed the Guardian himself wrote about these two institutions, the Guardianship and the Universal House of Justice:

"Not only have they (Bahá'u'lláh and 'Abdul-Bahá) *revealed all the directions required for the practical realisation of those ideals which the Prophets of God have visualized, and which from time immemorial have inflamed the imagination of seers and poets in every age. They have also, in unequivocal and emphatic language, appointed those twin institutions of the House of Justice and of the Guardianship as their chosen Successors, destined to apply the principles, promulgate the laws, protect the institutions, adapt loyally and intelligently the Faith to the requirements of progressive society and consummate the incorruptible inheritance which the Founders of the Faith have bequeathed to the world."*[10]

The Power of the Covenant

Referring in the *Kitáb-i-Aqdas* to the power of His Covenant, Bahá'u'lláh states:

"O My Branches! A mighty power and supreme potency is hidden and concealed in the world of Being."[11]

'Abdu'l-Bahá explains more fully:

"There is a power in this Cause—a mysterious power— far, far, far away from the ken of men and angels; that invisible power is the cause of all these outward activities. It moves the hearts. It rends the mountains. It administers the complicated affairs of the Cause. It inspires the friends. It dashes into a thousand pieces all the forces of opposition. It creates new spiritual worlds. This is the mystery of the Kingdom of Abhá!"[12]

To provide a Centre for the Cause of God is only part of the function of Bahá'u'lláh's Covenant. In the way that Covenants about the next Manifestation reveal their hidden power by causing certain things to happen towards the end of a Dispensation, so the Covenant of Bahá'u'lláh about His successor is gradually revealing now what lies within it. At first such a Covenant is but a seed whose inner efficacy is quite hidden from the eye of man; then it is a tender shoot, then a sapling and finally a strong and mighty tree. Hence 'Abdu'l-Bahá said:

"Through the power of the Divine Springtime, the downpour of the celestial clouds and the heat of the Sun of reality, the Tree of Life is just beginning to grow! Before long it will produce buds, bring forth leaves and fruits, and cast its shade over the East and the West. The Tree of Life is the Book of the Covenant."[13]

The roots of this tree are watered by the life-giving waters of the word of God, whence it acquires its strength. Thus the power of the Covenant is a reflection of the power of the Holy Spirit, exceeding all earthly power, or any the mind of man can conceive, 'Abdu'l-Bahá says:

> *"Know this for a certainty, that today the penetrative power in the arteries (and the nerves) of the world of humanity is the power of the Covenant.... There is no other power like unto this."*[14]

The power of the Covenant has already brought into being the Bahá'í Administrative Order* whose yearly growth it sustains; it has enabled the Cause of God to overcome, every obstacle; it has inspired the Bahá'ís to carry their Faith to more than 330 countries and significant territories; it has confounded the enemies of the Cause and so moved the hearts of the Bahá'ís that they gave their lives, their possessions, their all for the sake of God. Yet it is only just beginning to operate. When in the future its full potency becomes evident, the world will realise what a priceless treasure Bahá'u'lláh has bestowed upon mankind.

Firmness in the Covenant
Whatever is concealed in the Covenant will gradually become manifest. Bahá'u'lláh will fulfil His part in it and the Bahá'ís must fulfil theirs; again and again 'Abdu'l-Bahá stressed this supreme obligation. The Covenant is the greatest force for unity in the modem world; whoever is firm in it and obedient to it is blessed, whoever disobeys it is cut off from heavenly bounties and is spiritually as dead, 'Abdu'l-Bahá says:

> *"Today the most important affair is firmness in the Covenant, because firmness in the Covenant wards off differences."*[15]

> *Although in the body of the universe there are innumerable nerves, yet the main artery, which pulsates, energises and invigorates all beings, is the power of the Covenant. All else is secondary to this. Nobody is*

---

* See Chapter XV.

assisted and confirmed save that soul who is firm.
Consider it well that every soul who is firm in the
Covenant is luminous, like unto a candle which
emanates its light on those around it, while every
wavering soul is an utter failure, frozen, lifeless, dead-
yet moving. This one proof is sufficient."[16]

Those who achieve such firmness are abundantly rewarded.
God enables them to become stars that guide mankind, angels that
leaven humanity, channels for the flow of the spirit to creation,
'Abdu'l-Bahá says:

"Be ye assured with the greatest assurance that, verily,
God will help those who are firm in His Covenant in
every matter, through His confirmation and favour, the
lights of which will shine forth unto the East of the
earth as well as the West thereof. He will make them the
signs of guidance among the creation and as shining
and glittering stars from all horizons."[17]

"Whosoever is firm in the Covenant and Testament is
today endowed with a seeing eye, and a responsive
ear, and daily advances in the divine realm until he
becomes a heavenly angel."[18]

The Meaning of Firmness
What, then, does firmness in the Covenant consist in and what
must men do to attract such blessings to themselves and to mankind?
Since this Covenant is about a Successor, the paramount obligation
is to turn towards that Successor, an obligation Bahá'u'lláh refers
to in the passage already quoted from the *Kitáb-i-Aqdas,*
'Abdu'l-Bahá is 'The Centre of the Covenant'; He is both the Centre
towards Which all must turn and the Pivot round Which the
Covenant itself revolves. In a Tablet to 'Abdu'l-Bahá Himself,
Bahá'u'lláh summarises this:

"We have made Thee a shelter for all mankind, a shield
unto all who are in heaven and on earth, a stronghold

*for whosoever hath believed in God, the Incomparable,
the All-Knowing. God grant that through Thee He may
protect them, may enrich and sustain them, that He may
inspire Thee with that which shall be a well-spring of
wealth unto all created things, an ocean of bounty to
all men, and the dayspring of mercy unto all peoples.*"[19]

Turning towards the Centre of the Covenant means more than
mere obedience to Him. If one turns towards a light, one is illumined,
whereas if one turns away from it, the light is obstructed by one's
own body. Similarly in the spiritual realm, the self of anyone who
does not turn wholly towards the Centre of the Covenant intervenes
to veil his soul from the light of the Knowledge of God. Only those
can be said to be firm in the Covenant who so overcome their own
wishes and erroneous opinions as to direct their entire being towards
fulfilling the Divine commandments expressed by Bahá'u'lláh and
explained by 'Abdu'l-Bahá.

After the passing of 'Abdu'l-Bahá, the same wholehearted
loyalty that before was due to Him became due to the Guardian of
the Cause of God and after its formation to the Universal House of
Justice. Unreserved obedience to the Guardian and to the Universal
House of Justice is the second obligation incurred under the Covenant
of Bahá'u'lláh. Those who turn their spirit unreservedly towards
not only the Founder of the Faith and the Centre of His Covenant,
but also their twin successors, the Guardian and the Universal House
of Justice, receive the confirmation and blessings decreed for those
firm in the Covenant.

The Will and Testament of 'Abdu'l-Bahá

The momentous document in which 'Abdu'l-Bahá, appointed Shoghi
Effendi Guardian and commanded all Bahá'ís to turn towards the
Guardian's guidance is His Will and Testament. This document
contains much else of fundamental importance. Shoghi Effendi has
described it as *"the Child of the Covenant—the Heir of both the
Originator and the Interpreter of the Law of God"*;[20] firmness
in the Covenant requires obedience to its every clause.

The Will is pre-eminently the Charter which, in the words of Shoghi Effendi, "called into being, outlined the features and set in motion the processes of"[21] the Administrative Order[*] of Bahá'u'lláh. 'By leaving certain matters unspecified and unregulated in His Book of Laws,' he explains, "Bahá'u'lláh seems to have deliberately left a gap in the general scheme of Bahá'í Dispensation, which the unequivocal provisions of the Master's Will have filled."[22] The Administrative Order is one of the channels through which the power of the Covenant works; compliance with its provisions attracts the confirmation brought by obedience to the Covenant. Its institutions are the buds and leaves of the Tree of Life, which is eventually to cast its shade over East and West. Actions taken under the guidance of assemblies or other institutions of the Administrative Order are reinforced by the power of the Covenant; since Bahá'ís are eager for such spiritual reinforcement of their otherwise puny individual efforts, they take no step for the promotion of the Cause of Bahá'u'lláh without consulting the appropriate administrative body.

In the Will and Testament of 'Abdu'l-Bahá, the fundamental beliefs of the Bahá'í Faith are delineated. One who has fully accepted its contents is eligible for membership of the Bahá'í Community.[**] Besides instituting the Guardianship and calling into being the Administrative Order. 'Abdu'l-Bahá sets out in His. Will the stations of Bahá'u'lláh and the Báb, stresses the importance of the Kitáb-i-Aqdas, extols the virtues of the Covenant of Bahá'u'lláh. He also summons the Bahá'ís to arise unitedly to propagate the Cause of God, counsels them to demonstrate by their conduct its universality and high principles, and prescribes fidelity to all just rulers.

Covenant-breakers

A large part of the Will is about the misdeeds of those who disobeyed the Covenant of Bahá'u'lláh and who, although professing belief in Him, tried vainly to bring His decree to naught. 'Abdu'l-Bahá warns

---

[*] See Chapter XV.
[**] See pages 328-30.

the Bahá'ís in the strongest terms to avoid these people:

"For so grievous is the conduct and behaviour of this false people that they are become even as an axe striking at the very root of the Blessed Tree. Should they be suffered to continue they would, in but a few days' time, exterminate the Cause of God. His Word and themselves."[23]

These Covenant-breakers profess to accept the teachings of Bahá'u'lláh but they turn away from the central authority in the Cause to which all must turn and thereby they deny what they profess to accept. Disobedience to other teachings of Bahá'u'lláh is deplorable, but Covenant-breaking cuts man off from the very source of his spiritual life. It is a deep sin that comes only from exaltation of self above the Will of God. The documents appointing 'Abdu'l-Bahá, the Guardian and the Universal House of Justice are clear and decisive. Anyone who accepts that Bahá'u'lláh spoke for God, yet disobeys and opposes either 'Abdu'l-Bahá, the Guardian or the Universal House of Justice, deliberately sets his will against the power of the Covenant. Covenant-breaking is not mere apostasy, or denial of Bahá'u'lláh; it is a witting rebellion against the Sovereignty of God. 'Abdu'l-Bahá said:

"Carnal desires are the cause of difference, as it is the case with violators. They do not doubt the validity of the Covenant, but selfish motives have dragged them to this condition. It is not that they are ignorant of what they do; they are perfectly aware and still they exhibit opposition.."[24]

Such rebellion naturally carries with it spiritual penalties. As confirmation follows obedience to the Covenant, spiritual degradation follows resistance to it. One who breaks the Covenant is like a man who turns his back on the light—the light can no longer reach him; only if he once more turns towards it can he again be illumined. Similarly Covenant-breakers can regain spiritual illumination only if they turn once more to the Centre of the Cause.

Bahá'ís are told by both Bahá'u'lláh and 'Abdu'l-Bahá to avoid Covenant-breakers entirely. Bahá'u'lláh, speaking of the breakers of the Báb's Covenant, said:

"Therefore, to avoid these people will be the nearest path by which to attain the divine good pleasure; because their breath is infectious, like unto poison."[25]

And 'Abdu'l-Bahá wrote in His Will:

"One of the greatest and most fundamental principles of the Cause of God is to shun and avoid entirely the Covenant-breakers, for they will utterly destroy the Cause of God, exterminate His Law and render of no account all efforts exerted in the past."[26]

In explanation of this point He said on another occasion:

"If a consumptive should associate with a thousand safe and healthy persons, the safety and health of these thousand persons would not affect the consumptive and would not cure him of his consumption. But when the consumptive associates with those heavenly souls, in a short time the disease of consumption will infect a number of those healthy persons. This is a clear and self-evident question. Likewise, if a thousand magnanimous persons associate with a degraded one, the perfection of those souls will not affect this debased person. On the contrary, this mean person will be the cause of their going astray."[27]

Disobedience to assemblies,* is not Covenant-breaking. Such disobedience is a serious offence against the Law of Bahá'u'lláh and may even sometimes be a step towards breaking the Covenant; it isolates the offender from the spiritual power that comes through

_____

* See pages 306-307.

co-operation with Bahá'í administrative institutions; but it is not a deep sin like Covenant-breaking. The greatest penalty inflicted for such disobedience is deprivation of voting right, an administrative penalty only. Covenant breakers, on the other hand, are expelled from the Cause of God, a penalty that results from and confirms the veiling of a soul from the spiritual bounties showered on mankind in this age. Association with those deprived of their voting right is not forbidden and the National Assembly that took away the voting right may restore it at any time. Only the spiritual leprosy of Covenant-breaking calls for exclusion, proscription, and ostracism. Deliberate association with Covenant-breakers flouts the central authority in the Cause to which all must turn, and brings denunciation as a Covenant-breaker to the offender himself.

The Covenant as a Source of Unity

Covenant-breakers would utterly destroy the unity of the Cause of God if the power of the Covenant, creator and preserver of unity, did not cast them out, 'Abdu'l-Bahá says:

> *"The Covenant of God is like a vast and fathomless ocean. A billow shall rise and surge there from and shall cast ashore all accumulated foam."*[28]

Those whom self and desire for leadership cause to deviate from the straight path find sooner or later that the Covenant of God rids His Cause of their presence; for the purpose of the Covenant of Bahá'u'lláh is to promote unity. 'Abdu'l-Bahá explains:

> *"Be sure therefore that if the believers are not united in the Will of God, they will not be assisted. This is especially necessary because all of them are under the Tent of the Covenant in this Revelation. There is strength only in unity. Under one tent there is union and harmony. The Covenant of God in this day of Manifestation is a life-boat and Ark of Salvation. All true followers of the Blessed Perfection are sheltered and protected in this Ark. Whoever leaves it trusting in his own will and*

strength will drown and be destroyed. For the Blessed Perfection left no possibility for discord, disagreement and dissension. The Covenant is like the sea and the believers are as the fishes in the sea. If the fish leaves the water it cannot live. There is nothing to equal, nothing so effective as the Covenant of God to bring about arid continue unity."[29]

Such unity comes into being when individual Bahá'ís subordinate themselves to the power of the Covenant, and thus become recipients of the spiritual bounties that Bahá'u'lláh conferred to unite mankind. Unity like this is contagious; in the end, it is the only true means for uniting mankind. Plans for unity may be drawn up and the spirit of love may be preached, but only the power of the Covenant can weld divergent groups into a harmonious whole. Each man has his own desires and predilections; each group has its particular interests, history, and aspirations. A power above the will of man is needed to unite groups so multifarious and perverse—a power to which man's will and the aspirations of groups may be subordinated. The power of the Covenant is just such a power; for this purpose Bahá'u'lláh released it and to this end it is wholly directed. Therefore 'Abdu'l-Bahá says:

"It is evident that the axis of the oneness of the world of humanity is the power of the Covenant and nothing else."[30]

That is why firmness in the Covenant is so extraordinarily important. It is a Bahá'í duty whose performance attracts blessings and spiritual bounties to all mankind. Stressing its importance. 'Abdu'l-Bahá said:

"If it is considered with insight, it will be seen that all the forces of the universe, in the last analysis, serve the Covenant."[31]

No wonder He exhorts the believers:

"O ye beloved of God, know that steadfastness and firmness in this new and wonderful Covenant is indeed the spirit that quickeneth the hearts which are overflowing with the love of the glorious Lord; verily, it is the power which penetrates into the hearts of the people of the world! Your Lord hath assuredly promised His servants who are firm and steadfast to render them victorious at all times, to exalt their word, propagate their power, diffuse their lights, strengthen their hearts, elevate their banners, assist their hosts, brighten their stars, increase the abundance of the showers of mercy upon them, and enable the brave lions to conquer."[32]

CHAPTER XV

The Bahá'í Administrative Order

The Guardian of the Cause of God

Although the Guardian of the Cause of God was the Centre towards whom all Bahá'ís must turn, his nature was essentially human. He did not share 'Abdu'l-Bahá's station of stainless mirror perfectly reflecting the light of Bahá'u'lláh, nor could he claim to be a perfect exemplar of Bahá'u'lláh's Teaching: Shoghi Effendi himself clarified this point by saying: "There is a far, far greater distance separating the Guardian from the Centre of the Covenant than there is between the Centre of the Covenant and its Author... The fact that the Guardian has been specifically endowed with such power as he may need to reveal the purport and disclose the utterances of Bahá'u'lláh and 'Abdu'l-Bahá does not necessarily confer upon him a station co-equal with those Whose words he is called upon to interpret. He can exercise that right and discharge this obligation and yet remain infinitely inferior to both of them in rank and different in nature."[1]

Nevertheless, his station must not be underrated. 'Abdu'l-Bahá says of Shoghi Effendi in His Will:

> *"Well is it with him that seeketh the shelter of his shade that shadoweth all mankind."*[2]

Shoghi Effendi builds the Administrative Order

At the passing of 'Abdu'l-Bahá, Shoghi Effendi was a young man of 24 studying at Oxford University. Overcome with grief, he returned to Haifa to receive the shattering news that he was to be the Guardian of the Cause of God.

Many with more experience of the Cause than he tried to advise this young man so unexpectedly called to so responsible a position, but they soon found that he was indeed the Centre of the Cause, guided in his decisions by Bahá'u'lláh and endowed with just the characteristics needed to promote its development. He realised at once that two allied processes must advance simultaneously: the work of the Cause must come to be executed through proper administrative channels, and the believers must be emancipated both from the ties of their former religions and from the corrupt practices current in the modern world. He set himself to build a truly Bahá'í Community, operating truly Bahá'í institutions based on the principles of the *Kitáb-i-Aqdas* and the Will of 'Abdu'l-Bahá, brought into being and invigorated by the power of the Covenant, and worthy to form the pattern and the nucleus of the future World Order of Bahá'u'lláh.

Although local administrative institutions had existed in the time of 'Abdu'l-Bahá, they were loosely organised on lines that were neither clear nor uniform. National bodies had acted in Persia and the United States but for specific purposes only and with limited powers. Moreover, circumstances had made it right then for Bahá'ís to remain closely associated with their former religion; 'Abdu'l-Bahá Himself used to attend the Mosque regularly. There was a Bahá'í Movement, but the Bahá'í World Faith had not yet emerged from its swaddling clothes and the Bahá'í World Community had not yet been born.

The passing of 'Abdu'l-Bahá marked the end of the Heroic Age of the Faith and the beginning of the Formative Age. For nearly eighty years Bahá'u'lláh, the Báb, and 'Abdu'l-Bahá had radiated the spiritual power and expounded the precepts that were to create a new world. Now the time to form that world had come.

Its formation could not be completed overnight, nor in a year, nor a decade, nor a generation. Hundreds of years may pass before the Most Great Peace is here; but now is the beginning of its growth, and the beginning of any process is its most vital phase.

Shoghi Effendi saw that the Writings of the Central Figures of the Faith implied North America would cradle the Administrative Order, so he used the American Bahá'í Community as a prototype for other National Communities. Through a series of letters to the American National Spiritual Assembly, he brought into being national and local institutions capable of serving as channels for the power of the Covenant. For sixteen years he laboured; then the institutions in America were sufficiently developed to be used in an organised Plan for the spread of the Faith, the strikingly successful first Seven-Year Plan of the American Bahá'í Community.

With the completion of this Plan in 1944 at the Centenary of the Declaration of the Báb, the first epoch of the Formative Age came to an end. National and local administrative institutions were functioning adequately, if not perfectly, so Shoghi Effendi felt justified in turning his attention to the essential task of the second epoch of the Formative, building international Bahá'í institutions. For the next 9 years many National Assemblies were to co-operate in the successful prosecution of plans designed to promote the development of the Faith beyond the confines of the Western hemisphere. The internal consolidation and experience gained by these National Assemblies was utilised and mobilised by Shoghi Effendi through the launching of a Ten Year World Crusade in 1953. This global plan was to further accelerate the development of an emerging world community and witnessed the rise and steady consolidation of the World Centre of the Faith in Haifa. The culminating event of this epoch was the first world congress held in London and the election of the Universal House of Justice in 1963.

The period of the third epoch (1963-1986) was to encompass a further three world plans lasting nine, five and seven years respectively. Under the stewardship of the Universal House of Justice, these plans called the Bahá'ís to a yet more mature level of administrative functioning consistent with the vast increase in the size and diversity of the community and the extension of its influence in the world at large.

Among the key features of this epoch was the emergence of the Faith from obscurity, so clearly presaged by Shoghi Effendi, and the initiation of activities designed to foster the social and economic development of communities. Administrative evolution

Delegates attending an International Bahá'í Convention in 1983

The seat of the Universal House of Justice, Mount Carmel, Israel.

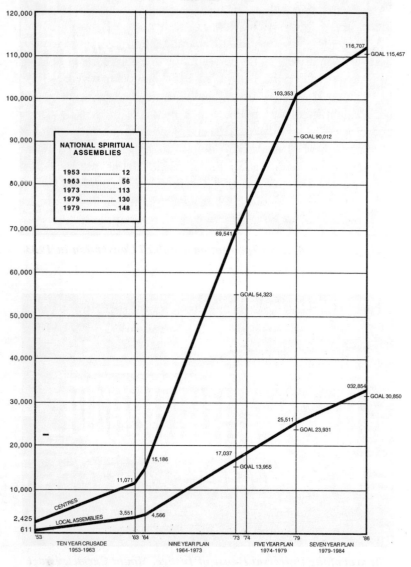

THE GROWTH OF THE BAHA'I FAITH
1953 - 1986

NATIONAL SPIRITUAL
ASSEMBLIES

1953 12
1963 56
1973 113
1979 130
1979 148

116,707
GOAL 115,457

103,353

GOAL 90,012

69,541

GOAL 54,323

032,854
GOAL 30,850

25,511
GOAL 23,931

17,037
GOAL 13,955

15,186

11,071

CENTRES

3,551
4,566

LOCAL ASSEMBLIES

2,425
611

'53   '63 '64   '73 '74   '79   '86

TEN YEAR CRUSADE
1953-1963

NINE YEAR PLAN
1964-1973

FIVE YEAR PLAN
1974-1979

SEVEN YEAR PLAN
1979-1984

continued with the institution of Continental Boards of Counsellors and the establishment of the International Teaching Centre. At the World Centre of the Faith, the historic construction and occupation of the Seat of the Universal House of Justice was a crowning event. At the passing of 'Abdu'l-Bahá, the Faith was represented in thirty-five countries; by the end of the first epoch of the Formative Age, organised teaching had increased the number to seventy-eight. In 1953, the start of the first global plan, nearly 2,500 centres had been established worldwide. Since then, the growth has been phenomenal. In April 1986, at the end of the third epoch, the number of communities had increased to almost 120,000 in over 200 countries and territories, with Bahá'í literature translated into over 750 languages. The rate of attracting new Bahá'ís leaped forward when the first Bahá'í Teaching Plan was organised, and again as intercontinental teaching gathered way. Further acceleration is to be expected as the international institutions of the Faith develop and assume their proper function.

The Teaching Plans that have achieved these successes have been inspired by the Tablets of the Divine Plan;[*] these provide yet another indication of the primacy of the American Bahá'í Community, to which they give a responsibility so weighty that 'Abdu'l-Bahá has said:

> "The moment this Divine Message is carried forward by the American believers from the shores of America and is propagated through the continents of Europe, of Asia, of Africa and of Australasia, and as far as the islands of the Pacific, this community will find itself securely established upon the throne of an everlasting dominion. Then will all the peoples of the world witness that this community is spiritually illumined and divinely guided. Then will the whole earth resound with the praises of its majesty and greatness."[3]

In the decades and centuries' ahead, the world will see the full

---

[*] See pages 342-43.

implication of the Tablets of the Divine Plan, both for the American believers and for mankind as a whole.

Source and Purpose of the Administrative Order

To appreciate the Bahá'í Administrative Order properly, it must be regarded as the forerunner of the World Order of Bahá'u'lláh, which has already been described.* This will be established only when the world as a whole is governed in the way prescribed by Bahá'u'lláh. The Administrative Order, on the other hand, is concerned with the affairs of the World Bahá'í Community; the Bahá'ís, first under the guidance of the Guardian during his lifetime, and now under that of the Universal House of Justice, are developing it patiently, in the firm conviction that the institutions of the Old Order will sooner or later be found utterly inadequate for mankind's new needs. Then the peoples of the world will become aware of the existence of a smoothly working Administrative Order, ready to be applied more widely and suited to the needs of the age, and they will freely choose to adopt it as their own.

Bahá'u'lláh Himself revealed its principles and established some of its institutions; gaps He left were filled by 'Abdu'l-Bahá in His Will and Testament, which Shoghi Effendi has described as the Charter of the New World Order. Thus the Bahá'í Administrative Order and the World Order of Bahá'u'lláh are firmly based on the written teachings of the Central Figures of the Faith. In this they differ from any administrative product of previous Dispensations. Although former Manifestations of God have revealed systems of laws, none has provided for an Administrative Order that can compare in scope or authority with the one now being established through the Covenant of Bahá'u'lláh.

Because the source of the Administrative Order is Bahá'u'lláh Himself, and because it is a child of the Covenant, its institutions must be regarded as channels for the outpouring of the Holy Spirit. Unless they are this, they are nothing. Shoghi Effendi said that the purpose of the Administrative Order is "to facilitate the flow of the

---

* See pages 81-83.

spirit of the Faith out into the world."[4] It does so partly by rational co-ordination and direction of available resources and partly by spiritual means; actions conforming to its principles are spiritually reinforced, whereas actions that disregard them have comparatively but slight effect. The Administrative Order ensures by the power of the Covenant that the efforts of Bahá'ís to spread the spirit of their Faith have the greatest possible influence on the hearts and souls of men.

Two Channels for the Outpouring of Spirit

The Administrative Order is supported by two pillars, the Guardianship and the Universal House of Justice. The Guardian was the Interpreter of the Holy Word and the Universal House of Justice legislates on matters not expressly revealed in the teachings. Bahá'u'lláh declares of it:

"It is incumbent upon the members of the House of Justice to take counsel together regarding those things which have not outwardly been revealed in the Book, and to enforce that which is agreeable to them. God will verily inspire them with whatsoever He willeth, and He verily is the Provider, the Omniscient."[5]

'Abdu'l-Bahá in His Will explains:

"Unto the Most Holy Book [the Kitáb-i-Aqdas) every one must turn, and all that is not expressly recorded therein must be referred to the. Universal House of Justice. That which this body, whether unanimously or by a majority doth carry, that is verily the Truth and the Purpose of God Himself. Whoso doth deviate therefrom is verily of them that love discord, hath shown forth malice, and turned away from the Lord of the Covenant."[6]

The Guardian was to be the permanent head of the Universal House of Justice with one vote, but no other legislative power; the two institutions thus being complementary in function, but different in significance. The Universal House of Justice handles the tasks of legislation, whereas the Guardian was the Authoritative Interpreter. Both institutions should have under them a system of subordinate institutions providing channels for the outpouring of the Holy Spirit.

Directly under the Guardian and appointed by him come the Hands of the Cause of God, 'Abdu'l-Bahá defines their duties thus:

> *"The obligations of the Hands of the Cause of God are to diffuse the Divine Fragrances, to edify the souls of men, to promote learning, to improve the character of all men and to be, at all times and under all conditions, sanctified and detached from earthly things."*[7]

And again:

> *"The Hands of the Cause of God must be ever watchful and So soon as they find anyone beginning to oppose and protest against the Guardian of the Cause of God cast him out from the congregation of the people of Bahá and in no wise accept any excuse from him. How often hath grievous error been disguised in the garb of truth, that it might sow the seeds of doubt in the hearts of men!"*[8]

In 1954 Auxiliary Boards were instituted to help the Hands of the Cause to discharge their duties of protection and propagation of the Faith.

Moreover in a message sent to the Bahá'ís of the world in October 1957 the Guardian named the Hands of the Cause 'the Chief Stewards of the Faith' and the inspired wisdom of this appointment became evident when on November 4, 1957, the Guardian, Shoghi Effendi, died leaving no heir. Without the body of the Hands of the Cause the Faith would have been left leaderless and without a visible centre but, having received the Guardian's message only a month before, the entire Bahá'í world turned to the Hands of the Cause for guidance and they became the focal point of the Faith for nearly six years during which the worldwide teaching crusade given to the Bahá'í community by the Guardian in 1953 was triumphantly completed.

Having made sure that the tasks already set by the Guardian would be completed, the Hands made preparations for a further tremendous step forward in the development of the Faith and of its Administrative Order, namely the election for the first time of the Universal House of Justice. A world convention was called in April, 1963, at which the members of the various National Spiritual Assemblies then existing, in accordance with the provisions of 'Abdu'l-Bahá's Will and Testament, elected the first Universal House of Justice, that body of which Bahá'u'lláh promised that its decisions would be without error. From then on the Hands of the Cause of God, with the administration of the Faith in the firm hands of the House of Justice, continued to carry out their work of supervision and encouragement of teaching and protection of the Cause and the spiritualisation of mankind.

As mentioned above, at the death of Shoghi Effendi there was no possibility of fulfilling the conditions laid down by 'Abdu'l-Bahá's Will in regard to Shoghi Effendi's successor. After the election of the Universal House of Justice, that body consulted at length on this question, making a prayerful and careful study of the Holy Texts bearing on it, but finally concluded that 'there is no way to appoint or to legislate to make it possible to appoint a second Guardian to succeed Shoghi Effendi.'

Since the Hands of the Cause, according to 'Abdu'l-Bahá's Will, must be appointed by the Guardian, it follows that no further Hands can now be appointed and that as from time to time one of them passes on, their number will decrease. It has already been reduced from twenty-seven at the time of Shoghi Effendi's death to eight at the time of publication. In order both to supplement their efforts and to ensure that their work of teaching and protection shall be adequately continued as the body of the Hands grows smaller the Universal House of Justice in 1968, having the authority to legislate on those matters not provided for in the Sacred Texts, inaugurated a new institution called the Continental Boards of Counsellors. These are bodies appointed by the Universal House of Justice, one board in each continent, who have responsibility for the protection of the Faith and for the encouragement and stimulation of its propagation in the area, working with the National Spiritual Assemblies and supervising the Auxiliary Boards, as the Hands had hitherto done. The Hands were at the same time freed from the responsibility for a particular continent and made free to go wherever in the world their services might be helpful.

Under the Universal House of Justice, now so firmly established and vigorously exercising its functions, comes a network of national and local Spiritual Assemblies. Later on they will be known in the World Order of Bahá'u'lláh as Houses of Justice, but they will at no time achieve infallibility. Each Assembly has at present nine members, elected by Bahá'ís of the area aged twenty-one or more. To help its work an Assembly may appoint specialised committees, whose members need not be members of the Assembly. The function and mode of operation of these Assemblies will be discussed later in this chapter.

Spiritual Assemblies

Wherever as many as nine Bahá'ís aged 21 or more live in an area of local government, a Bahá'í Spiritual Assembly is formed, by joint declaration if there are nine only and by election if there are more than nine. These Assemblies form the bedrock upon which the Administrative Order stands.

Where enough local Spiritual Assemblies exist in a country and the believers are sufficiently mature, a National Spiritual Assembly is formed with jurisdiction over all Bahá'ís and local Assemblies in its area. Responsibility for directing the Bahá'í activity of the area is centralised in this body.

Appeal to the National Assembly against decisions of a local Assembly is permissible, as is appeal to the World Centre of the Faith against decisions of a National Assembly. Normally, however, only National Assemblies and Hands of the Cause correspond directly with the World Centre.

Bahá'ís from Balsal Village, Panama, gathered outside their local centre.

Grassroots development at a Bahá'ís vocational institute for women, Indore, India.

A Bahá'í Primary School at Singtam, Sikkim, in the Himalayas. In April, 1986, some 600 other Bahá'í Schools were in operation in different parts of the world.

Shoghi Effendi has summarised the duties of local Assemblies as follows:

"The matter of teaching [the Faith], its direction, its ways and means, its extension, its consolidation, essential as they are to the interests of the Cause, constitute by no means the only issue which should receive the full attention of these Assemblies....

"It is incumbent upon them to be vigilant and cautious, discreet and watchful, and protect at all times the Temple of the Cause from the dart of the mischief-maker and the onslaught of the enemy.

"They must endeavour to promote unity and concord amongst the friends, efface every lingering trace of distrust, coolness and estrangement from every heart, and secure in its stead an active and wholehearted co-operation for the service of the Cause.

"They must do their utmost to extend at all times the helping hand to the poor, the sick, the disabled, the orphan, the widow, irrespective of colour, caste and creed.

"They must promote by every means in their power the material as well as the spiritual enlightenment of youth, the means for the education of children, institute whenever possible Bahá'í educational institutions, organise and supervise their work and provide the best means for their progress and development.

"They must make an effort to maintain official, regular and frequent correspondence with the various Bahá'í centres throughout the world, report to them their activities, and share the glad tidings they receive with all their fellow-workers in the Cause.*

---

* This is now done by National Spiritual Assemblies.

"They must encourage and stimulate by every means at their command, through subscription, reports and articles, the development of the various Bahá'í magazines.

"They must undertake the arrangement of the regular meetings of the friends, the feasts and the anniversaries, as well as the special gatherings designed to serve and promote the social, intellectual and spiritual interests of their fellow-men.

"They must supervise, in these days when the Cause is still in its infancy, all Bahá'í publications and translations, and provide in general for a dignified and accurate presentation of all Bahá'í literature and its distribution to the general public."[11]

The Assembly allocates human and financial resources to these various objects at its own discretion. In the present stage of the development of the Faith. Bahá'ís feel their most important work is to lay a foundation upon which the World Order of Bahá'u'lláh can be erected, and they allocate resources accordingly. Later, it will be possible to devote a larger proportion of them to education and to social welfare work.

Bahá'í Elections
Local Assemblies are elected each year on the First Day of Riḍván* (April 21st). All Bahá'ís of 21 years or more who reside in the Assembly's area of jurisdiction have the right to vote and to serve on the Assembly if elected. There are no candidates or nominations, and canvassing is forbidden.

The voters gather to vote in a spirit of prayer for the nine members of the Community who they consider "best combine the necessary qualities of unquestioned loyalty, of selfless devotion, of a well-trained mind, of recognised ability and mature experience"[10]

* See pages 325-26.

The nine members receiving the most votes are considered elected, whether they have an absolute majority or not.

A similar procedure is used in electing delegates to the National Convention and by these delegates in electing the National Assembly. Shoghi Effendi has commented: "Every Assembly elected in that rarified atmosphere of selflessness and detachment, is in truth appointed of God."[11]

The same principles govern the election of the members of the Universal House of Justice, who are elected by the members of all the National Spiritual Assemblies.

National Conventions
National Assemblies are elected at National Conventions at present held annually during Riḍván.*

The delegates to the Convention constitute the electorate. They are elected regionally in well-developed national communities like that of the United States, where State Conventions are held and State delegates elected, and by local communities in less developed national communities where Regional Conventions are not yet practicable.

The National Convention has a double function: as well as electing the National Assembly for the year, the delegates consult with the outgoing and incoming National Assemblies. They make recommendations, which the incoming Assembly must study carefully although it need not do what is recommended if for any reason it considers this unwise.

Only delegates and outgoing and incoming National Assembly members have the right to speak at the National Convention, but Bahá'ís who are not delegates attend as visitors and may ask a delegate to raise a point on their behalf.

Nineteen-Day-Feasts
Consultation between the Local Assembly and its community takes place every nineteen days at a gathering called a Nineteen Day-Feast. This has three parts: devotional, business and social.

---

* See pages 325-26.

The devotional part is conducted in the manner already described.* The business part consists in reports from the Local Assembly and its committees, followed by discussion. The social part provides an opportunity for members of the Community to meet each other and to take food together.

Nineteen-Day-Feasts are the heart of local Bahá'í activity. Regular attendance, although not obligatory, is an important Bahá'í duty, and only Bahá'ís may attend. At these Feasts, the members of the Community get to know each other better; the Community learns what the Assembly is doing, and the Assembly learns what the Community thinks. Anyone with a suggestion, query, or criticism not of a personal nature can convey it to the Assembly at a Nineteen-Day-Feast under conditions that disclose how many think likewise. The Local Assembly must carefully study resolutions passed in these business sessions, although it may use its discretion whether or not to act upon them.

'Abdu'l-Bahá has explained the significance of these Feasts thus:

> *"The Nineteen-Day-Feast was inaugurated by the Báb and ratified by Bahá'u'lláh in His Holy Book, the Aqdás, so that people may gather together and outwardly show fellowship and love, that the Divine mysteries may be disclosed. The object is concord, that through this fellowship hearts may become perfectly united, and reciprocity and mutual helpfulness be established. Because the members of the world of humanity are unable to exist without being banded together, co-operation and helpfulness is the basis of human society. Without the realisation of these two great principles no great movement is pressed forward."*[12]

Consultation

The principle underlying Bahá'í administration is consultation. This comprises not merely discussion with others, but discussion in a

_____
* See page 147.

proper spirit, such as 'Abdu'l-Bahá describes in a passage on the conditions for satisfactory Assembly consultation:

"The first condition is absolute love and harmony amongst the members of the Assembly. They must be wholly free from estrangement and must manifest in themselves the Unity of God, for they are the waves of one sea, the drops of one river, the stars of one heaven, the rays of one sun, the trees of one orchard, the flowers of one garden. Should harmony of thought and absolute unity be non-existent, that gathering shall be dispersed and that Assembly be brought to naught. The second condition: They must, when coming together, turn their faces to the Kingdom on High and ask aid from the Realm of Glory. They must proceed with the utmost devotion, courtesy, dignity, care and moderation to express their views. They must in every matter search out the truth and not insist upon their own opinion, for stubbornness and persistence in one's views will lead ultimately to discord and wrangling and the truth will remain hidden. The honoured members must with all freedom express their own thoughts, and it is in no wise permissible for One to belittle the thought of another, nay, he must with moderation set forth the truth, and should differences of opinion arise a majority of voices must prevail, and all must obey and submit to the majority. It is again not permitted that anyone of the honoured members object to or censure, whether in or out of the meeting, any decision arrived at previously, though that decision be not right, for such criticism would prevent any decision from being enforced. In short, whatsoever thing is arranged in harmony and with love and purity of motive, its result is light, and should the least trace of estrangement prevail the result shall be darkness upon darkness."[13]

Consultation in this spirit should permeate the workings of all Bahá'í institutions.

The principle of consultation requires also that no Bahá'í activity should be undertaken without the Spiritual Assembly or its appropriate Committee being first consulted; for example, teaching the Faith is organised by Spiritual Assemblies through Teaching Committees, so individual efforts to spread the Faith are rendered fruitful by consulting the Teaching Committee. Suggestions and criticisms should be made through the channels the Administrative Order provides—Nineteen-Day-Feasts, Local Assemblies and Conventions. Moreover, Bahá'ís often seek the advice of their Spiritual Assembly about matters that do not affect the Faith directly, believing they can thereby tap unseen sources of spiritual power. Should two Bahá'ís dispute, they take their dispute to the Spiritual Assembly to settle, and it sometimes happens in the East that non-Bahá'ís bring a dispute before a Bahá'í Assembly, because they know that they can rely upon the Assembly to judge justly.

Initiative and Obedience

Authority in the Bahá'í Administrative Order rests with the institutions of the Cause, but power and initiative with the individual believer. Interaction of these principles releases the spiritual energy the Administrative Order provides. Only when individuals act, and act in consultation with the appropriate body, can this be achieved. Upon the initiative of the individual believer all else depends.

The Administrative Order nicely blends freedom and authority. It provides ample opportunity for individuals to express their views and to choose the members of the Assembly in which authority rests; if they do not like the action of the Assembly, they may say so at a Nineteen-Day-Feast and are free to elect other members the next year. But the authority of the Assembly must be recognised. Its decisions must be respected, and its instructions obeyed. Any Bahá'í who flouts the authority of an Assembly is liable to have his National Assembly take away his Bahá'í voting right, which means that he loses an privileges of membership of the Bahá'í Community, such as the right to attend Nineteen-Day-Feasts, to contribute to

'Ishqábád—the first Bahá'í House of Worship

Wilmette, Illinois—the Mother temple of the West.

the Fund, or to be introduced as a Bahá'í to other Bahá'í Communities, besides losing his right to vote at Bahá'í elections.

The Institution of the Mashríqu'l-Adhkár

The words Mashríqu'l-Adhkár mean literally 'Dawning-place of the praise of God.' The Central Edifice of a Mashríqu'l-Adhkár is a House of Worship, nine-sided and domed, and dedicated to the worship of God as manifested by Bahá'u'lláh.

Round it will be built social institutions such as an old people's home, an orphanage, a hospital, and a college of science; administrative buildings will cluster near it. The life of every community in the World Order of Bahá'u'lláh will centre in its Mashríqu'l-Adhkár.

As yet, few are being built and those begun have national, or even continental, rather than local significance. All of them, however, are buildings worthy of their noble purpose; they are like cathedrals rather than parish churches. The time has not yet come for every local Bahá'í community to be thinking of building its House of Worship; for the present, local communities worship in their administrative buildings, or rent a Bahá'í Centre in which to-hold meetings of all kinds.

Two Mashríqu'l-Adhkár are of special importance. The first in the world was constructed in 'Ishqábád, Turkistan, in the time of 'Abdu'l-Bahá. In 1938 it was taken over by the Soviet authorities who converted it into an art gallery. It was subsequently destroyed by an earthquake.

The second, the Mother Temple of the West, is at Wilmette, a suburb of Chicago, 'Abdu'l-Bahá Himself laid the foundation stone and approved the architect's design. This beautiful temple was dedicated in 1953, since when well over 4 million visitors from all over America and beyond have flowed to it. Its first dependency, a Bahá'í Home for the Aged, was opened in 1959 and, in 1978, the United States Government designated the temple as a National Historic Place, 'One of the nations cultural resources worthy of preservation.'

Frankfurt, Germany.

Kampala, Uganda.

Sydney, Australia.

Panama, Central America.

Samoa, Pacific.

New Delhi, India.

Six other Bahá'í Houses of Worship have since been constructed in different parts of the world and sites for over 100 others purchased.

FRANKFURT, Europe: SYDNEY, Australia: KAMPALA, Africa: PANAMA, Central America: SAMOA, Pacific: NEW DELHI. India.

Each one of these is a mother temple for a continent or region and each one symbolises the Bahá'í teachings of peace, harmony and brotherhood. Open to people of every race, background and belief, the Mashríqu'l-Adhkár with its nine doors facing every direction, is a focal point of unity. Here followers of all religions and those with none are welcomed to share silence, meditate, pray or attend the regular services Here the sacred scriptures of all the world's revealed religions are read side by side.

The Institution of the Ḥazíratu'l-Quds

Ḥazíratu'l-Quds means 'The Sacred Fold.' It is the name given to the administrative headquarters of the Faith in an area if these are housed in property owned by the Assembly. Shoghi Effendi explains its function as follows: "Complementary in its functions to those of the Mashríqu'l-Adhkár an edifice exclusively reserved for Bahá'í worship—this institution, whether local or national, will, as its component parts, such as the Secretariat, the Treasury, the Archives, the Library, the Publishing Office, the Assembly Hall, the Council Chamber, the Pilgrim's Hostel, are brought together and made jointly to operate in one spot, be increasingly regarded as the focus of all Bahá'í administrative activity, and symbolise, in a befitting manner, the ideal of service animating the Bahá'í Community in its relation alike to the Faith and to mankind in general."[14]

He has explained further that although a Ḥazíratu'l-Quds is primarily an administrative centre, it should also, through suitable social and intellectual activities, be made a centre for teaching the Faith.

At present, more Ḥazíratu'l-Quds are purchased than built. Most National Assemblies have one, and a number of Local assemblies also.

Summer Schools and Teaching Conferences

In areas where there are a sufficient number of believers. Summer Schools open both to Bahá'ís and non-Bahá'ís are held to provide facilities for studying the Faith. Bahá'ís regard these as forerunners of future Bahá'í universities; Shoghi Effendi has defined their present function as "to foster the spirit of fellowship in a distinctly Bahá'í atmosphere, to afford the necessary training for Bahá'í teachers, and to provide facilities for the study of the history and teachings of the Faith, and for a better understanding of, its relation to other religions and to human society in general."[15]

Regional or national Teaching Conferences are gatherings with a more specialised purpose than the Summer Schools, held for consultation on the problems of teaching the Faith in an area and for instruction of those who wish to teach. Usually, Bahá'ís only may attend them.

The Bahá'í Fund

Each Assembly has a Bahá'í Fund supported solely by voluntary contributions from members of the Bahá'í Community. Contributions to it are in no circumstances accepted from non-Bahá'ís, except for charitable undertakings.

Shoghi Effendi has described the money flowing through the Bahá'í Fund as the life-blood of the Administrative Order. Nevertheless, he stressed that all contributions must be wholly voluntary: "It should be made clear and evident to everyone that any form of compulsion, however slight and indirect, strikes at the very root of the principle underlying the formation of the Fund ever since its inception. While appeals of a general character carefully worded and moving and dignified in tone are welcome under all circumstances, it should be left entirely to the discretion of every conscientious believer to decide upon the nature, the amount, and purpose of his or her own contribution for the propagation of the Cause."[16]

Of the attitude Bahá'ís should have to the Bahá'í Fund, he writes: "We must be like the fountain or spring that is continually emptying itself of all that it has and is continually being refilled from an invisible source. To be continually giving out for the good of our fellows undeterred by the fear of poverty and reliant on the unfailing bounty of the Source of all wealth and all good—that is the secret of right living."[17]

Shoghi Effendi has particularly stressed the importance of the National Fund, to which believers should contribute direct as well as through their local Fund: "It is the sacred obligation of every conscientious and faithful servant of Bahá'u'lláh who desires to see His Cause advance, to contribute freely and generously for the increase of that Fund.... Contribution to this fund constitute, in addition, a practical and effective way whereby every believer can test the measure and character of his faith, and prove in deeds the intensity of his devotional and attachment to the Cause."[18]

Both individuals and Assemblies give also to the International Bahá'í Fund, and to Continental Funds devoted to the work of the Continental Boards of Counsellors and their Auxiliar Boards.

Bahá'ís in the East contribute money, known as Ḥuqúqu'lláh (Right of God), or Ḥuqúq for short, to be used in whatever way will most help the Cause. Such contributions are ordained the Kitáb-i-Aqdas, although it is a provision of that Book Western Bahá'ís are not, at the time of writing, expected to comply with.

World Centre of the Faith

Ḥuqúq is an institution that will link all believers with the World Centre of the Faith, the nerve centre to "which Bahá'í turn to become receptive to the Faith's regenerative spirit and from which the affairs of the Cause are directed.

At first the Guardianship alone was established there, but other institutions have gradually appeared. From 1952 some of the Hands of the Cause were resident there to assist the Guardian and after his passing in 1957 nine of them reside there, under the Hands' function of 'Chief Stewards of the Faith', dealing with the affairs of the Cause, until in 1963 till first Universal House of Justice was elected and took up its seat in the Holy Land. Soon after this event the number (Hands resident at the World Centre was reduced to four. In 1968 the Hands in the Holy Land became the focal point for the work of the Continental Boards of Counsellors throughout the world. In 1973 a new institution was established at all World Centre, the International Teaching Centre, which comprises all the Hands of the Cause but especially those resident there together with a number of distinguished Bahá'í holding the rank of Counsellor who work with them in the International Teaching Centre.

Little by little, the future glory of the World Centre of the Faith is being unveiled. As well as forming the institutions, its material development is being promoted, a visible sign of splendour that is already evident enough to thrill the pilgrims who flow to Haifa in a steady stream.

The Shrine of the Báb and its gardens were described earlier.[*] Around it eventually will be erected an arc of buildings related to the institutions and the work of the Faith. The International Archives was the first to be built and the magnificent building for the seat of the Universal House of Justice was completed in 1982. Later there will be others. A little way off, also on Mount Carmel, is land Shoghi Effendi bought for the erection of the Mashríqu'l-Adhkár of the World Centre, the design for which he approved during his lifetime.

The Shrine of Bahá'u'lláh is established a few miles from Haifa, at Bahji, where Bahá'u'lláh spent the last years of His life. It is set in beautiful gardens bordering the Mansion He inhabited, now a Bahá'í museum. Several other places in Israel associated with Bahá'u'lláh or 'Abdu'l-Bahá are also owned by the Cause and visited by those making the pilgrimage to the World Centre of the Faith.

Bahá'u'lláh has extolled the greatness of the World Centre and particularly of Mount Carmel in a very important prophetic Tablet in which He says:

"Haste thee, O Carmel, for lo, the light of the Countenance of God... hath been lifted upon thee.... Rejoice, for God hath, in this Day, established upon

---

[*] See pages 257-58.

thee His throne, hath made thee the dawning-place of His signs and the dayspring of the evidences of His Revelation. Well is it with him that circleth around thee, that proclaimeth the revelation of thy glory, and recounteth that which the bounty of the Lord thy God hath showered upon thee."[18]

The Significance of the Administrative Order

Enough has been said in this brief outline of the Administrative Order of Bahá'u'lláh for it to be clear that His Order is quite distinct from any political or religious system the world has known.

That the Bahá'í Faith has no clergy at once distinguishes it from most religious systems; that its Guardian should be recognised as the supreme head of the Cause on earth, yet have no legislative function except as a member of the Universal House of Justice; distinguishes it from them still more sharply; but its most decisive distinguishing feature is that the Manifestation of God for the age has, in the words of Shoghi Effendi. Himself "revealed its principles, established its institutions, appointed the person to interpret His Word and conferred the necessary authority on the body designed to supplement and apply His legislative ordinances."[20]

The administration of no Christian Church is based on clearly defined administrative ordinances unambiguously given by Jesus Christ. The authority assumed by the leaders of no sect of either Christianity or Islm was given to them in unchallengeable written statements by the Founder of their Faith. To liken the Guardian of the Bahá'í Faith to the Caliph or the Pope, or to liken the Universal House of Justice to any of the governing councils of other religious sects, proclaims gross misunderstanding of the nature of these Bahá'í institutions.

Nor is there any parallel to the Bahá'í Administrative Order in political systems. It contains within itself the best elements of democracy, autocracy and aristocracy, while avoiding their unfavourable features. This was very clearly stated by Shoghi Effendi:

"Nor is the principle governing its operation similar to that which underlies any system, whether theocratic or otherwise, which the minds of men have devised for the government of human institutions. Neither in theory nor in practice can the Administrative Order of the Faith of Bahá'u'lláh be said to conform to any type of democratic government, to any system of autocracy, to any purely aristocratic order, or to any of the various theocracies, whether Jewish, Christian or Islámic which mankind has witnessed in the past. It incorporates within its structure certain elements which are to be found in each of the three recognised forms of secular government, is devoid of the defects which each of them inherently possesses, and blends the salutary truths which each undoubtedly contains without vitiating in any way the integrity of the Divine verities on which it is essentially founded."[21]

Nevertheless, it must always be remembered that the Administrative Order is only a framework, a static, inert thing, whose function is to provide channels for the spirit of life. Although necessary for the proper functioning of the Cause, it is insufficient in itself to produce any result. Shoghi Effendi summarises its significance thus: "Should we build up the Administrative World Order to a point of absolute perfection but at the same time allow it to be hampered or disconnected from the channels within, through which channels the Holy Spirit of the Cause pours forth, we would have nothing more than a perfected body out of touch with and cut off from the finer promptings of the soul and spirit. If, on the other hand, the influxes and goings forth of the spirit are scattered, diffused and subjected wholly to the more or less imperfect guidance and interpretation of individual believers, lacking both the wisdom secured through consultation and also the lights of real unity which shine through consultative action and obedience there to a disordered and disorganised activity would be witnessed, which would but dimly reflect the divine purpose for this age, which is no less than the establishment of the reign of divine love, justice and wisdom in the world, under and in conformity to the Devine Law."[22]

The immediate purpose of the Administrative Order is to spread the Faith of Bahá'u'lláh but its inner purpose is to facilitate the diffusion of the Divine Fragrance itself, which is the food of the spirit. When this Fragrance has been sufficiently diffused, the Administrative Order will change; the peoples of the world will adopt it as the Order of their choice and ceasing to be for Bahá'ís only, it will be transformed into the World Order of Bahá'u'lláh. This tremendous event lies sometime in the far, far distant future; until then, the Formative Age of the Faith will continue to witness the steady evolution of an expanding Bahá'í Administrative Order.

CHAPTER XVI

Laws, Obligations
and Teaching the Faith

The Laws of Bahá'u'lláh

Every religion, including the Bahá'í Faith, has a code of laws. All except the Bahá'í Faith, however, have irretrievably confused later additions of human origin with the Laws given by the Founder of the Faith.

The statement that Christ gave Laws surprises some Christians; nevertheless the Gospels record His revealing certain Laws explicitly, such as that concerning divorce, and others by implication, such as that concerning baptism as practised by the early Church. Our record of His Teaching is unfortunately not full enough for us to be sure which of the laws of the early Church he originated.

The standing of the Jewish and the Muslim Law differs little from the standing of the Christian. Although Moses undoubtedly revealed Laws. Priests and Rabbis have added so much to them that it is impossible to know which are authentic. Muslim Law is better recorded, but thirteen hundred years' attention from Muslim divines has distorted this also, until it is no longer recognisable as the Law of Muhammad.

The Laws of Bahá'u'lláh, on the other hand, are both authentically recorded and associated with an administrative system that can be relied on to preserve their purity. Moreover, He has provided for the Universal House of Justice to ordain anew according to the needs of each period the many laws that should not remain unchanged throughout a whole Dispensation.

The chief repository of His Laws is the Kitáb-i-Aqdas revealed in 'Akká, a brief Arabic exposition crammed with delectable fruit.

Of it Bahá'u'lláh says:

*"In such a manner hath the Kitáb-i-Aqdas been revealed
that it attracteth and embraceth all the divinely
appointed Dispensations. Blessed those who peruse it!
Blessed those who apprehend it! Blessed those who
meditate upon it! Blessed those who ponder its meaning!
So vast is its range that it hath, encompassed all men
ere their recognition of it. Ere long will its sovereign
power, its pervasive influence and the greatness of its
might be manifested on earth."*[1]

Much of the Book has been translated into English, but not yet
those parts of it in which the Laws are given. Shoghi Effendi has
listed these and some moral precepts of the Book as follows: "He…
prescribes the obligatory pruyers; designates the time and period of
fasting; prohibits congregational prayer except for the dead; fixes
the Qiblih;* institutes Ḥuqúqu'lláh (Right of God): formulates the
law of inheritance; ordains the institution of the Mashriqu'l-Adhkár;
establishes the Nineteen-Day-Feasts, the Bahá'í festivals and the
Intercalary Days:** abolishes the institution of priesthood; prohibits
slavery, asceticism, mendicancy, monasticism, penance, the use of
pulpits and the kissing of hands; prescribes monogamy; condemns
cruelty to animals, idleness and sloth, backbiting and calumny;
censures divorce; interdicts gambling, the use of opium, wine and
other intoxicating drinks; specifies the punishments for murder, arson,
adultery and theft; stresses the importance of marriage and lays
down its essential conclitions; imposes the obligation of engaging in
some trade or profession, exalting such occupation to the rank of
worship; emphasises the necessity of providing the means for the
education of cilildren ; and lays upon every person the duty of writing
a testament and of strict obedience to one's government."[2]

---

* The point on the earth's surface to which Bahá'ís turn in certain prayers is the
Shrine of Bahá'u'lláh at Bahjí. The Muslim Qiblih is Mecca, that of the Jews,
Jerusalem.
** See Pages 324-326.

Details of a few only of these laws are available to the Western Bahá'ís. "Others," Shoghi Effendi explains, "have been formulated in anticipation of a state of society destined to emerge from the chaotic conditions that prevail today."[3]

Bahá'í Marriage

Bahá'u'lláh says in the *Kitáb-i-Aqdas:*

> *"Enter into wedlock, O people, that ye may bring forth one who will make mention of Me."*[4]

In this sentence He both encourages Bahá'ís to marry and affirms that the chief purpose of marriage is procreation.

For Bahá'ís, marriage is no mere temporary bond to be taken on or cast off according to the desire of the moment. Extracts from various Tablets of 'Abdu'l-Bahá show its status:

> *"They must show forth the utmost attention and become informed of one another's character and the firm covenant made between each other must become an eternal binding, and their intentions must be everlasting affinity, friendship, unity and life... The marriage of the Bahá'ís means that both man and woman must become spiritually and physically united, so that they may have eternal unity throughout all the divine Worlds and improve the spiritual life of each other... When relationship, union and concord exist between the two from a physical and spiritual standpoint, that is the real union, therefore everlasting. But if the union is merely from the physical point of view, unquestionably it is temporal and at the end separation is inevitable. Consequently when the people of Bahá desire to enter the sacred union of marriage, eternal connection and ideal relationship, spiritual and physical association of thoughts and conceptions of life must exist between them, so that in all the grades of existence and all the worlds of God this union may continue for ever and*

ever, for this real union is a splendour of the light of the love of God."[5]

To promote unity and avoid friction, Bahá'u'lláh ordained that before marrying, a Bahá'í must obtain the consent of all of the four parents that are living and sane. Bahá'u'lláh gives no exceptions to this rule; it applies whatever the age of the Bahá'í and even though a parent object on grounds that are prejudiced or otherwise unreasonable. Parents do not, however, have the right to choase a spouse for their child; consent of both parties is the first requirement of Bahá'í marriage.

On marriages between Bahá'ís and non-Bahá'ís, Shoghi Effendi's secretary wrote on his behalf: 'If a Bahá'í marries a non-Bahá'í who wishes to have the religious ceremony of his own sect carried out, it must be quite clear that, first, the Bahá'í partner is understood to be a Bahá'í by religion and not to accept the religion of the other party to the marriage through having his or her religious ceremony; and, second, the ceremony must be of a nature which does not commit the Bahá'í to any declaration of faith in a religion other than his own.'

"Under these circumstances, the Bahá'í can partake of the religious ceremony of his non-Bahá'í partner. The Bahá'í should insist on having the Bahá'í ceremony carried out before or after the non-Bahá'í one, on the same day."[6]

Two Bahá'ís, of course, always have a Bahá'í ceremony; in countries where Bahá'í marriages are not yet recognised as legal, they also have a civil wedding.

Bahá'í weddings are conducted under the auspices of Bahá'í Assemblies. There is no set form at present. The wedding culminates in the bride and groom saying in turn, 'We will all, verily, abide by the Will of God.'

In addition, there are whatever prayers and readings from Bahá'í and other Holy Writings the bride and groom please, or the Assembly chooses at their request. A particular prayer revealed by Bahá'u'lláh for marriages is usually included, but even this is not obligatory.

Divorce

The Bahá'í attitude to divorce has been expressed thus by 'Abdu'l-Bahá:

> *"The friends must strictly refrain from divorce unless something arises which compels them to separate because of their aversion for each other; in that case, with the knowledge of the Spiritual Assembly, they may decide to separate. They must then be patient and wait one complete year. If during this year harmony is not re-established between them, then their divorce may be realised... The foundation of the Kingdom of God is based upon harmony and love, oneness, relationship and union, not upon differences, especially between husband and wife. If one of these two become the cause of divorce, the one will unquestionably fall into great difficulties, will become the victim of formidable calamities and experience deep remorse."*[7]

Since Bahá'ís approach marriage in so serious a frame of mind, and since each Bahá'í on marriage hopes the union will prove eternal, it is inevitable that divorce should be regarded with disfavour. Nevertheless, Bahá'í law recognises that mistakes are sometimes made; it does not seek to force two incompatibles to live together in mutual hatred. The sanction that keeps the frequency of divorce low amongst Bahá'ís is spiritual, not legal, and is proving extremely effective.

A Bahá'í contemplating divorce consults his Spiritual Assembly, which may try to reconcile the couple. Its procedure if it decides reconciliation is impossible varies from country to country, since the Bahá'í law of divorce is applied only to the extent consistent with the current civil law.

Burial

Bahá'ís bury their dead within one hour's journey of the place of death. Cremation is forbidden, 'Abdu'l-Bahá said that: 'The body of man, which has been formed gradually, must similarly be decomposed gradually. This is according to the real and natural order and Divine Law.'

A Bahá'í funeral service is arranged in much the same way as any other Bahá'í devotional programme of prayers and readings, but always includes a particular prayer.

To resolve any possible doubt relatives might have, Bahá'ís often state in their Wills that they want to be buried according to Bahá'í law and custom and specify that they should not be cremated.

The Bahá'í Calendar

Each religion, and the civilisation based on it, has its own calendar. The Bahá'í calendar was given by the Báb and confirmed by Bahá'u'lláh. It uses a solar year divided into nineteen months of nineteen days each, with four intercalary days to make up the year, except in Leap Years at four-year intervals, when a fifth intercalary day is added. Each day is deemed to start at sunset.

The names of the months and the Gregorian dates of their first days are given below:

Month	Arabic Name	Translation	First Day
1st	Bahá	Splendour	March 21st
2nd	Jalál	Glory	April 9th
3rd	Jamál	Beauty	April 28th
4th	'Azamat	Grandeur	May 17th
5th	Núr	Light	June 5th
6th	Rahmat	Mercy	June 24th
7th	Kalimát	Words	July 13th
8th	Kamál	Perfection	August 1st
9th	Asmá'	Names	August 20th
10th	'Izzát	Might	September 8th
11th	Mashíyyat	Will	September 27th
12th	'Ilm	Knowledge	October 16th
13th	Qudrat	Power	November 4th
14th	Qawl	Speech	November 23rd
15th	Masá'il	Questions	December 12th
16th	Sharaf	Honour	December 31st

17th	Sulṭán	Sovereignty	January 19th
18th	Mulk	Dominion	February 7th
19th	'Alá'	Loftiness	March 2nd

Ayyám-i-Há (Intercalary Days) February 26th-March 1st, inclusive.

The nineteen days of each month bear the same names in the same order as the nineteen months. Nineteen-Day-Feasts are normally held on the first day of each month, but may exceptionally be held on some other day.

The days of the week are named as follows:

Day	Arabic Name	English	Translation
1st	Jalál	Saturday	Glory
2nd	Jamál	Sunday	Beauty
3rd	Kamál	Monday	Perfection
4th	Fiḍál	Tuesday	Grace
5th	'Idál	Wednesday	Justice
6th	Istijlál	Thursday	Majesty
7th	Istiqlál	Friday	Independence

The Bahá'í Era dates from the Declaration of the Báb in 1844, so its hundredth year was completed on March 20, 1944.

Feasts and Anniversaries

The Bahá'í Anniversaries and annual Feasts are listed below, with any time of day specially commemorated:

Feast of Riḍván (the First, Ninth and
Twelfth Days, on April 21st, 29th and
May 2nd specially. The First Day at
3.0 p.m.) ... ... April 21st-May 2nd
Declaration of the Báb (two hours and
eleven minutes after sunset on May 22nd) May 23rd
Ascension of Bahá'u'lláh (3.0 a.m.) ... May 29th
Martyrdom of the Báb (12.0 noon) ... July 9th
Birth of the Báb ... ... October 20th

Birth of Bahá'u'lláh	November 12th
Day of the Covenant	November 26th
Ascension of 'Abdu'l-Bahá (10 a.m.) ...	November 28th
Feast of Naw-Rúz	March 21st

Most of these are explained by their names. The twelve days of Riḍván commemorate the twelve days Bahá'u'lláh spent in the Riḍván garden before leaving Baghdád, during which period He declared His Mission. The Day of the Covenant is dedicated to 'Abdu'l-Bahá, the Centre of the Covenant, whose birthday is celebrated as the anniversary of the Declaration of the Báb. Naw-Rúz is the Bahá'í New Year, a day both joyous and holy. Its date is determined by the spring equinox; should this fall before sunset on March 20th or after sunset on March 21st, the date of Naw-Rúz (and of Naw-Rúz only) is changed accordingly.

Bahá'ís are forbidden to work on nine Holy Days each year: the First, Ninth, and Twelfth Days of Riḍván, the other anniversaries relating to Bahá'u'lláh or the Báb, and Naw-Rúz. Shoghi Effendi has conveyed through his secretary the following instruction: "Believers who have independent businesses or shops should refrain from working on these days. Those who are in government employ should, on religious grounds, make an effort to be excused from work; all believers, whoever their employers, should do likewise. If the government, or other employers, refuse to grant them these days off, they are not required to forfeit their employment, but they should make every effort to have the independent status of the Faith recognised and their right to hold their own religious Holy Days acknowledged."[8] Work is not suspended on the two anniversaries relating to 'Abdu'l-Bahá, or on the nine days of Riḍván not specially celebrated.

Intercalary Days, entitled the Ayyám-i-Há, although neither Feasts nor Anniversaries, are days of hospitality, charity and the making of gifts, as well as preparation for the Fast. Bahá'ís do not observe such holidays as Christmas and New Year in relation to each other. Their festival gatherings are held instead at Naw-Rúz and on the Intercalary Days.

Laws of Prayer and Fasting

Each Manifestation of God has ordained laws of prayer and fasting. Shoghi Effendi says of these observances: "As regards fasting, it constitutes, together with the obligatory prayers, the two pillars that sustain the revealed Law of God. They act as stimulants to the soul, strengthen, revive, and purify it, and thus insure its steady development."[9]

The laws of prayer and fasting are sometimes symbolised in Holy Writings by the sun and the moon. At the beginning of each Dispensation, when these laws are changed, the sun and moon of the earlier Dispensation cease to shine.

Each Manifestation of God has enjoined prayer. Bahá'u'lláh's own general comments on praying have been mentioned earlier in this book.* He ordained also that three prayers should be obligatory, in the sense that one of them should be said each day by all Bahá'ís who have reached the age of 15, except 'those who are weak from illness or age.' Shoghi Effendi writes: "The daily obligatory prayers are three in number. The shortest one consists of a single verse which has to be recited once in every twenty-four hours at midday. The medium [prayer] has to be recited three times a day, in the morning, at noon and in the evening. The long prayer which is the most elaborate of the three has to be recited once in every twenty-four hours, and at any time one feels inclined to do so. The believer is entirely free to choose anyone of these three prayers, but is under the obligation of reciting either one of them, and in accordance with any specific directions with which they may be accompanied. These daily obligatory prayers, together with a few other specific ones, such as the Healing Prayer, the Tablet of Aḥmad, have been invested by Bahá'u'lláh with a special potency and significance, and should therefore be accepted as such and be recited by the believers with unquestioned faith and confidence, that through them they may enter into a much closer communion with God, and identify themselves more fully with His laws and precepts."[10]

---

* See pages 144-147.

Each Manifestation of God has also enjoined fasting for a set period according to set laws. Shoghi Effendi explains the significance of the Fast thus: "It is essentially a period of meditation and prayer, of spiritual recuperation, during which the believer must strive to make the necessary readjustments in his inner life, and to refresh and reinvigorate the spiritual forces latent in his soul. Its significance and purposes are, therefore, fundamentally spiritual in character. Fasting, is symbolic, and a reminder of abstinence from selfish and carnal desires."[11]

The Bahá'í fasting period is the month of 'Alá', which lasts from March 2nd to March 20th and is immediately followed by the Feast of Naw-Rúz. On each of the nineteen days of 'Alá', Bahá'ís fast from sunrise to sunset. People more than 70 or less than 15 years old, and people who are travelling, or ill, or pregnant, or suckling a child, are excused from fasting.

Conditions of Membership

Membership of the Bahá'í Community is open to all who believe in the Bahá'í Faith. A person who wishes to become a member applies to the local Spiritual Assembly in whatever way the local Assembly requests; if the Assembly is satisfied that he sincerely believes the tenets of the Bahá'í Faith, it accepts him. These tenets have been expressed by Shoghi Effendi as follows: "Full recognition of the station of the Forerunner, the Author, and the True Exemplar of the Bahá'í Cause, as set forth in 'Abdu'l-Bahá's Testament; unreserved acceptance of, and submission to, whatsoever has been revealed by their Pen loyal and steadfast adherence to every clause of our Beloved's sacred Will; and close association with the spirit as well as the form of the present-day Bahá'í administration throughout the world."[12]

On Labelling Oneself

Some people are surprised when they hear that the Bahá'í Community is an organisation with members; they say they do not want to label themselves. Bahá'ís sympathise with the dislike such people have of accepting wholly the teaching of any organisation founded by men. No set of ideas of human origin can be wholly right; anyone who thinks the Bahá'í Community is an organisation founded by men promulgating ideas of human origin should certainly not seek to join it.

But for anyone who believes the Bahá'í Faith to have been revealed by a Manifestation of God, the objection fades. Such a person knows that the Glory of God, Possessor of the Most Great Infallibility, revealed nothing but truth. If one believing this refrains from labellihg himself a Bahá'í, it is pride and attachment to the world that deters him; he is seeking the esteem of men at the cost of sincerity. The Messenger of God thought fit to label Himself and His followers Bahá'ís; by what right can a man who acknowledges this say he will not be labelled?

Membership of other Organisations

Membership of the Bahá'í Community is incompatible with membership of any organisation whose programme or policy cannot be wholly reconciled with the tenets of the Bahá'í Faith. Being a member of another religious sect is therefore inconsistent with being a Bahá'í. The outworn creeds, ceremonies, and institutions of non-Bahá'í ecclesiastical organisations are completely at variance with the fundamental assumptions of the Cause of Bahá'u'lláh.

For a Bahá'í to belong to an organisation, religious or secular, membership of which implied holding beliefs or approving aims out of harmony with the teachings of Bahá'u'lláh, would amount either to a denial of faith in those teachings or to open insincerity. Anyone applying for membership of the Bahá'í Community who is unwilling to relinquish membership of such an organisation proves by his unwillingness that he has not fully understood the Bahá'i teachings, and consequently he is unacceptable. For the same reason, a Bahá'í who insists on joining such an organisation after his Assembly has warned him not to is liable to be deprived of his voting right in the Bahá'í Community.[*]

There are very few organisations whose beliefs and aims are

_____

[*] See page 306.

wholly consistent with the Bahá'í teachings. Virtually all religious organisations, except perhaps a few concerned with comparative religion, require some kind of belief to which a Bahá'í cannot subscribe. Most other organisations also include among their objects or methods some to which a Bahá'í cannot commit himself. Association with such organisations is permissible, but to become a member of one would be a denial of faith.

The object of the Bahá'ís is to establish the Most Great Peace. Although there are many praiseworthy objects less comprehensive than this, supported by organisations that have the sympathy of all members of the Bahá'í Community, no Bahá'í can feel justified in sacrificing what is greater to what is less, in taking action that hinders the establishment of the Most Great Peace in order to achieve more quickly some minor goal.

The Bahá'í Faith and Politics

These arguments apply with still greater force to membership, or even active support, of political parties and programmes. No political party in any country has aims wholly consistent with the teachings of Bahá'u'lláh, nor can the good that might superficially appear to result from political support by Bahá'ís of some particular aim of some particular party outweigh the grave harm such support would do to the Cause of Bahá'u'lláh.

Should Bahá'ís dabble in politics, Bahá'í unity could not be preserved; support of one party would inevitably arouse the distrust and opposition of sympathisers of the others; political pressures might be brought to bear upon a Bahá'í Community because of the actions of Bahá'ís in another country; misunderstanding might even lead Bahá'ís to advocate opposing policies in the mistaken belief that they were furthering the aims of the Faith.

The Bahá'í Community is in no way concerned with politics; it is concerned with establishing the Most Great Peace. In their explanation of the moral and social principles of the Faith. Bahá'ís carefully avoid making comments that could be misconstrued as support for any political faction. At political elections they vote only if they are convinced that they can vote on the merit of an individual without identifying themselves with any party—a condition rarely fulfilled.

Nevertheless Bahá'ís are alive to the welfare of their country and to their sacred obligation to promote its best interests by methods consistent with the high standards of their Faith. Their aims are spiritual, not political, and will be achieved by the power of the Spirit and not by political agitation. Unless the power of the Holy Spirit confirms their efforts, the Bahá'ís will never be successful; if they attract this confirmation, no political power can stop them. The Bahá'ís have therefore no need to join political factions to achieve their ends.

Relations with the United Nations
Support of recognised international organisations like the United Nations is an entirely different matter. Bahá'ís are encouraged to work in close association with such organisations as are truly international and not vehicles for imposing the views of a particular group of nations on others. The Bahá'í International Community is accredited to the United Nations and has enjoyed consultative status with the Economic and Social Council (ECOSOC) since 1970. Other affiliations with U.N. bodies, such as U.N.I.C.E.F. (U.N. Childrens Fund) and U.N.E.P. (U.N. Environment Programme) have increased the number of opportunities for Bahá'ís to make known their interest in the goals of the United Nations Charter. Increasingly, the Bahá'í International Community has been able to explain that its concern for world peace, universal human rights and the full social and economic development of the peoples of the planet, is rooted firmly in the Bahá'í teachings and to demonstrate that the principles and laws now being practiced by Bahá'í communities around the globe offer a lasting solution to the world's problems.

This developing relationship has also enabled the Bahá'í world community as a whole to lend significant support to the work of the United Nations Agencies in many countries. Bahá'ís have made important contributions to such campaigns as International Decade for Women, Year of the Child, International Youth Year and more recently International Year of Peace. Such efforts to promote justice and secure the rights of others, particularly the rights of oppressed groups and minorities, have earned praise and respect from statesmen throughout the international community.

Bahá'ís have themselves often been the victims of persecution and oppression and successful appeals have been made by the Bahá'í world community to both the League of Nations and the United Nations to secure the application of their influence against, such extremes of injustice.

The appeal to the League of Nations was for the return of the House of Bahá'u'lláh in Baghdád, which had been seized by the Shí'ih Muslims of 'Iraq, then a Mandated Territory. The League urged that the property should be returned, but the 'Iraqi Government failed to implement the recommendations made by both the League Council and the Permanent Mandates Commission. Bahá'u'lláh had prophesied this House would be expropriated when He wrote:

> *"Grieve not, O House of God, if the veil of thy sanctity be rent asunder by the infidels. God hath, in the world of creation, adorned thee with the jewel of His remembrance. Such an ornament no man can, at any time, profane. Towards thee the eyes of Thy Lord shall, under all conditions, remain directed."*[13]

Persecution of Bahá'ís in Írán

The history of the Bahá'í Faith is punctuated with outbreaks of fanatical persecution of its followers, especially in the land of its birth, Írán. In 1955, the Bahá'í International Community appealed to the United Nations to intervene against the latest outbreak of persecutions in Írán. This appeal was sympathetically received both by the Secretariat and the member nations and international pressure gradually relieved the situation.

In 1979, the revolutionary regime in Írán initiated yet another full-scale persecution of the Bahá'í community. This latest pogrom developed into the most severe onslaught of this century against the Bahá'í Faith, its members, endowments, holy places and institutions. By April 1983 well over 100 Bahá'ís had been martyred. The wave of persecutions threatened to intensify overnight, swelling the number of deaths from hundreds to thousands. Government leaders talked of a 'final solution'. The desecration and confiscation of Bahá'í holy places and properties was combined with the systematic 'asset stripping' of the entire Bahá'í community. Bahá'ís were dismissed from their jobs, their children were expelled from school, many aged were deprived of their pensions or cast out from homes and hospitals. Homes and businesses were appropriated or looted, bank accounts seized and many Bahá'ís who had worked as Government officials were ordered to repay their entire salaries. Such crimes against property were matched with even greater crimes of violence against the Bahá'ís themselves. Men, women, children, even the elderly and infirm became victims of violence and cruelty. Prominent Bahá'ís were imprisoned, tortured and executed or simply 'disappeared'. Others were left open to the abuse of the mob with no protection offered from the law. Even previous generations of Bahá'ís became targets of hostility as Bahá'í cemeteries were desecrated and bulldozed. Almost overnight the Bahá'í community of Írán was outwardly deprived of five generations of external development. The anguish experienced can, in human terms, barely be estimated, but throughout their ordeal, the Bahá'ís of Írán have displayed courage and self-sacrifice of heroic proportions.

This demonstration of faith and fortitude has released tremendous spiritual energy which has galvanised the entire Bahá'í world and spurred them to even greater efforts in the proclamation and teaching of their Faith. To appreciate the providential outcome of this new persecution of the Íránian Bahá'ís for the growth of the Bahá'í Faith as a whole, one can do no better than study the observations Shoghi Effendi made on the pogrom of 1955, observations which seem even more apposite today:

"...this fresh ordeal that has, in pursuance of the mysterious dispensations of Providence, afflicted the Faith, at this unexpected hour, far from dealing a fatal

blow to its institutions or existence, should be regarded as a blessing in disguise, not a ... "calamity" but a "providence" of God...

"Whatever its outcome, this sudden commotion that has seized the Bahá'í world, that has revived the hopes and emboldened the host of the adversaries of the Faith intent on quenching its light and obliterating it from the face of the earth, has served as a trumpet call in the sounding of which the press of the world, the cries of its vociferous enemies, the public remonstrances of both men of good will and those in authority have joined, proclaiming far and wide its existence, publicizing its history, defending its verities, unveiling its truths, demonstrating the character of its institutions and advertising its aims and purposes."

Emancipation of the Faith

Gradually the Faith is achieving recognition as the independent world religion that it is. Failure to realise that it is more than sect of Islám was perhaps understandable in the days of 'Abdu'l-Bahá, before the Bahá'í Community had taken form, but in these days only ignorance or malice can hinder the realisation.

How can a Faith that recognises the Founders of all the great religions as Manifestations of God and accords the same status to its own Founder be considered a sect of any other religion? The highest Muslim ecclesiastical authorities in Egypt have themselves circulated a judgment of the Appellant Muslim Court that states unequivocally: "The Bahá'í Faith is a new religion, entirely independent, with beliefs, principles and laws of its own, which differ from, and are utterly in conflict with, the beliefs, principles and laws of Islám. No Bahá'í, therefore, can be regarded a Muslim or vice versa, even as no Buddhist, Brahmin, or Christian can be regarded a Muslim or vice versa."[14]

In 1929 the Palestine authorities accorded to the Bahá'í Community full powers to administer its own affairs, as a result of which certificates of marriage issued by the Bahá'ís in Israel are recognised as legal. Bahá'í Holy Places are exempted from tax, and branches in Israel of various National Assemblies are enabled to hold property as 'religious societies.' The Ministry of Religious Affairs of the State of Israel has established a separate Bahá'í Department to handle matters relating to the Bahá'í Faith.

Since 1929 the number of countries in which Bahá'í marriage certificates are recognised has slowly grown. The number of incorporated Bahá'í Assemblies has grown more rapidly. In most countries where a Bahá'í National Assembly exists it is incorporated in whatever way is customary for religious bodies in that country. Many Local Assemblies are also incorporated and thus able to hold property; the value of property held by Bahá'í Assemblies throughout the world runs into millions of pounds.

Although some time may pass before the whole world accords the Bahá'í Faith its rightful place as the youngest of the great religions, its prestige is mounting yearly. Gradually it is being recognised that a new religion has been born, whose institutions are founded upon rock, and whose spirit is fed by the water of life. As decades go by, it will become ever plainer that its progress is of a kind that could be achieved only by the Eternal Faith of God.

Opposition to the Faith

Before universal recognition of the Faith is achieved. Bahá'ís expect to meet much opposition. Bigoted members of those institutions, political or religious, that have ceased to be just and to transmit the Spirit of Eternal Life will become alarmed at the vitality of the Bahá'í Community and will rise against it.

"How great, how very great is the Cause! How very fierce the onslaught of all the peoples and kindreds of the earth. Ere long shall the clamour of the multitude throughout Africa, throughout America, the cry of the European and the Turk, the groaning of India and China, be heard from far and near. One and all, they shall arise with all their power to resist His Cause. Then

shall the knights of the Lord, assisted by His grace from
on high, strengthened by faith, aided by the power of
understanding, and reinforced by the legions of the
Covenant, arise and make manifest the truth of the
verse: "Behold the confusion that hath befallen the
tribes of the defeated."[16]

Bahá'ís are convinced that such attacks will be impotent to resist the advance of the Cause of God, whose motive power is the power of the Covenant. Rather they will release spiritual forces that will hasten its advance and speed the downfall of the institutions that attack it. Though all the peoples, nations, and religions of the world rise against the Cause of Bahá'u'lláh, they cannot change by one iota God's Plan for the ultimate triumph of His Cause.

Nor can those who from time to time shall seek to disturb the unity of the Cause from within succeed in hindering its growth. Of these Shoghi Effendi has said: "Viewed in the light of past experience, the inevitable result of such futile attempts however persistent and malicious they may be, is to contribute to a wider and deeper ecognition by believers and unbelievers alike of the distinguishing features of the Faith proclaimed by Bahá'u'lláh. These challenging criticisms, whether or not dictated by malice, cannot but serve to galvanise the souls of its ardent supporters, and to consolidate the ranks of its faithful promoters. They will purge the Faith from those pernicious elements whose continued association with the believers tends to discredit the fair name of the Cause, and to tarnish the purity of its spirit. We should welcome, therefore, not only the open attacks which its avowed enemies persistently launch against it, but should also view as a blessing in disguise every storm of mischief with which they who apostatise their faith or claim to be its faithful exponents assail it from time to time. Instead of undermining the Faith, such assaults, both from within and without, reinforce its foundation, and excite the intensity of its flame. Designed to becloud its radiance, they proclaim to all the world the exalted character of its precepts, the completeness of its unity, the uniqueness of its position, and the pervasiveness of its influence."[16]

No need to detail the failure of the various abortive efforts to undermine the Cause of God from within that have recurred since the time of Bahá'u'lláh. The Bahá'í Community stands firm and united, incontrovertible evidence that they failed. Even the defection of all surviving descendants of Bahá'u'lláh other than Shoghi Effendi caused no cleavage. The vast and fathomless ocean of the Covenant surged and cast ashore the accumulated foam of the Covenant-Breakers. So it will continue to cast out those who seek to disturb its unity in the future.

Means of Spreading the Faith

Like all great religions in their youth, the Bahá'í Faith is a missionary religion, that is, Bahá'ís seek to attract others to their Faith.

The teaching is organised by Spiritual Assemblies, usually through committees, but it is individuals who teach. Every Bahá'í considers he has an obligation to offer the treasure he has found, the Cause of God, to others; if they are interested, he is eager to tell them more; if they are not interested, he leaves them to go their own way.

In an area where there is a Bahá'í Local Spiritual Assembly, meetings and publicity are arranged by the Assembly. To it, individual Bahá'ís refer any suggestion they may have for spreading the Faith that involves, either directly or indirectly, more than their own personal teaching activity.

Teaching in areas where there is no Local Assembly is organised by the National Assembly through national and regional teaching committees, which also arrange interchange of teachers between areas and help weak local communities. National Assemblies, through appropriate committees, are responsible for publication of Bahá'í literature.

The Faith is spread to new areas by concerted effort. Usually one or more Bahá'ís settle in the area to pioneer the Faith, supported by visits from teachers resident in other areas and assisted by the National Assembly in whatever way is suitable. Sometimes an existing Community will form a new one by extending its teaching to a nearby area after consultation with the appropriate national committee. There have even been instances of Communities being formed by correspondence alone.

All this activity requires great zeal on the part of the Bahá'ís. To pioneer to a new area may involve great sacrifice; much time and much money is needed to promote and execute organised teaching. Except for the work of a very few paid administrative workers, everything is done without payment by people engaged in daily activities similar to those of the rest of mankind; that they are willing to give so much time and money to teaching the Bahá'í Faith is another proof of its divine origin. Not every one can contribute equally, either time, or money, or service, but participation in Bahá'í activity to whatever extent is possible is regarded by every true Bahá'í as his most important action; for it is his contribution to the Cause of God, than which no cause can be greater. To have the opportunity to make such a contribution is regarded by Bahá'í as a great privilege.

Teaching the Cause of God
The source of their zeal is the Word of Bahá'u'lláh. Among the many passages in His Writings about teaching the Cause of God, the following is typical:

> *"Gird up the loins of thine endeavour, that haply thou mayest guide thy neighbour to the law of God, the Most Merciful, such an act, verily, excelleth all other acts in the sight of God, the All-Possessing, the Most High. Such must be thy steadfastness in the Cause of God, that no earthly thing whatsoever will have the power to deter thee from thy duty. Though the powers of earth be leagued against thee, though all men dispute with thee, thou must remain unshaken.*
>
> *Be unrestrained as the wind, while carrying the Message of Him Who hath caused the Dawn of Divine Guidance to break.Consider how the wind, faithful to that which God hath ordained, bloweth upon all the regions of the*

earth, be they inhabited or desolate. Neither the sight of desolation, nor the evidences of prosperity, can either pain or please it. It bloweth in every direction, as bidden by its Creator. So should be every one that claimeth to be it lover of the one true God. It behoveth him to fix his gaze upon the fundamentals of His Faith, and to labour diligently for its propagation. Wholly for the sake of God he should proclaim His Message, and with that same spirit accept whatever response his words may evoke in his hearer. He who shall accept and believe, shall receive his reward; and he who shall turn away, shall receive none other than his own punishment."[17]

'Abdu'l-Bahá in His Will tells the believers:

"Of all the gifts of God the greatest is the gift of Teaching. It draweth unto us the Grace of God and is our first obligation. Of such a gift how can we deprive ourselves? Nay our lives, our goods, our comforts, our rest, we offer them all as a sacrifice for the Abhá Beauty and teach the Cause of God."[18]

Qualifications of a Bahá'í Teacher

There is but one essential qualification for a teacher of the Bahá'í Faith—an upright and praiseworthy character. Bahá'u'lláh commands:

"Whoso ariseth among you to teach the Cause of His Lord, let him, before all else, teach his own self, that his speech may attract the hearts of them that hear him. Unless he teacheth his own self, the words of his mouth will not influence the heart of the seeker. Take heed, O people, lest ye be of them that give good counsel to others but forget to follow it themselves. The words of such as these, and beyond the words the realities of all things, and beyond these realities the angels that are

nigh unto God, bring against them the accusation of falsehood.

Should such a man ever succeed in influencing anyone, this success should be attributed not to him, but rather to the influence of the words of God, as decreed by, Him Who is the Almighty, the All-Wise. In the sight of God he is regarded as a lamp that imparteth its light, and yet is all the while being consumed within itself."[18]

Shoghi Effendi has advised those especially concerned with teaching, either as teachers or administrators, that they must "thoroughly familiarise themselves with the various aspects of the history and teachings of their Faith. In their efforts to achieve this purpose they must study for themselves, conscientiously and painstakingly, the literature of their Faith, delve into its teachings, assimilate its laws and principles, ponder its admonitions, tenets and purposes, commit to memory certain of its exhortations and prayers, master the essentials of its administration, and keep abreast of its current affairs and latest developments."[20] He also urges them to study Islám, the Qur'án, and 'those institutions and circumstances that are directly connected with the origin and birth of their Faith, with the station claimed by its Forerunner, and with the laws revealed by its Author.'

Making Teaching Effective

Bahá'u'lláh's instructions to teachers are clear as pure water in a deep well:

"O wayfarer in the path of God! Take thou thy portion of the ocean of His grace, and deprive not thyself of the things that lie hidden in its depths...With the hands of renunciation draw forth from its life-giving waters, and sprinkle therewith all created things, that they may be cleansed from all man-made limitations and may approach the mighty seat of God, this hallowed and resplendent spot.

Be not grieved if thou performest it thyself alone. Let God be all sufficient for thee. Commune intimately with His Spirit, and be thou of the thankful. Proclaim the Cause of Thy Lord unto all who are in the heavens and on the earth. Should any man respond to thy call, lay bare before him the pearls of the wisdom of the Lord, thy God, which His Spirit hath sent down unto thee, and be thou of them that truly believe. And should anyone reject thy offer, turn thou away from him, and put thy trust and confidence in the Lord, thy God, the Lord of all worlds. By the righteousness of God! Whoso openeth his lips in this Day and maketh mention of the name of his Lord, the hosts of Divine inspiration shall descend upon him from the heaven of My name, the All-Knowing, the All-Wise. On him shall also descend the Concourse on High, each bearing aloft a chalice of pure light. Thus hath it been foreordained in the realm of God's Revelation, by the behest of Him Who is the All-Glorious, the Most Powerful."[21]

These heavenly hosts, rather than the Bahá'ís, spread the Bahá'í Faith; the Bahá'ís are merely the instruments through which the divine fragrances are diffused. Hence Bahá'u'lláh says:

"Should any man, in this Day, arise and, with absolute detachment from all that is in the heavens and all that is on the earth, set his affections on Him Who is the Day Spring of God's holy Revelation, he will, verily, be empowered to subdue all created things, through the potency of one of the Names of the Lord, his God, the All-Knowing, the All-Wise. Know thou of a certainty that the Day Star of Truth hath, in this Day, shed upon the world a radiance, the like of which bygone ages have never witnessed. Let the light of His glory. O people, shine upon you, and be not of the negligent."[22]

Pioneering in Foreign Lands

To leave one's homeland to teach the Faith in a foreign country has especial merit. Bahá'u'lláh says of people who do this:

"They that have foresaken their country for the purpose

of teaching our Cause—these shall the Faithful Spirit strengthen through its power. A company of Our chosen angels shall go forth with them, as bidden by Him Who is the Almighty, the All-Wise. How great the blessedness that awaiteth him that hath attained the honour of serving the Almighty. By my life! No act, however great, can compare with it, except such as have been ordained by God, the All-Powerful, the Most Mighty. Such a service is, indeed, the prince of all goodly deeds, and the ornament of every goodly act. Thus hath it been ordained by Him Who is the Sovereign Revealer, the Ancient of Days.

Whoso ariseth to teach our Cause must needs detach himself from all earthly things, and regard, at all times, the triumph of our Faith as his supreme objective. This hath, verily, been decreed in the Guarded Tablet. And when he determineth to leave his home, for the sake of the Cause of his Lord, let him put his whole trust in God, as the best provision for his journey, and array himself with the robe of virtue. Thus hath it been decreed by God, the Almighty, the All-Praised.

If he be kindled with the fire of His love, if he forgoeth all created things, the words he uttereth shall set on fire them that hear him. Verily, thy Lord is the Omniscient, the All-Informed. Happy is the man that hath heard Our voice, and answered Our call. He, in truth, is of them that shall be brought nigh unto Us. "[23]

The Tablets of the Divine Plan

All efforts to spread the Bahá'í Faith are governed by principles revealed in a series of Tablets, known as the Tablets of the Divine Plan, which 'Abdu'l-Bahá revealed for the American believers in 1916-17. Bahá'ís believe the revelation of these to have released spiritual forces that take effect through detailed Plans adopted from time to time to guide and stimulate the growth of the Faith in all parts of the world.

These Plans demonstrate the power of the Bahá'í Administrative Order to combine in harmonious unity, multitudinous individual efforts to spread the Faith; no other system has ever inspired and harmonised so well the efforts of so varied a collection of people scattered over so wide an area. The potent forces concealed within the Cause of God are demonstrated in many ways by the Bahá'í Teaching Plans. Over and overagain Bahá'ís prosecuting them report experiences that can be satisfactorily explained only by reference to spiritual forces beyond human comprehension.

Recounting such experiences does not adequately convey the impression they make on the people who experience them. The neophyte who finds himself imparting wisdom he did not know he possessed, the administrator who witnesses an Assembly reach a satisfactory solution to an apparently insoluble problem, the veteran pioneer who feels himself led to the one man who seems equipped beyond all others to promote the Faith in his area—these and countless others participating in Bahá'í Teaching Plans encounter proof, incontrovertible for them, that, they are taking part in God's own Great Plan for the spread of His Cause. Teaching, 'Abdu'l-Bahá tells us, 'draweth unto us the Grace of God.' Those who teach the Bahá'í Faith in accordance with the Divine Plan of 'Abdu'l-Bahá know from personal experience how true this statement is.

The Divine Plan has as its object establishing the Most Great Peace, the Kingdom of God on earth; it will not be completed quickly. Decades and centuries must pass before the Most Great Peace is here. During these centuries, the Bahá'ís will be working to speed the day when mankind acknowledges what God has spread abroad for its edification, organisation, and salvation. As yet the Bahá'í Community is quite small; through the execution of the Divine Plan it will grow continuously in size and importance, scope and influence. It will traverse many phases; from obscurity, it will pass through, persecution to emancipation and recognition. Then it will be adopted by a number of states as their state religion, and finally the peoples of the world will see that only by following the Teaching of Bahá'u'lláh can their age-long dreams of a heavenly kingdom be realised on earth. Final victory may lie in the far, far distant future, but only in the light of that future glory can the Teaching Plans the Bahá'ís are now executing be appreciated at their true worth as part of a great Divine Plan predestined to culminate in the establishment of the Most Great Peace.

CHAPTER XVII

The Greatness of This Day

The way to the Most Great Peace lies through suffering. Without suffering, little is achieved in this world and nothing is created. The peoples of the earth have turned aside from the Messenger of God; wrapped in veils of idle fancy and hidden in the depths of worldly desire, they have failed to recognise the One for Whose coming they have prayed for hundreds, even thousands of years. Only suffering can open hearts thus shut against the bounties of the Lord.

All men share to some degree the common blindness. Each may feel himself well-meaning and blameless, but he cannot avoid the influence of the standards of his time. The spirit of the Christian martyrs, of the companions of the Prophet, is beyond the reach of most men in our day.

This is the spirit that inspires the members of the Bahá'í Community. Martyrdom seems to them a path to grace that some may still tread, even though the Heroic Age of the Faith with its twenty thousand martyrs is gone. Enduring hardship to teach the Cause of God, sacrificing worldly pleasures to finance it, renouncing rest and ease to administer its affairs, they diffuse the same divine fragrance as was diffused by the saints of old.

The foundation of the World Order of Bahá'u'lláh is now being laid. Although the helpers are still, few and the work very great, Bahá'ís are confident of success because the motive power that is irresistibly establishing the new world order comes from God, not man. His is the ultimate Plan that will ensure the triumph of His Cause. Even 'Abdu'l-Bahá's Divine Plan is subordinate to the Plan of God, which works through Bahá'í and non-Bahá'í alike. All that happens in the world is subject to its influence, the influence of the Covenant of God. The acceleration of scientific discovery, the unrest of the peoples of the earth, the products of genius, and the blunders of politics all form part of a gigantic, world-embracing panorama that portrays the Will of God. Certain elements in this panorama were singled out by Bahá'u'lláh for inclusion in His Tablets to the kings and the leaders of religion;* other elements can be dimly distinguished in the bright light of His teachings.

Among the Writings of Bahá'u'lláh appear references to a great calamity that the world must experience, from which it will emerge purified. A few of these references, taken from a selection made by Shoghi Effendi, follow:

> "Great, great is the Cause! The hour is approaching when the most great convulsion will have appeared. I swear by Him Who is the Truth! It shall cause separation to afflict everyone, even those who circle around Me.' 'O ye that are bereft of understanding! A severe trial pursueth you, and will suddenly overtake you. Bestir yourselves, that haply it may pass and inflict no harm upon you.' 'O ye peoples of the world! Know, verily, that an unforeseen calamity is following you, and that grievous retribution awaiteth you. Think not the deeds ye have committed have been blotted from My sight.' 'Grieve thou not over those that have busied themselves with the things of this world, and have forgotten the remembrance of God, the Most Great. By Him Who is the Eternal Truth! The day is approaching when the wrathful anger of the Almighty will have taken hold of them. He, verily, is the Omnipotent, the All-Subduing, the Most Powerful. He shall cleanse the earth from the defilement of their corruption, and shall give it for an heritage unto such of His servants as are nigh unto Him."[1]

Bahá'ís expect this calamity to produce a great spiritual change in mankind, whose destined pangs will be the pangs of birth as well

---

* See Chapter III.

as death; the old order is dying, but a new order is being born. Bahá'u'lláh has proclaimed:

"The whole earth is now in a state of pregnancy. The day is approaching when it will have yielded its noblest fruits, when from it will have sprung forth the loftiest trees, the most enchanting blossoms, the most heavenly "blessings. Immeasurably exalted is the breeze that wafteth from the garment of thy Lord, the Glorified! For lo, it hath breathed its fragrance and made all things new! Well is it with them that comprehend."[2]

And 'Abdu'l-Bahá explained:

"The Call of God, when raised, breathed a new life into the body of mankind, and infused a new spirit into the whole creation. It is for this reason that the world hath been moved to its depths, and the hearts and consciences of men been quickened. Erelong the evidences of this regeneration will be revealed, and the fast asleep will be awakened."[3]

The Bahá'í World Civilisation

The process of establishing, the new world order will be a gradual one. First the Lesser Peace will come, when, the nations enforce the general principles of Bahá'u'lláh without as yet realising their source. While this is being created and consolidated, the local, national, and international institutions of the Bahá'í Administrative Order will be evolving. In the fullness of time, during the Golden Age of the Faith, both Lesser Peace and Bahá'í Administrative Order will attain their final consummation in the Most Great Peace when the peoples and governments of the world call into being the World Order of Bahá'u'lláh. Thus will the Kingdom, of God be established on earth, as Jesus prophesied.

But this will not end the story. Bahá'u'lláh affirms:

"All men have been created to carry forward an ever-advancing civilisation."[4]

The Most Great Peace will usher in a Bahá'í civilisation inspired by the spirit flowing through the institutions of the World Order of Bahá'u'lláh, that is, through the very institutions whose embryos are now developing as part of the Bahá'í Administrative Order. This civilisation, which Shoghi Effendi has described as "divinely inspired, unique in its features, world, embracing in its scope, and fundamentally spiritual in its character,"[5] will continue, to grow and flower through many future Dispensations, for the influence of Bahá'u'lláh will not end when His Dispensation ends. That is why this Day of God is so very, very great. His is no ordinary Dispensation, but one which lies at a crucial stage in the history of mankind. All previous Revelations prepare for this Day of unity; all subsequent Revelations for ages and cycles to come will lie in its shadow and promote the world civilisation to which the World Order of Bahá'u'lláh will give rise.

The Greatness of the Bahá'í Cycle

Some of the sayings of Bahá'u'lláh about the greatness of this Day have already been quoted,* but these do not give the full measure of its greatness. He has said:

"I testify before God to the greatness, the inconceivable greatness of this Revelation. Again and again have We in most of our Tablets borne witness to this truth, that mankind may be roused from its heedlessness."[6]

'Abdu'l-Bahá comments:

"The mere contemplation of the Dispensation inaugurated by the Blessed Beauty would have sufficed to overwhelm the saints of bygone ages—saints who longed to partake for one moment of its great glory."[7]

No wonder Bahá'u'lláh exclaims:

"The world of being shineth in this Day with the resplendency of this Divine Revelation. All created

* See pages 47-50 and 248-249

things extol its saving grace and sing its praises. The universe is wrapt in an ecstasy of joy and gladness. The Scriptures of past Dispensations celebrate the great jubilee that must needs greet this most great Day of God. Well is it with him that hath lived to see this Day and hath recognised its station."[8]

Something of the true greatness of the Revelation of Bahá'u'lláh can be gleaned from the following extracts from a Tablet by 'Abdu'l-Bahá:

"Thou hast written that in the sacred books of the followers of Zoroaster it is written that in the latter days, in three separate Dispensations, the sun must needs be brought to a standstill. In the first Dispensation, it is predicted, the sun will remain motionless for ten days; in the second for twice that time; in the third for no less than one whole month. The interpretation of this prophecy is this: the first Dispensation to which it refers is the Muḥammadan Dispensation during which the Sun of Truth stood still for ten days. Each day is reckoned as one century. The Muḥammadan Dispensation must have, therefore, lasted no less than one thousand years, which is precisely the period that has elapsed from the setting of the Star of the Imámate to the advent of the Dispensation proclaimed by the Báb. The second Dispensation referred to in this prophecy is the one inaugurated by the Báb Himself, which began in the year 1260 A.H. and was brought to a close in the year 1280 A.H. As to the third Dispensation—the Revelation proclaimed by Bahá'u'lláh—inasmuch as the Sun of Truth when attaining that station shineth in the plenitude of its meridian splendour its duration has been fixed for a period of one whole month, which is the maximum*

---

* i.e. of the Muslim Calendar, which is reckoned from. the Hegira, the flight of Muḥammad from Mecca to Medina.

time taken by the sun to pass through a sign of the Zodiac. From this thou canst imagine the magnitude of the Bahá'í cycle—a cycle that must extend over a period of at least five hundred thousand years."[9]

Universal Cycles

The key to this last extraordinary statement is given in another explanation made by 'Abdu'l-Bahá, Who said:

"A universal cycle in the world of existence signifies a long duration of time, and innumerable and incalculable periods and epochs. In such a cycle the Manifestations appear with splendour in the realm of the visible, until a great and universal Manifestation makes the world the centre of His radiance. His appearance causes the world to attain to maturity, and the extension of His cycle is very great. Afterwards other Manifestations will arise under His shadow, who according to the needs of the time will renew certain commandments relating to material questions and affairs, while remaining under His shadow. We are in the, cycle which began with Adam, and its Universal Manifestation is Bahá'u'lláh."[10]

Of the cycle before the present one no trace or record remains; we know nothing of the life, thoughts, feelings of the men of twenty thousand years ago. Because no complicated tools or ruins of imposing buildings have been found, we rate the men of that time as much inferior to ourselves; but we cannot be sure even of this. Our supposedly primitive ancestors might have possessed a spiritual life far superior to our own that was not allied to so great a control over the material environment. Such things are beyond our knowledge, and speculation is unprofitable. That there is a mystery about these early men is strongly suggested by this comment of 'Abdu'l-Bahá:

"Each of the Divine Manifestations has... a cycle, and

*during the cycle His laws and commandments prevail
and are performed. When His cycle is completed by the
appearance of a new Manifestation, a new cycle begins.
In this way cycles begin, end, and are renewed, until a
universal cycle is completed in the world, when
important events and great occurrences will take place
which entirely efface every trace and every record of
the past; then a new universal cycle begins in the world,
for this universe has no beginning."*[11]

Archaeology leaves no doubt that some six thousand years ago
man entered a new phase of his existence. Bahá'ís believe this to
be a sign that a new universal cycle had begun, a cycle that has
been marked by the development of the arts and sciences of
civilisation. When asked why no records are to be found concerning
the Prophets Who preceded Adam or the kings who lived in their
days, Bahá'u'lláh replied:

*"Know thou that the absence of any reference to them
is no proof that they did not actually exist. That no
records concerning them are now available should be
attributed to their extreme remoteness, as well as to the
vast changes which the earth hath undergone since their
time.*

*Moreover such forms and modes of writing as are now
current amongst men were unknown to the generations
that were before Adam. There was even a time when
men were wholly ignorant of the art of writing, and
had adopted a system entirely different from the one
they now use. For a proper exposition of this an
elaborate explanation would be required.*

*Consider the differences that have arisen since the days
of Adam. The diverse and widely known languages now
spoken by the peoples of the world were originally
unknown, as were the varied rules and customs*

prevailing amongst them. The people of those times spoke a language different from those now known. Diversities of language arose in a later age...

Witness, therefore, how numerous and far-reaching have been the changes in language, speech, and writing since the days of Adam. How much greater must have been the changes before Him!" [12]

Bahá'u'lláh as Universal Manifestation

These explanations enable us to see, very dimly and indistinctly, the relation of Bahá'u'lláh to former Manifestations of God. Before Adam, there were other Universal Cycles of which all record has been lost. They will have followed the same pattern as the present one: some calamity or series of calamities will have erased all trace of the previous cycle; a Manifestation of God will then have come to inaugurate a new cycle and set the spirit of men on a new track; other Manifestations of God will have succeeded Him and man will have progressed spiritually under their guidance; the cycle will eventually have culminated in the appearance of a Universal Manifestation of God in whose shadow all following Manifestations appeared until the cycle was completed; then a great convulsion will have erased all traces of it and a new universal cycle will have begun, to repeat the theme once more.

These earlier cycles may have appeared superficially to be very different from our own. Material civilisation, means of communication, even the physical characteristics of man were quite other than ours. But the inner spiritual development in each universal cycle will have followed a similar pattern, just as the cycle of each Manifestation of God follows a similar pattern in spite of superficial differences.

What happened to conclude the universal cycle before our own we cannot know; perhaps it ended in the climatic changes following an ice age, perhaps in calamities brought about by the heedlessness of man, or perhaps a major change in physical conditions resulted, in some way we do not understand, from man's spiritual degradation.

Nor can we know how the new cycle started, nor whether Adam came before, during, or after these final calamities. All we know is that He inaugurated the universal cycle in which we now live, of which the Universal Manifestation is Bahá'u'lláh. The early religious history of this cycle has come down to us scrappily and in a confused way in the Book of Genesis, which presents spiritual truths allegorically in the form of ancient legends. The Qur'án also deals allegorically with those times.

From the Bible, the Gospel, and the Qur'án it can be seen that within the universal cycle is a smaller prophetic cycle that began with Adam and ended with the Báb, during which all Manifestations of God have prophesied the coming of the Day of the Universal Manifestation, Bahá'u'lláh. Their promise has conveyed the Eternal Covenant of God, which is now being fulfilled. Shoghi Effendi says of this prophetic cycle 'The Faith of Bahá'u'lláh should indeed be regarded, if we wish to be faithful to the tremendous implications of its message, as the culmination of a cycle, the final stage in a series of successive, of preliminary and progressive revelations. These, beginning with Adam and ending with the Báb, have paved the way and anticipated with an ever-increasing emphasis the advent of that Day of Days in which He Who is the Promise of All Ages should be made manifest."[13]

Nevertheless, Bahá'ís always bear in mind that no distinction may be made between the Manifestations of God.

> *"Nay, all the Prophets of God, His well-favoured, His holy and chosen Messengers are, without exception, the bearers of His names and the embodiments of His attributes. They only differ in the intensity of their revelation, and the comparative potency of their light."[14]*

The stage of development mankind has reached, not the superiority of Bahá'u'lláh's person, is the cause of the unsurpassed intensity of His Revelation.

After the prophetic cycle comes the cycle or cycles of fulfilment, during which world civilisation will come into being and develop. During the Dispensation of Bahá'u'lláh, before the appearance of the next Manifestation of God. His New World Order will be formed, whose emergence is the essential prerequisite for the growth of the new civilisation. For aeons thereafter, during the Dispensations of countless Manifestations of God, that civilisation will grow to maturity. We are as yet quite incapable of visualising the development that will take place in mankind during these ages over a period whose duration will far exceed the time that has elapsed since Adam; still less are we capable of visualising the more distant developments that will take place after world civilisation has reached its maturity. Yet all the Manifestations of God during this seemingly endless period will come in the shadow of Bahá'u'lláh. On the building of the World Order of Bahá'u'lláh in this age the future civilisation in its manifest splendour will depend. This age is the culmination of the cycle; it stands associated with a Revelation that Bahá'u'lláh has said is *"unparalleled in the annals of the past, nor will future ages witness its like."*[15] Such is its sublime glory; to live in this age is the immeasurable bounty bestowed upon every human being now alive. In the words of 'Abdu'l-Bahá:

> *"Centuries, nay ages, must pass away ere the Day-Star of Truth shineth again in its mid-summer splendour, or appeareth once more in the radiance of its vernal. How thankful must we be for having been made in this Day the recipients of so overwhelming a favour! Would that we had ten thousand lives that we might lay them down in thanksgiving for so rare a privilege, so high an attainment, so priceless a bounty."*[16]

POSTSCRIPT ON

The Next Manifestation
of God

Many centuries will elapse before another Manifestation of God comes to the earth. Lest any man should be tempted to claim a Revelation from God before the Bahá'í World Order is established Bahá'u'lláh issued the following clear warning:

> *"Whoso layeth claim to a Revelation direct from God, ere the expiration of a full thousand years, such a man is assuredly a lying impostor. We pray God that he may graciously assist him to retract and repudiate such a claim. Should he repent, God will, no doubt, forgive him. If, however, he persisteth in his error, God will, assuredly, send down one who will deal mercilessly with him. Terrible, indeed, is God in punishing! Whosoever interpreteth this verse otherwise than its obvious meaning is deprived of the Spirit of God and of His mercy which encompasseth all created things. Fear God, and follow not your idle fancies. Nay, rather follow the bidding of your Lord, the Almighty, the All-Wise."* [1]

Only after a thousand years will such a claim be worthy of consideration. Then the people of the world must be watchful, for at any time God might manifest Himself again.

As each previous Manifestation of God scattered through His Teachings indications and warnings about the condions that would obtain at the coming of the Manifestation Who would succeed Him, so also has Bahá'u'lláh. Shoghi Effendi draws attention to this clear statement:

> *"I am not apprehensive for My own self. My fears are*

*for Him Who will be sent down unto you after Me—
Him Who will be invested with great sovereignty and
mighty dominion.*"[2]

One of the most beautiful passages in all the Writings of
Bahá'u'lláh seems to refer to the conditions of that Day:

*"Step out of Thy holy chamber, O Maid of Heaven,
inmate of the Exalted Paradise! Drape thyself in
whatever manner pleaseth Thee in the silken Vesture of
Immortality, and put on, in the name of the All-Glorious,
the broidered Robe of Light. Hear the sweet, the
wondrous accent of the Voice that cometh from the
Throne of Thy Lord, the Inaccessible, the Most High.
Unveil Thy face, and manifest the beauty of the black-
eyed Damsel, and suffer not the servants of God to be
deprived of the light of Thy shining countenance. Grieve
not if Thou hearest the sighs of the dwellers of the earth,
or the voice of the lamentations of the denizens of
heaven. Leave them to perish on the dust of extinction.
Let them be reduced to nothingness, inasmuch as the
flame of hatred hath been kindled within their breasts.
Intone, then, before the face of the peoples of earth
and heaven, and in a most melodious voice, the anthem
of praise, for a remembrance of Him Who is the King
of names and attributes of God. Thus have We decreed
Thy destiny. Well able are We to achieve Our purpose.*

*Beware that Thou divest not Thyself, Thou Who art the
Essence of Purity, of Thy robe of effulgent glory. Nay,
enrich Thyself increasingly, in the kingdom of creation
with the incorruptible vestures of Thy God, that the
beauteous image of the Almighty may be reflected
through Thee in all created things and the grace of Thy
Lord be infused in the plenitude of its power into the
entire creation.*

If Thou smellest from anyone the smell of the love of

Thy Lord, offer up Thyself for him, for We have created Thee to this end, and have covenanted with Thee, from time immemoial, and in the presence of the congregation of Our well-favoured ones, for this very purpose. Be not impatient if the blind in heart hurl, down the shaft of their idle fancies upon Thee. Leave them to themselves, for they follow the promptings of the evil ones.

Cry out before the gaze of the dwellers of heaven and earth: I am the Maid of Heaven, the Offspring begotten by the Spirit of Bahá. My habitation is the Mansion of His Name, the All-Glorious. Before the Concourse on high I was adorned with the ornament of His names. I was wrapt within the veil of an inviolable security, and lay hidden from the eyes of men. Methinks that I heard a Voice of divine and incomparable sweetness, proceeding from the right hand of the God of Mercy, and lo, the whole Paradise stirred and trembled before Me in its longing to hear its accents, and gaze on the beauty of Him that uttered them. Thus have We revealed in this luminous Tablet, in the sweetest of languages, the verses which the Tongue of Eternity was moved to utter in the Qayyumu'l-Asma'*."[3]

We cannot understand, and it would not be profitable for us to attempt to understand, all that is implied by this statement. When the next Manifestation of God comes. He will no doubt Himself explain the significance of such passages; they will provide the pure in heart with evidence that the Maid of Heaven has come; but speculation now about their significance would only hasten the errors of interpretation the blind in heart will foster, and thus add force to the idle fancies they hurl down on the Messenger of God.

---

* See pages 223-224.

List of References

In this list, U.S.A. means a book published by the Bahá'í Publishing Trust of the United States of America: U.K. means a book published by the Bahá'í Publishing Trust of the United Kingdom. Certain books are published in various editions; where possible reference has been made to chapters, verses, and sections of these, enabling the passage to be located without difficulty in any edition. Roman numerals have been used for such references and arabic numerals for references to pages of particular editions. (C) means that the book is a compilation of Writings of some or all of the Central Figures of the Bahá'í Faith or of Shoghi Effendi.

1. BAHÁ'Í BOOKS REFERRED TO

Abbreviations	*Full Title*
A.D.J.	*Advent of Divine Justice,* by Shoghi Effendi: Wilmette: Bahá'í Publishing Trust, 1974
B.B.R.	The *Bábí and Bahá'í Religions,* 1844-1944, compiled by Moojah Momen, Oxford, George Ronald, 1981
B.N.E.	*Bahá'u'lláh and the New Era,* By J. E. Esslemont, London, Bahá'í Publishing Trust, 1974
B.P.	*Bahá'í Prayers,* London, Bahá'í Publishing Trust, 1975
B.R.	*Bahá'í Revelation,* London Bahá'í Publishing Trust, 1955
B.W.F.	*Bahá'í World faith,* Wilmette, Bahá'í Publishing Trust, 1976
C.B.	*The Covenant of Bahá'u'lláh,* London, Bahá'í Publishing Trust, 1963
C.H.	*The Chosen Highway,* by Lady Blomfield, Wilmette, Bahá'í Publishing Trust, 1975
D.	*The Dawnbreakers,* by Nabíl-i-A'zam: UK 1953 Edward Granville Browne and the Bahá'í Faith, by H. M. Balyuzi, Oxford, George Ronald, 1980
E.S.W.	*Epistle to the Son of the Wolf,* by Bahá'u'lláh, translated by Shoghi Effendi, Wilmette, Bahá'í Publishing Trust, 1979
G.	*Gleanings from the Writings of Bahá'u'lláh,* translated by Shoghi Effendi, London, Bahá'í Publishing Trust,

LIST OF REFERENCES

	rev. ed. 1978
G.P.B.	*God Passes By*, by Shoghi Effendi, Wilmette, Bahá'í Publishing Trust, 1979
H.W.	*The Hidden Words of Bahá'u'lláh*, translated by Shoghi Effendi, London, Bahá'í Publishing Trust, 1975
K.I.	*The Kitáb-i-Íqán: The Book of Certitude*, revealed by Bahá'u'lláh, translated by Shoghi Effendi, London, Bahá'í Publishing Trust, 1982
M.F.	*Memorials of the Faithful*, by 'Abd'ul-Bahá, translated by Marzieh Gail, Wilmette, Bahá'í Publishing Trust, 1975
P.B.	*The Proclamation of Bahá'u'lláh* to the Kings and Leaders of the World, Haifa, Bahá'í World Centre, 1967
P.B.A.	*Principles of Bahá'í Administration*: a compilation, London, Bahá'í Publishing Trust, 4th ed. 1976
P.D.C.	*The Promised Day is Come*, by Shoghi Effendi, Wilmette, Bahá'í Publishing Committee, 1941
P.F.	*Portals to Freedom*, by Howard Colby Ives, Oxford, George Ronald, 1943
P.M.	*Prayers and Meditations*, by Bahá'u'lláh, London, Bahá'í Publishing Trust, 1975
P.T.	*Paris Talks*, by 'Abdu'l-Bahá, London, Bahá'í Publishing Trust, 11th ed.1972
P.U.P.	*The Promulgation of Universal Peace*, by 'Abdu'l-Bahá, Wilmette, Bahá'í Publishing Trust, 2nd ed. 1982
S.A.Q.	*Some Answered Questions*, by 'Abdu'l-Bahá, collected and translated by Laura Clifford Barney, London, Bahá'í Publishing Trust, 1971
S.C.K.A.	*A Synopsis and Codification of the Laws and Ordinances of the Kitáb-i-Aqdas*, Haifa, Bahá'í World Centre, 1973
S.D.C.	*The Secret of Divine Civilization*, by 'Abdu'l-Bahá, Wilmette, Bahá'í Publishing Trust, 1979
S.V.	*The "Seven Valleys and the Four Valleys*, by Bahá'u'lláh, Wilmette, Bahá'í Publishing Trust, 1975
S.W.	*Star of the West*, Chicago, reprinted by George Ronald, Oxford, 1978, in eight volumes
S.W.A.B.	*Selections from the Writings of 'Abdu'l-Bahá*, Haifa, Bahá'í World Centre, 1978
S.W.B.	*Selections from the Writings of the Báb*, Haifa, Bahá'í World Centre, 1978
T.B.	*Tablets of Bahá'u'lláh, revealed after the Kitáb-i-Aqdas*, Haifa, Bahá'í World Centre, 1978

T.D.P.	*Tablets of the Divine Plan*, by 'Abdu'l-Bahá, Wilmette, Bahá'í Publishing Trust, 1977
T.F.	'Tablet from 'Abdu'l-Bahá to August Forel', in *For the Good of Mankind*, by John Paul Vader, Oxford, George Ronald, 1984, pp.70-80
T.H.	'Tablet to the Hague', by 'Abdu'l-Bahá, in *Bahá'í Revelation*, London, Bahá'í Publishing Trust, 1955
W.O.B.	*World Order of Bahá'u'lláh*, by Shoghi Effendi, Wilmette, Bahá'í Publishing Trust, 1969
W.T.	*Will and Testament of 'Abdu'l-Bahá*, Wilmette, Bahá'í Publishing Trust, 1971

2. BOOKS OF OR ABOUT OTHER RELIGIONS

The Bible, Authorised Version.

The Qur'án, translated by J. M. Rodwell

'The Digha Nikaya', in *Dialogues of the Buddha*, Translated by C. A. F. Rhys Davids, London, Henry Froude, 1895, vol. 2.

The Bhagavad-Gita, translated by Annie Besant, Madras, Theosophical Publishing House, 1924.

The Dinkárd, the passage quoted was translated from the Persian by H. M. Balyuzi for this book.

The Rise of Christianity, by Ernest William Barnes, London, Longmans Green, 1947.

References

Chapter I: *Introducing the Bahá'í Faith*

(1) Matt. x. 29. (2) Bahá'u'lláh, quoted in P.D.C. 8. (3) Col Edward Alexander Stanton, quoted in G.P.B. 313-314. (4) Quoted in G.P.B. 290. (5) P.T. 56-7.

PART I

THE TEACHINGS

Chapter II: *The Oneness of God and of Religion*

(1) G. XCIX. (2) G. LXXXII. (3) G. LII. (4) T.F. 75. (5) G. XXVI. (6) T.F. 75. (7) P.T. 58-9. (8) G. CXI. (9) P.U.P. 126. (10) P.U.P. 365-366. (11) S.A.Q. 74-76. (12) PT. 130. (13) G. XXI. (14) P.M. LVIII. (15) G. XXII. (16) G. XXIV. (17) B.P. 212. (18) G. CIX. (19) G. LXXIV. (20) John xvi. 12-13. (21) Matt. xxii. 14. (22) G. XVI.

Chapter III: *The Proclamation of Bahá'u'lláh*

(1) G.P.B. 212. (2) P.B. 5-6. (3) P.B. 57. (4) John xvi. 13. (5) G. CXVI (6) Matt. xxiv. 12. (7) Zachariah xiv. 9. (8) G. XI. (9) G. XXV. (10) G. VII (11) G. XlV. (12) P.B. 9. (13) P.B. 20-21. (14) P.B. 39. (15) P.D.C. 37 (16) P.B. 27. (17) FB. 43. (18) P.B. 51. (19) Bahá'u'lláh, 'Lawḥ-i-Ra'ís' quoted in P.D.C. 62, (20) Bahá'u'lláh, 'Kitáb-i-Aqdas', quoted in P.D.C. 40. (21) P.B. 59. (22) The Báb, 'Qayyúmú'l-Asmá', quoted in P.D.C. 68. (23) P.B. 83. (24) Bahá'u'lláh, quoted in P.D.C. 72. (25) Bahá'u'lláh, quoted in P.D.C. 115. (26) K.I. 15. (27) K.I. 165-166. (28) Bahá'u'lláh, quoted in P.D.C. 83. (29) T.B. 213. (30) P.B. 93. (31) Bahá'u'lláh, quoted in P.D.C. 78-79.

Chapter IV: *The Oneness of Mankind*

(1) E.S.W. 14. (2) Malachi ii. 10. (3) Matt. xxiii. 8-9. (4) Q. II. 209. (5) S.W.A.B. 31-32. (6) G. CXII. (7) P.B.A. 54. (8) W.T. 13-14. (9) P.T. 38. (10) P.T. 138-9. (11) S.W.A.B. 291. (12) B.R. 210-Tablet to The Hague. (13) G. XLIII. (14) G. CXVII. (15) G. XLIII. (16) B.R. 210-211-Tablet to The Hague. (17) G. CXVII. (18) G. CXII. (19) Bahá'u'lláh, quoted in A.D.J. (20) 'Abdu'l-Bahá, quoted in A.D.J. (21) 'Abdu'l-Bahá, quoted in A.D.J. (22) E.S.W. 15. (23) P.T. 16. (24) P.T. 21-2. (25) G. XLIII. (26) G. CVII. (27) G. LXXII. (28) 'Abdu'l-Bahá, quoted in W.O.B. 164-165.

ALL THINGS MADE NEW

Chapter V: *World Unity*

(1) G XVI. (2) G LXI. (3) G LXX (4) Bahá'u'lláh, quoted in W.O.B. 186-187. (5) W.O.B. 203-4. (6) G CXIX (7) S.D.C. 64-65. (8) B.R. 25-16-Tablet to The Hagne. (9) W.O.B. 40-1. (10) G CVI. (11) G CXVII. (12) E.S.W. 89. (13) Bahá'u'lláh, 'Lawh-i-Sulṭán', quoted in P.D.C. 75. (14) E.S.W. 91-92. (15) P.B. 34. (16) G CX (17) G CLXIII. (18) G CLIX (19) G CXVIII. (20) G CII. (21) Matt. xxii. 21. (22) W.T. 8. (23) Isaiah XI. 9. (24) G CXIX

Chapter VI: *Social and Economic Teachings*

(1) P.U.P. 174-176. (2) S.C.D. 109-11. (3) T.H. 213. (4) E.S.W. 27. (5) P.U.P. 329-330. (6) T.B. 68. (7) T.B. 51-52. (8) H.W. Persian LXXX (9) P.T. 176-7. (10) P.T. 151-3. (11) 'Abdu'l-Bahá, quoted in 'The Social Teachings of the Bahá'í Movement', compiled by George O, Latimer, S.W. vol. VII. no. 15, Dec. 12, 1916 pp. 147-148. (12) S.A.Q. 274-276. (13) H.W. Persian XLIX (14) 'Abdu'l-Bahá, quoted in 'The Economic Teaching of 'Abdu'l-Bahá', by Mary Hanford Ford, S.W. vol. VIII. no. I, March 21, 1917, pp. 4-5. (15) B.N.E. 149. (16) B.N.E. 153-154. (17) S.A.Q. 268-272. (18) T.B. 39-40. (19) P.U.P. 109-110.

Chapter VII: *Personal Conduct*

(1) T.B. 156. (2) Galen, quoted in S.A.Q. 303. (3) Matt. vii. 16-20. (4) G CXXVI. (5) H.W. Persian LXXVI. (6) P.U.P. 185. (7) G CXXX (8) H.W. Arabic XXXVI. (9) T.B. 155. (10) H.W. Arabic XXXI. (11) W.T. 14. (12) B.N.E. 76-77. (13) H.W. Arabic V. (14) H.W. Arabic VII. (15) G CLIII. (16) H.W. Persian XL. (17) G CXXVIII. (18) G CLXIII. (19) T.B. 129. (20) P.T. 159-60. (21) 'Abdu'l-Bahá, quoted in A.D.J. 24. (22) H.W. Arabic II. (23) K.I. 124. (24) 'Abdu'l-Bahá, quoted in A.D.J. 24. (25) S.A.Q. 269. (26) T.B. 26. (27) T.B. 37. (28) S.A.Q. 215-216. (29) G CXXVI. (30) H.W. Arabic I. (31) Bahá'u'lláh, quoted in A.D.J. 27. (32) Bahá'u'lláh, quoted in A.D.J. 27. (33) S.W.A.B. 146-147, (34) H.W. Persian LVI. (35) H.W. Persian VIII. (36) T.B. 130. (37) G.V. (38) G CXL V. (39) H.W. Arabic XXVII. (40) K.I. 124. (41) K.I. 123-4. (42) G.V. (43) P.B. 20. (44) 'Abdu'l-Bahá, quoted in B.R. 302-303. (45) 'Abdu'l-Bahá, quoted in A.D.J. 27. (46) G CXXXI. (47) G II.

Chapter VIII: *Science and the Knowledge of God*

(1) P.U.P. 221-222. (2) P.U.P. 292-293. (3) P.U.P. 107. (4) P.U.P. 311-312. (5) P.T. 143. (6) G XC. (7) T.B. 156. (8) K.I. 123. (9) S.V. 36. (10) G CLIII. (11) G CLIII. (12) G CLX. (13) P.T. 175. (14) P.B. 95. (15) H.W. Arabic XVI. (16) 'Abdu'l-Bahá, quoted in B.W.F. 368. (17) H.W. Arabic XVIII. (18) G CXXXVI.

REFERENCES

(19) H.W. Persian LVI. (20) G. I. (21) T.B. 156. (22) G. CLIII. (23) G. CXXXII. (24) B.P. 61. (25) P.M. XXIII. (26) P.M. XXVI. (27) P.M. CLXVIII. (28) B.P. 79-80. (29) B.P. 75-76. (30) P.M. LVII. (31) P.M.I. (32) P.M. LI. (33) P.M. XCII.

Chapter IX: Man and the Universe

(1) G. LXXVII. (2) S.A.Q. 248. (3) P.T. 60-1. (4) G. CII. (5) G. CXXXVI. (6) G. CXXXIV. (7) P.U.P. 307-8. (8) P.U.P. 226. (9) S.A.Q. 209. (10) S.A.Q. 214-6. (11) G. LXXXI. (12) G. LXXXI. (13) 'Abdu'l-Bahá, quoted in B.N.E. 178. (14) S.A.Q. 252. (15) S.A.Q. 283. (16) P.T. 178. (17) P.T. 110-11. (18) P.T. 51. (19) H.W. Arabic I. (20) S.A.Q. 257-8. (21) T.A.B. 587. (22) S.A.Q. 239. (23) P.M. CLXX. (24) S.A.Q. 238. (25) S.A.Q. 195-6. (26) S.A.Q. 132. (27) P.U.P. 240-241. (28) P.U.P. 358-9. (29) S.A.Q. 188. (30) G. XXVII. (31) G. XC. (32) G. XXVI. (33) G. XIX.

Chapter X: The Relation of the Bahá'í Faith to other Religions

(1) G. III. (2) Isaiah vi. 10. (3) Matt. xxiv. 37-9. (4) P.T. 54—6. (5) Joel ii. 10: (6) Isaiah ix. 6. (7) Matt. x. 34. (8) Isaiah xi. I. (9) Isaiah ii. 4. (10) Isaiah xxxv. 1-2. (11) Matt. xxiv. 14. (12) Matt. xxiv. 26-7. (13) Matt. vii. 15-20. (14) K.I. 46. (15) Matt. xxiv. 44. (16) Q. XXI: 104. (17) Q. II: 206.(18) Q. XXXIX: 67-71. (19) Q. LXXIX: 6. 13. (20) Bhagavad Gita, Fourth Discourse. (21) Digha Nikaya III: 75-6. (22) Dinkird. (23) Matt. viii. 22. (24) P.U.C. 113. (25) G. XXXVI. (26) S.A.Q. 85. (27) S.A.Q. 88. (28)]ohn vi. (29) S.A.Q. 91-2. (30) The Rise of Christianity, 170. (31) S.A.Q. 97. (32) K.I. 104. (33) G. LXX.

PART II

HISTORICAL

The whole of this part is based upon the accounts in G.P.B. and D

Chapter XI: The Báb

(1) G.P.B. 13. (2) M.F. 7. (3) The Báb, quoted in G.P.B. 30. (4) The Báb, quoted in G.P.B. 30. (5) The Báb, quoted in G.P.B. 30. (6) The Báb, quoted in G.P.B. 30. (7) The Báb, quoted in G.P.B. 25. (8) The Báb, quoted in G.P.B. 23. (9) Bahá'u'lláh, quoted in W.O.B. 124. (10) S.WB. 12. (11) K.I. 155-6. (12) The Báb, quoted in G.P.B. 29-30.

Chapter XII: Bahá'u'lláh

(1) 'Abdu'l-Bahá, quoted in B.N.E. 23-4. (2) Captain Alfred von Gumoenz, quoted in B.B.R. 133. (3) E.S.W. 20-1. (4) E.S.W. 11.(5) E.S.W. 21. (6) Bahá'u'lláh, quoted in G.P.B. 101. (7) K.I. 159. (8) K.I. 160. (9) K.I. 160. (10)

'Abdu'l-Bahá, quoted in G.P.B. 133. (11) Nabil, quoted in G.P.B. 134. 137. (12) Bahá'u'lláh, quoted in G.P.B. 155. (13) Bahá'u'lláh, quoted in G.P.B. 154. (14) Nabil, quoted in G.P.B. 156-7. (15) Bahá'u'lláh, quoted in-G.P.B. 169. (16) Bahá'u'lláh, quoted in G.P.B. 188. (17) 'Abdu'l-Bahá, quoted in G.P.B. 193. (18) Edward Granville Browne, quoted in E.G.B. 56-57. (19) P.M. 302. (20) Bahá'u'lláh, quoted in W.O.B. 103-4. (21) Bahá'u'lláh. quoted in W.O.B. 107. (22) G.P.B. 94. (23) W.O.B. 100.

Chapter XIII: *'Abdu'l-Bahá*

(1) G.P.B. 242. (2) Bahá'u'lláh, quoted in W.O.B. 135-6.(3) Bahá'u'lláh, 'Súriyi-Ghusn', quoted in W.O.B. 135. (4) W.O.B. 132. (5) 'Abdu'l-Bahá, quoted in W.O.B. 133. (6) Túbá Khánum, quoted in C.H. 99-103. (7) G.P.B. 269. (8) G.P.B. 275. (9) C.H. 150-1. (10) Retold from C.H. 161-2. (11) P.F. 119-20. (12) P.F. 98. (13) C.H. 185. (14) Isabel Fraser, 'Abdu'l-Bahá at the Salvation Army Shelter', S.W. Feb. 7, 1913, Vol. III. no. 18: p.8-9.

PART III

THE BAHÁ'Í COMMUNITY

Chapter XIV: *The Covenant of Bahá'u'lláh*

(1)'Abdu'l-Bahá, quoted in W.O.B. 146. (2) G. CLV. (3) 'Abdu'l-Bahá, quoted in C.B. 70. (4) E.S.W. 160. (5) S.C.K.A. 24. (6) T.B. 221. (7) W.T. II. (8) W.T. II. (9) W.O.B. 149. (10) W.O.B. 19. 20. (11) T.B. 221. (12) 'Abdu'l-Bahá, 'This is a Mystery of the Kingdom of Abhá', S.W., Nov. 23, 1920, Vol. II. no. 14, p. 243. (13) 'Abdu'l-Bahá, 'The Tree of Life is just beginning to grow…', S.W., Mar. 21, 1922, Vol. 13, no. I, p. 19. (14) S.W. XI. 12. (15) 'Abdu'l-Bahá, 'The Center of the Covenant', S.W. Nov. 23, 1921, Vol. 12. no. 14, p. 227. (16) 'Abdu'l-Bahá, 'Tablet to'Mr. and Mrs. Killiuz', S.W. Feb. 7, 1921, Vol. II, no. 18, p. 308. (17) T.A.R 83. (18) 'Abdu'l-Bahá, 'Tablet to Ella Quant', S.W. Nov. 4, 1919, Vol. 10, no. 13, p. 250-1. (19) Bahá'u'lláh, quoted in W.O.B 135-6. (20) W.O.B 144. (21) G.P.R 325. (22) W.O.B 4. (23) C.R 114-W.T. (24) 'Abdu'l-Bahá 'Tablet to Corine True', S.W. Nov. 4, 1919, Vol. 10, no. 13, P.246. (25) B.R. 192-Last Tablet to America. (26) W.T. 25. (27) S.W. IV. 242. (28) 'Abdu'l-Bahá, 'The Covenant of God' is like unto a vast and fathomless ocean', S.W. Aug. I. 1919, Vol. 10, no. 8, p. 153. (29) European Teaching Conference Manual, 1948, 50. (30) T.D.P. 45. (31) 'Abdu'l-Bahá, 'This, like unto a magnetic power', S.W. Nov. 23, 1920, Vol. II, no. 14, pp. 240-242. (32) 'Abdu'l-Bahá, quoted in BW.F. 357.

Chapter XV: *The Administrative Order*

(1) W.O.B. 151. (2) W.T. 3. (3) 'Abdu'l-Bahá, quoted in W.O.B 78. (4) Shoghi Effendi, quoted in P.B.A 2. (5) TR 68. (6) W.T. 19-20. (7) W.T. 13. (8) W.T. 12. (9) Shoghi Effendi, quoted in P.B.A. 39-40. (10) P.B.A. 77-8. (11) P.B.A. 66. (12) 'Abdu'l-Bahá, quoted in P.BA 52. (13) S.W.A.R 87-88. (14) G.P.R 339-40. (15) G.P.R340. (16) Shoghi Effendi, quoted in P.B.A 92. (17) P.B.A 95. (18) P.B.A. 95. (19) TR 3-4. (20) W.O.B. 145. (21) G.P.R 326. (22) P.B.A 1.

Chapter XVI: *Laws, Obligations, and Teaching the Faith*

(1) Bahá'u'lláh, quoted in G.P.R 216. (2) G.P.R 214. (3) P.B.A 18. (4) S.C.K.A 17. (5) 'Abdul-Bahá, quoted in B.W.F. 372-373. (6) Shoghi Effendi, letter to N.S.A. U.S.A., June 20, 1954. (7) B.N.E. 183-184. (8) P.B.A. 55. (9) P.B.A. 8. (10) P.B.A 7. (11) P.B.A. 9. (12) P.B.A. 17. (13) G. LVII. (14) G.P.R 365. (15) 'Abdu'l-Bahá, quoted in W.O.B 17. (16) W.O.B 15-16. (17) G. CLXI. (18) W.T. 25. (19) G. CXXVIII. (20) A.D.J. 41. (21) G. CXXIX (22) G. CXLIX (23) G. CL VII.

Chapter XVII: *The Greatness of This Day*

(1) Bahá'u'lláh, quoted in A,D.J. 68-69. (2) Bahá'u'lláh, quoted in W.O.B 164. (3) 'Abdu'l-Bahá, quoted in W.O.B. 169. (4) G. CIX (5) Shoghi Effendi, Letter to N.S.A. U.S.A. Nov. 27, 1954. (6) Bahá'u'lláh, quoted in W.O.B 103. (7) 'Abdul-Bahá, quoted in W.O.B. II 0. (8) Bahá'u'lláh, quoted in W.O.B 108. (9) 'Abdul-Bahá, quoted in W.O.B. 101-102. (10) S.A.Q. 148. (11) S.A.Q. 147. (12) G. LXXXVII. (13) W.O.B. 103. (14) G. XIX. (15)' A.D.J. 65. (16) 'Abdu'l-Bahá, quoted in W.O.B. 110.

Postscript on *The Next Manifestation of God*

(1) G. CLXV. (2) Bahá'u'lláh, quoted in W.O.B. 117. (3) G. CXXIX.

INDEX

Spirit of, 3, 4, 7, 178-83
Transformation of human nature, 3-4, 81
Manifestations of God
  Cause of Progress, 5, 43, 162
  Cause of Unity, 81
  Divine Physician, 37
  Intermediaries between God and man, 31, 37-8
  Next Manifestation, 352-54
  Obedience to Commandments of, 128, 131, 141, 273
  Oneness of, 37-40, 192, 222, 350
  Opposition to, 5, 33-4, 66
  Regenerative Power, 30, 33-5, 81, 101-02, 183-84
  Station of, 37-40, 95
Mankind—
  Love for, 72-73, 117, 120
  New powers of, 4, 81, 344
  Oneness of, 70-82
  Progress of, 1-6, 41-42, 80-1, 101-102, 345, 350
  Service to, 76, 91, 102
  Unification of, 4, 71, 73-74, 80, 85
Manúchihr-Khán, 112
Marriage, 320, 321-22, 334
Mashríqu'l-Adhkár, 259, 263, 316, 320
Materialism, 133-35
Medicine, 176-77
Meditation, 127, 141-42, 144
Mercy, 124
Mihdi, 48, 226
Miracles, 196-97
Moderation, 91, 92, 102, 123
Monarchy, 90
Monks, 142, 209
Moral Conduct, 116, 118
Moses, 23, 33-4, 40, 275

Most Great Peace, 96-7, 190, 269, 289, 342, 345
Muhammad, 23, 40, 49, 195, 201, 275-76
Muhammad-'Alí, Mírzá, 256-57, 261
Muhammad, Siyyid, 230, 232, 238, 239, 240
Muslim Doctrines and Law, 202, 309
Mysticism, 122, 142-43
Napoleon III of France, 57-8, 142
Násiri'd-Dín, Sháh of Írán, 62-63, 244
Nationalism, 71, 74, 75
Nineteen Day Feasts, 305-06, 307, 308, 314, 320
Noah, 34
Orientalists, 8
Pantheism, 183
Parliament, 90-92
Patriotism, 75
Peace, 74-86, 133
Penance, 320
Persia, 62
Peter, Primacy of, 199, 276
Philanthropic works, 303-04
Pilgrims, 236, 243, 252, 315
Pioneering, 339, 341
Politics, 330-31
Poor, The, 93, 105, 108, 303
Pope Pius IX, 62
Prayer—
  Communal worship, 144-45
  Communion with God, 126, 142
  Obligatory Prayers, 320, 326-27
  Supplication, 133-4, 141
  Work is worship, 104
Prayers of Bahá'u'lláh and 'Abdu'l-Bahá, 144, 146-48, 177
Prehistoric Times, 1, 2-3, 348-50
Prejudice, 74-75, 134
Press, The, 86-113